CHALLENGES TO SOCIAL POLICY

HV
244
.C38
1985

Challenges to Social Policy

Edited by
RICHARD BERTHOUD

Gower

GOSHEN COLLEGE LIBRARY
GOSHEN, INDIANA

© Policy Studies Institute 1985

All rights reserved. No part of this publication may be reproduced, stored in a retrieval system, or transmitted in any form or by any means, electronic, mechanical, photocopying, recording or otherwise without the prior permission of Gower Publishing Company Limited.

Published by
Gower Publishing Company Limited,
Gower House,
Croft Road,
Aldershot, Hants GU11 3HR,
England

and

Gower Publishing Company,
Old Post Road,
Brookfield,
Vermont 05036,
U.S.A.

British Library Cataloguing in Publication Data

Challenges to social policy.
   1. Public welfare--Government policy--Great Britain
   2. Great Britain--Social policy
   I. Berthoud, Richard
   361.6'0941   HV248

Library of Congress Cataloging-in-Publication Data

Challenges to social policy.
   Includes index.
   1. Great Britain--Social policy--Congresses.
   2 Public welfare--Great Britain--Congresses.
   I. Berthoud, Richard.
   HV244.C38 1985   361.6'1'0941   85-14699

ISBN 0 566 05011 0

Printed in Great Britain at the University Press, Cambridge

Contents

Foreword

THE RIGHT HON. SIR PATRICK NAIRNE

The Leeds Castle seminar of September 1984 was born, as all good seminars should be, in a mood of self-questioning and in a spirit of hope.

The Joseph Rowntree Memorial Trustees rounded off their mid-summer meeting of 1983 with a working dinner at the Policy Studies Institute, at which Sir Kenneth Stowe, Permanent Secretary of the Department of Health and Social Security, was their sole guest. In the discussion round the dinner table the tentative possibility was aired of holding a conference or seminar, as a joint venture between the JRMT and the DHSS, which would enable the Trustees to review their research strategy and the Department to review its policy strategy. Was it perhaps time to take stock of the received wisdom? Might not a meeting of minds - if it was a good 'mix' of minds - produce new and timely insights into intractable problems?

A steering committee (which I was asked to chair) was assembled, composed of representatives of the Trustees and of the Department of Health and Social Security - meeting in the Policy Studies Institute and blessed with the capable and energetic support of Richard Berthoud of the Institute and the shrewd guidance of Robin Guthrie of the Trust. The steering committee gave birth to a proposal which put forward the case for the seminar - for the substantial effort of preparation; for the demands it would make on the busy men and women to be invited; and for the significant cost which would be borne primarily by the Trust. The proposal highlighted the urgent need to define the relevant demographic, technological, social, and economic factors and trends more clearly, and then to consider what must now be done to crystallize the aims of social policies over the next decade, to assess potential resources, and to set in hand what was likely to be the most fruitful research.

From the outset the Trust and the steering committee sought to maintain close contact with those members of the Economic and Social Research Council who were convening an academic conference in June 1984 at the University of Bath on 'Social Policy and the Economy'. It was obviously important that that conference and the seminar should, so far as possible, complement each other since they would need to attract at least some of the same participants. To this end Michael O'Higgins of the University of Bath played a particularly valuable part through assisting in organising the Bath conference and also presenting the opening paper at Leeds Castle on 'Social policy needs and resources: the prospects for the 1990s'. The opening words of that paper set the tone for both Bath and Leeds Castle:

> 'For better or worse, the central issue in any debate about needs and resources for social policy in the 1990s is the level of public expenditure which will be available for social welfare, the services which this can purchase and the extent to which these services will be more or less adequate in meeting social needs than those we have at present.'

In short, a sombre theme - and a theme that perhaps made the participants somewhat more conscious of (or self-conscious about) the rich and rare setting of Leeds Castle, where the seminar was held through the courtesy of the Leeds Castle Foundation. The venue was important. The seminar brought together six Permanent Secretaries and a senior supporting cast from Whitehall departments, a galaxy of academic talent, and a strong team of Trustees. As the early autumn storms lashed the castle walls, the warm and informal atmosphere of a country house party rapidly promoted the flow of ready and lively talk round the room on which the success of the seminar depended. We owe a large debt of gratitude to those who contributed so freely to the discussion, and particularly to those who prepared the seminar papers which are now presented to a wider audience.

But what does the 'success of the seminar' mean? Academic papers of high quality were written and presented; views and counterviews were vigorously expressed; friendships were renewed, and new contacts were made. All that was to the good. As to a further and more lasting harvest, I warmly commend this book, composed of Richard Berthoud's perceptive Introduction and the Leeds Castle papers in permanent form.

Patrick Nairne
February 1985

Contributors and participants

Donald Acheson - Chief Medical Officer at the Department of Health and Social Security.

Sir Lawrence Airey - Chairman of the Board of Inland Revenue.

A.B. Atkinson - Professor of Economics at the London School of Economics and Political Science, and Director of the International Centre for Economics and Related Disciplines.

John Banham - Controller of the Audit Commission for Local Authorities in England and Wales.

Peter Barclay - solicitor; Chairman of the National Institute for Social Work; trustee of the Joseph Rowntree Memorial Trust.

Sir Donald Barron - Chairman of the Midland Bank; Chairman of the Joseph Rowntree Memorial Trust.

Richard Berthoud - Senior Fellow of the Policy Studies Institute.

Ann Bowtell - Under Secretary at the Department of Health and Social Security responsible for the Coordinating Unit for the social security reviews.

Jonathan Bradshaw - Professor of Social Administration at the University of York, and Director of the Social Policy Research Unit.

Ian Byatt - Deputy Chief Economic Adviser at the Treasury.

Sir Charles Carter - Chairman of the Research Committee of the Policy Studies Institute; Vice-chairman of the Joseph Rowntree Memorial Trust.

Nicholas Deakin - Professor of Social Policy and Administration at the University of Birmingham.

David Donnison - Professor of Town and Regional Planning at the University of Glasgow.

Christopher France - Deputy Secretary at the Department of Health and Social Security responsible for health and personal social services development.

Roy Griffiths - Deputy Chairman and Managing Director of Sainsbury's; Chairman of the recent Management Inquiry into the use of resources in the National Health Service.

Robin Guthrie - Director of the Joseph Rowntree Memorial Trust.

Sir Douglas Hague - Chairman of the Economic and Social Research Council.

Graham Hart - Deputy Secretary at the Department of Health and Social Security responsible for NHS management.

Geoffrey Hulme - Deputy Secretary and Principal Finance Officer at the Department of Health and Social Security.

Margot Jefferys - formerly Professor of Medical Sociology and Director of the Social Research Unit at Bedford College, London.

William Jeffrey - Assistant Secretary in the Criminal Department of the Home Office.

John Kay - Director of the Institute for Fiscal Studies; Fellow of St. John's College, Oxford.

Jeremy Knight - Assistant Secretary in the Community Services Division of the Department of Health and Social Security.

Alan Maynard - Professor of Economics and Director of the DHSS-ESRC Centre for Health Economics at the University of York.

Sir Peter Middleton - Permanent Secretary at the Treasury.

Patrick Minford - Edward Gonner Professor of Applied Economics at the University of Liverpool.

Sir George Moseley - Permanent Secretary at the Department of the Environment.

Sir Patrick Nairne - Master of St. Catherine's College, Oxford; trustee of the Joseph Rowntree Memorial Trust; Permanent Secretary at the Department of Health and Social Security, 1975 to 1981.

T.E. Nodder - formerly Deputy Secretary at the Department of Health and Social Security responsible for health and personal social services development.

Michael O'Higgins - Reader in Social Policy at the University of Bath.

Robert Pinker - Professor of Social Work Studies at the London School of Economics and Political Science.

Sir Michael Quinlan - Permanent Secretary at the Department of Employment.

Clive Smee - Chief Economic Adviser to the Department of Health and Social Security.

Sir Kenneth Stowe - Permanent Secretary at the Department of Health and Social Security.

W.B. Utting - Chief Social Work Officer at the Department of Health and Social Security.

Alan Walker - Reader in Social Policy at the University of Sheffield.

Joseph Ward - Under Secretary at the Department of Health and Social Security responsible for pensions policy.

Adrian Webb - Professor of Social Administration and Director of the Centre for Research in Social Policy at the University of Loughborough.

Malcolm Wicks - Director of the Family Policy Studies Centre.

Alan Williams - Professor of Economics at the University of York.

Introduction

RICHARD BERTHOUD

Everyone seems to agree: the welfare consensus is over. According to the newly received wisdom, the development of social policy along post-war lines has come under attack from two directions. First, the long-run growth of public expenditure on social provision (as on other aspects of government activity) has run up against a halt in the previously steady growth in the economy, and against attempts by governments to restrict budgets. At the same time, the methods and even the objectives of current social policy have increasingly been called into question.

It is no coincidence that these two types of pressure should have arisen together, since the budgetary and political issues are closely entwined. They have come up in country after country over the past ten years, to be dubbed the 'crisis of the welfare state'. There is undoubtedly a crisis of confidence. How serious the problems are, and how likely to affect the various elements of the welfare system, may be open to debate. There is no doubt, however, that it is more important than ever before to be clear about the aims of policy, to re-examine the means of achieving them, and to take stock of the resources available to meet need.

These considerations have engendered an international flow of books, articles and conferences on the future of the welfare state. In this country, the Economic and Social Research Council sponsored a conference at the University of Bath in June 1984 on the theme of Social Policy and the Economy (Klein and O'Higgins, 1985). The purpose of that conference was to examine the general relationship between economic and social policies, test the effect of a variety of economic, demographic and policy assumptions, and discuss the influence of social policy strategies on a broad front.

While the public and academic debate is in progress, those responsible for the management of social policy need to take account of three types of influence which may bear on their ability to meet future requirements. One of these factors is institutional: the public service has a current stock of staff, buildings, policies and commitments which cannot be wound down or transferred rapidly. A second type of factor consists of circumstances beyond the direct influence of social policy decisions, which may affect the balance between needs and resources: the state of the economy as a whole may have an important bearing on the funds available for social services and also on the needs that have to be met; the number of 'clients' of different programmes may vary with demographic swings. Third, the managers of social policy need to be able to anticipate likely political trends, and to know the probable effects of alternative options.

It was with these considerations in mind that the Joseph Rowntree Memorial Trust determined to organise a seminar on the theme of 'Social Policy: Aims and Resources for the 1990s'. The meeting took place in impressive surroundings at Leeds Castle, near Maidstone, Kent, on September 19th, 20th and 21st, 1984. The format was unusual: in effect, a meeting was arranged between some of the leading independent experts on social policy, and some of the most senior officials responsible for the development and implementation of social policy. Ten senior officials of the Department of Health and Social Security, covering the whole range of its responsibilities, took part in the meeting. So did senior officials from four other government departments whose responsibilities are relevant to social policy.

The aim for the seminar was to review the issues likely to affect the planning of social policy over the next five to ten years. The immediate focus was on the responsibilities of the DHSS, but factors and policies relevant to the DHSS task were also to be covered. The theme - aims and resources for the 1990s - was summarised as follows:

It is rapidly becoming clear that if current trends in the structure of the population continue, our economic performance remains near its present level, and existing social policies are maintained, the difficulties of providing social services, by whatever means, may increase substantially by the end of this decade.

For the purpose of these discussions, it may be useful to consider the aims of social policy in terms of the ordering of resources among the members of society to meet their various needs. It is necessary to take account of all kinds of resource: what people do for themselves, and for each other; private resources that may be drawn into social care in competition with other businesses; as well as what public agencies provide.

During the coming decade, need is expected to grow faster than the economy. Resources to meet that need will not emerge of their own accord. The challenge for the seminar will be to find them.

Seven papers were commissioned to provide the basis for the discussions. Five addressed specific policy fields: two on the distribution of incomes (of the elderly and of the working population); two on social services (to the elderly and to the family); and one on health policy. Consideration of these specific services was, however, preceded by discussion of wider issues: one paper examined the arithmetic of public expenditure over the next ten years; the other reviewed some of the alternative approaches to the provision of welfare. These two papers were designed to introduce some of the ideas and conclusions of the ESRC conference, and to lay a basis for the more detailed discussions of policy areas to follow.

This book presents the seven essays prepared for the seminar, as subsequently amended by the authors. The views expressed in each paper are, of course, the sole responsibility of each author. In view of the official position of many of the participants in the seminar, it must be emphasised that the papers cannot be interpreted as in any way a reflection of the views of the seminar members; the reader will learn here, in effect, what was said to the meeting, but not the reply.

In the remainder of this introduction, however, the editor's essay reviews some of the major themes from the papers, in the light of the debates that took place at the seminar. This does not represent the decisions of the group: decisions were neither expected nor achieved. Some members of the seminar later wrote in, either with a precis of a message they had hoped to get across, or with a review of some of the lessons they had learnt in the discussion. These, combined with the author's notes of the discussion itself, provide useful material for the essay, but it is to be stressed that it is simply one individual's view of the issues, having listened to the views of others. There is probably no issue on which all the delegates would be unanimous; nor will there be any other delegate who agrees with all the views expressed here. In particular, it has to be stressed again that the presence of senior public officials at the meeting should not be taken to imply agreement by them with any opinion recorded in this volume.

Caveats aside, it is hoped that these essays will provide a useful statement of the art of social policy planning. The meeting itself was valuable, as indicated perhaps by the warmth with which the members commended the Joseph Rowntree Memorial Trust for its initiative. It enabled senior officials to discuss large issues outside the press of daily business; it helped academics to recognise some of the practical aspects of policy planning. Readers of this book cannot take part directly in this interchange, but the papers may nevertheless help them to focus on the aims and implications of social policy at a level somewhere below abstract theory or ideal-world proposals, but somewhere above administrative management. Great though the achievements of the welfare state have been, the social problems to be addressed are still great: a search for new solutions is urgent.

Financial prospects

In 1955, the total of public expenditure in the United Kingdom was one-third of the gross domestic product. Over the next 20 years, the economy grew steadily, if unspectacularly by comparison with that of other nations. Since 1975, the growth has been far from steady, but the signs are still that the general upward trend may continue. This increase in the prosperity of the country as a whole has enabled governments to provide a better level of public services, higher social security payments and so on. But the growth in public expenditure has been more rapid than the growth in GDP: instead of remaining at one third, the ratio of public expenditure to GDP has tended, taking one period with another, to rise by about one percentage point every two years. As a result, it is now approaching a half. Put another way, while a third of the 1955 GDP passed through the public purse, about three-fifths of the subsequent growth has done so.

To some commentators, these trends, which have not been confined to this country, have been an unmitigated disaster: an indication of the economy being sucked dry by the public sector leech, of the extension of the deadening hand of bureaucracy, of an enervating dismantling of incentives to personal initiative. To other commentators, the same trends have been welcome: according to this view, the deployment of growth on collective expenditure on common goals has provided an opportunity to narrow inequality and to aid those whose needs would otherwise have gone unmet.

Even at a more immediately practical level of analysis, there are conflicting aspects of the growth of public expenditure to be taken into consideration. With inevitable exceptions, the services provided have been of genuine value, and social security payments have met genuine need. Moreover, that part of public expenditure which directly purchases goods or pays wages (i.e. transactions which are not simply a transfer of income from one person to another) is a familiar economic activity, whose direct contribution to the nation's economic growth should be considered as relevant as the indirect restraint on growth produced by the taxes which finance it. The method of relating the public expenditure total to the GDP can, indeed, create an exaggerated impression. Only about half of public expenditure is the kind of consumption or capital formation which appears in the national accounts as a part of the national product: in this light the public sector is not responsible for nearly half the economy, but less than a quarter - leaving the other three-quarters to be accounted for by the private sector.

But while it is true that different elements of public expenditure play different economic roles, they all need to be funded out of taxation or borrowing; an increase in public expenditure above the rate of economic growth will sooner or later require an increase in taxation. There is no evidence of a specific limit above which taxation should not rise, but it may be suggested as a general proposition that each slice of increased taxation may have more harmful side-effects on the economy than the last one, and will be less popular among taxpayers. It is a political decision where a line should be drawn. At the same time, while the increasing cost of many public programmes accurately reflects necessary improvements or extensions to the services provided, the difficulty of controlling costs and of weeding out activities no longer urgently required, means that a part of the natural increase in expenditure may be wasted.

These factors have meant that those responsible for the public budget have to keep the brake on almost permanently in order to restrain spending. The figures for the mid-1960s and mid-1970s remind us that even when a government generally committed to public provision has come to power, it has been able to raise public expenditure only once, before having to apply the brake as vigorously, and on one occasion more successfully, than the current government with its abhorrence of state expenditure. Because there is no natural restraint provided by a market, a planning restraint has to be substituted. It may be suggested, at least in principle, that failure to control expenditure could be the worst enemy of a viable welfare service - the more funds devoted to non-essential programmes, the less would be available for those that are required most urgently.

All this sounds a good deal more straightforward when considered at the level of the aggregate of public expenditure, than when it has to be applied in practice to the curtailment of particular programmes. Table 1 provides a very broad outline of how the major social policy budgets changed between 1955 (the year when the PE/GDP ratio was at its post-war low) to 1975 (the post-war peak); and from 1975 to the most recent figures, a period of unprecedented budgetary restraint, but also of unprecedented increase in unemployment-led demands on welfare. 'Social expenditure' took up a very large proportion of the general growth during the expansionary period, although it is worth noting that public social services - health, education and so on - accounted for only about one-seventh of the domestic product even in the peak year of 1975; another ninth of the national income was redistributed from its original earners to those who lacked earning power. Put this way, the welfare state may not seem so all-pervasive as is sometimes suggested. Since 1975, social transfer payments have had to be increased, in spite of various reductions in detail, to meet the basic needs of increasing numbers of pensioners, and a rising tide of unemployed. The total budget for social services has, however, been cut back, almost entirely because government (net) funding of housing programmes has dwindled so rapidly.

The present stance (HM Treasury, 1984) is that a reduction in taxation takes priority over any expenditure requirements; the total of expenditure is intended to be fixed at its current (real) level for at least five years, followed by a further five year period when its growth, if any, will be restricted to 1 per cent each year. The purported reasoning behind this target is that a decision should be taken about the total that can be afforded without regard for the desirability of the objectives that are to be achieved or foregone. When you think about it, this attractive doctrine cannot be applied to a very serious analysis. No one can decide in abstract how much they want to spend on, say housing, without considering the family's housing needs in relation to food, clothing and other necessities, and without taking account of the cost of

Table 1   Analysis of public expenditure; 1955, 1975 and 1983

	1955	1975	1983
£ billion, 1983 prices			
Social Services			
Health	4.5	12.8	15.9
Education	4.0	13.6	12.7
Housing	2.5	5.2	0.7
Personal social services	na	2.5	3.0
Others	0.7	2.8	3.0
Total	11.7	36.9	35.3
Social transfers			
Social security	7.3	20.9	32.2
Others	2.1	9.4	11.0
Total	9.4	30.3	43.2
Non-social services	18.1	31.0	34.1
Non-social transfers	9.2	30.0	25.7
As a percentage of GDP			
Social services	8.4%	14.0%	11.7%
Social transfers	6.7%	11.5%	14.3%
Non-social services	13.0%	11.7%	11.3%
Non-social transfers	6.6%	11.4%	8.5%

Notes: 'Services' defined for this table as 'current expenditure on goods and services' plus 'gross domestic fixed capital formation'. These are the elements of public expenditure which are part of the gross domestic product.

'Transfers' are all other items of public expenditure, not part of the gross domestic product.

'Social' - includes housing and employment services in addition to the items officially listed under social services.

Source: Central Statistical Office, National Income and Expenditure (Blue Book), 1960 and 1984, HMSO.

housing in relation to other prices. Indeed, to take the principle to its limit, discounting the value of goods or services altogether could only lead to a decision to spend nothing. The doctrine is a tactic much used by domestic budget-managers, for drawing the line <u>here</u> - 'I don't care how much you need a pair of shoes, we're not spending any more!' Similarly, the decision to hold public expenditure at its current level can hardly be a statement that the current level is optimum - quite apart from the impossibility of identifying some optimum figure, there is no doubt that the government actually thinks the amount is far too high and would reduce it at a stroke if it could. The fixed total is, therefore, a tactical target, en route to the real objective which is a reduction in the proportion of GDP passing through Treasury hands.

Having declared the objective, however, the government still has to investigate the means by which it might be achieved. Do forecasts for the next ten years suggest that the pressure of demands on public programmes will make the target easy or difficult to achieve? If difficulties are foreseen, what are the alternative options available for making the savings that appear to be required? What would be the various effects of each of those alternatives, and what sorts of people would be affected for good or ill? How do the good effects compare with the ill effects? The true objective of economic policy is not concerned with the various intermediate indicators of inflation, public expenditure, currency, productivity or even growth rates - the aim of economic policy, as of social policy, is the welfare of the people. Examination of the actual consequences of a policy proposal for the welfare of the people is therefore an essential part of its evaluation. One of the possible outcomes of the investigation of the means of achieving a freeze on public expenditure might be a decision that the best imaginable consequences of the freeze could be worse than any possible ill-effects of an increase in spending.

It became increasingly apparent to this observer at the Leeds Castle meeting that we are a hundred miles away from an accurate forecast of demand for public services, a thousand miles from a clear analysis of the options available for social policy, and a million from any prognosis of the effects of different policies on different people. It would be a pipe-dream to expect to establish a precise and all-embracing analysis, but it is vital, nonetheless, that such considerations are brought to bear as far as possible on policy planning. The very advantage of public services - the ability to provide on the basis of collective planning - would be lost if governments were obliged simply to continue with the programmes they inherited.

Michael O'Higgins's analysis of the prospects for public expenditure on particular programmes, in his contribution to the earlier ESRC conference (O'Higgins and Patterson, 1985) as well as to the Leeds Castle seminar (chapter 1), fills in a major gap in the argument. By estimating the resources required to fulfil existing commitments to meet known needs, he has approached the public expenditure question from the other end, in order to suggest likely impacts of alternative decisions about the total. Naturally such predictions are sensitive to many of the assumptions that have to be made, but in his paper in this volume, O'Higgins has matched the Treasury assumptions in order to reach conclusions which may be compared directly with the Green Paper. The message is fairly easily summarised:

- If it were decided to 'carry on' with existing policies, without a direct attempt to limit expenditure, then the total of public expenditure would float upwards nearly, though not quite, at the same rate as the assumed growth in the economy.
- If it were decided to constrain the cost of existing programmes so as to maintain 'constant' levels of benefits and services, but without actually cutting back on commitments, then the PE/GDP ratio would fall from year to year; but the growth in need (for instance, increasing numbers of elderly and very elderly people) would still force the absolute amount of public expenditure (in real terms) to rise.
- The present aim of holding public expenditure at its existing level could only be achieved, therefore, by making actual cuts in benefit rates, and/or in pay levels and/or in service provision, over and above the relative cuts involved in the 'constant' projection.

These prognostications about the next ten years are not dissimilar from the patterns of the last ten. The response has been surprisingly varied. On one interpretation, the message is 'don't panic'. The prospect of irresistible demographic forces driving public expenditure through the roof seems to recede. Governments need not apply severe restraint; present welfare commitments could be maintained; the rate of growth anticipated by the Treasury would accommodate them without an increase in the proportion of income required for taxation. No-one could use this arithmetic to claim that large cuts were inevitable to forestall national bankruptcy.

This view is based on the assumption that the maintenance of a constant PE/GDP ratio is the appropriate fiscal target. The analysis undoubtedly shows that there is room for manoeuvre between policy options, and therefore blocks any attempt to foreclose debate on 'there is no choice' grounds. But even on its assumption of a constant ratio, this interpretation of the figures seems over-optimistic. In the first place, it can hardly be wise to rely on the achievement of the growth rates assumed for the purpose of the calculations. 2 per cent every year for ten years was normal in the fifties and sixties, but has been rare even for individual years since the mid-seventies. The present government's first five years saw growth averaging $\frac{3}{4}$ per cent per year. Some of the anticipated pressure for increasing public expenditure is directly caused by growth - the demand for real increases in benefits and public sector pay to keep pace with the national average - but even so, a shortfall of economic performance would immediately undermine the optimistic outcome of the calculations. As one member of the seminar pointed out, it would be unwise to commit ourselves to spending extra money provided by growth until we are more confident that it will reach our pockets.

Even if our economic performance were to live up to the expectations implicit in the calculations, there is another ground for concern about the social policy prospects under a constant-ratio target. O'Higgins's 'carry on' prospect channels the whole of the tax-yield of economic growth into maintaining the output of current services, the wage rate parity of the public sector and the share of increased prosperity due (according to one way of thinking) to the portion of the population that happens to be economically inactive at any time. No government can feel excited at the prospect of merely maintaining existing policies, and no electorate can be wooed from such a platform; nor can anyone concerned with social problems feel that the present set of policies has achieved anything like enough towards the elimination of disadvantage, or the provision of care. From either point of view, the prospect is a dismal one: if the only resources available for improvements to existing services or the provision of new ones have to be found through a constant attrition of the current programme, then the hopes for new developments are slim and the confidence and morale of the public sector can only be expected to decline.

All of this, remember, is based on the optimistic view of the public expenditure options! O'Higgins showed that it is not imperative that the government should scale down its activities; but the same analysis shows that a determination nominally to hold them constant actually requires a level of attrition more severe than can probably be maintained over a ten-year period, and positive cuts on a substantial scale over and above that. It is all very well discovering that one goal is reasonably obtainable, if it turns out that the goal-posts have been placed somewhere else. The outlook for programmes dependent on public expenditure is quite frightening if this really is the target; some rapid thinking is required. A delegate to the seminar managed to chill the hearts of officials from all of the executive departments represented, by surmising that the strategy would require either an effective cut in DHSS funding equivalent to about one-sixth of its budget - or a transfer of that sum from the budgets of other departments! In place of the irresistible force that had threatened to drive public expenditure up, we have found an immovable object set to drag it down. If no way of meeting this situation can be put forward, then the message may be 'do panic' after all.

Is there a better way?
The fiscal prospects just outlined suggest that current, essentially sterile, short-term arguments about the budgets for specific services and benefits are likely to become more frequent, more intense and more bitter. The parallel agenda for Leeds Castle was, therefore, a review of the options that might be available to social policy planners to achieve their objectives a better way.

The unanimity with which the welfare state was welcomed in the late 1940s by all sections of society, anxious to share hardships in peace as in war, may well have been exaggerated by present day commentators. Nevertheless, by comparison with current analyses, it is fair to characterise post-war developments in terms of general agreement about the basic objectives and principles of policy: that the needs of ordinary people, subject to ordinary ups and downs, were best met by collective arrangements for income insurance, health care, education and, in part, for housing. On the assumption that the fifth great social/economic problem could also be solved, so that virtually all those in a position to work could have a job, the same ordinary people making use of these arrangements could be largely responsible for funding them. People might be net contributors at one period, and net withdrawers at another; if some people were forced to rely on the collective arrangements more than others over the course of their lives, that was entirely desirable in alleviating what would otherwise have been severe hardship. Programmes specifically to identify and relieve hardship of individuals, one at a time, were not, however, central to the philosophy (or, at least, to modern interpretations of it); the welfare state was not designed to succour particular people who had failed to provide for themselves, but provided for everybody.

Perhaps few participants in these developments articulated so elaborate a philosophy underlying the new or improved services. Nevertheless, the services themselves were popular, and policy issues in the 1950s and '60s were more concerned with which public programmes should attract the larger share of increasing budgets, than with questions about what the role of the state should be. In those days, a politician who promised expansion of his programme 'when resources allow' meant this year or next year; now he means sometime or never.

The early manifestation of disenchantment with the welfare state came, ironically enough, from social researchers who began to find, in the late 1960s and early '70s, that it was not achieving its objectives as successfully as had been supposed. Poverty was 'rediscovered'; social inequalities in health and education had not been wiped out by free services; unemployment was found to be on a long-run upward trend (there was even scare-talk of it reaching the million mark!); an ever-increasing number of elderly people were found still to be suffering isolation and hardship. It seemed that while the spending of money could solve or relieve some problems, it also exposed more needs. The conclusion usually drawn by the discoverers of these problems was the need for a further expansion of public services in favour of a particular client group. There could be a logical justification for such an approach - we have achieved much, but there is much still to be achieved, and we must not rest on our laurels. On the other hand the implications could be taken a step further. Many critics of the failures of the welfare state were saying, or appeared to be saying, that the achievements were illusory, that no progress had been made at all. The policy prescription - more resources to be devoted to services which were allegedly useless - was scarcely logical. But by so exaggerating the short-comings and playing down the successes of public provision, these critics may have had the opposite effect to the one intended - other critics appeared who were prepared to call into question the whole philosophy of collective action. Since the mid-'70s the uncertainty of economic growth, the increasing pressure on budgets and above all the arrival of mass unemployment, have led to a transformation in views of the welfare state. Even though the vast majority of citizens are recent, current or prospective participants in its services, suddenly the principle of collective action appears to have been replaced with a view that public provision involves 'us' being obliged to help 'them'. This has led to a two-stage attack on welfare: first, it is argued that state provision should be confined to those in particular circumstances of need; second, it becomes clear that those selected for such specialised services are getting 'too much' in comparison with those who provide for themselves.

The strength of this pressure for the marginalisation and isolation of the welfare state and of the people who rely upon it clearly varies between different policy sectors and different client groups. Nevertheless it appears to have had some effect on all aspects of social policy discussion. Our collective memory of the extremes of inequality that used to exist has faded to the extent that some commentators appear happy to contemplate a return to the old order. They have tended to divert attention from some of the more immediate issues facing social policy. The seminar for which these papers were commissioned was based on a set of assumptions which were not compatible with such a rejectionist philosophy. The needs of people are real, and require to be met. Some of the current arrangements for meeting need are satisfactory, others are not and may need to be either extended or revised. The state is involved in some of those arrangements, and cannot withdraw suddenly without ensuring a satisfactory replacement. But the scale of unmet need greatly exceeds the immediate prospect of further resources for direct state involvement. It is therefore necessary to examine current arrangements carefully, in order to see whether other resources might be deployed to cover some of the needs the state currently meets or fails to meet.

Adrian Webb's clear and unemotional analysis of alternative approaches to welfare (chapter 2) is based on this essentially pragmatic need to review policy - not so as to abandon mutual obligations but to meet them more effectively by whatever means, direct or indirect, which may prove satisfactory. Webb's task was to consider the options, rather than to argue the case for any particular solution. It is likely, in any case, that different types of solution may be found most appropriate or effective for different aims. Indeed, a unitary 'welfare state' based on public finance, public production and public allocation was never achieved in practice, and the very concept is already an anachronism. Social policy analysis has moved on to what is fashionably described as a 'mixed economy of welfare' - the phrase 'welfare state' is now used to describe current schemes mostly by people seeking to exaggerate and denigrate the direct role of public institutions. Webb discounted the possibility that there would or could be a very substantial shift in aims and methods in the immediate future, and this seemed to be reflected in the subsequent discussions of separate policy fields. According to one member's end-of-seminar summary, there was no prospect of a new 'grand design' for social policy equivalent to that developed in the 1940s; change to the existing set of policies would be incremental, the suitability of any approach being examined in the light of its potential role for each particular task.

This remains the general view, even though a case for a major withdrawal of the state from the welfare sector is now being put forward. According to this hypothesis, markets could provide for the majority of the needs currently handled by public services more efficiently and therefore more effectively. The proposition is not convincing. It seems to the present writer that the reasons for the failure to come to close grips with this issue lie both in the proposition and in the opposition. One difficulty is in the concept of the value of goods and services as residing in the price which people will pay for them; this market-based standard seems remote and uncertain in the context of public services deliberately provided to people whose income does not match their needs. A second set of assumptions which are not shared, concerns the extent to which transactions in a complex society can be predicted by market-based economic theory, without direct empirical confirmation. Belief in the operation of markets appears, in some contexts, to have become a faith.

When the case against public sector involvement is overstated, the counter-reaction may prevent a proper analysis of the pros and cons of different approaches for different policies. It may also be suggested that people professionally committed to a social policy more or less along the lines of that developed over the past forty years will not give any radical alternative a serious hearing. The failure of the proponents of the current mixed economy of welfare to develop a strongly argued response to the coherent radicalism of the Right, and the complete absence of any convincing formula from a radical Left, are at the heart of the 'crisis of confidence' of the welfare state. The criticisms from the Right need to be considered seriously: if these criticisms are ill-founded, the misunderstandings need to be cleared up, but (more fruitfully) the real shortcomings of existing services need to be identified, and new solutions tested.

'Things change when they have to', said one member of the seminar at about this point in the discussion, 'and when the existing ways of doing things are discredited.' Both these conditions, he implied, were becoming true. Whether he intended it or not, this could be taken as a comforting message – that new policies would emerge as they became needed. But what if no better way of doing things became apparent? Might not things change for the worse, if the point of decision arrived before an adequate response had been developed? If no comprehensive formula for a 'better way' appears likely, it is that much more important that medium term policy planning should be used to identify the modifications to the present system that will be essential if it is to continue to meet its objectives.

It may be a mistake, in any case, to see the policy choices in terms of the 'planning' of 'public services'. It is easy for the debate about budgets to be simplified into an assumption of a given set of 'needs' or 'demands' which the state must either meet or deny. In fact, of course, there is a wide range of policy implements available to government. One of the reasons for the disenchantment with the growth of the public sector has been the extension of the state's direct influence over the everyday lives of ordinary citizens. During the period when massive institutions were being built up to achieve specific social objectives it was natural, and perhaps essential, for a professionally administered central government, wielding multi-million pound budgets, to take more and more decisions about what was good for us. The outcomes may indeed have been good, on the whole, but there has also been a change in the relationship between public authorities and individual people. Depending on your angle of view, it has meant a loss of personal self reliance, as people have looked to the state to solve their problems; or it has meant a loss of individual autonomy, as decisions have been taken by remote authorities, and as access to services has been made conditional on approved social behaviour.

The increasing subordination of the individual to the state, brought about by the extension of public welfare services, is of recent origin, but there is no point in looking forward to a return to a 19th century laissez-faire model of the relationship between governors and governed. Nor is it appropriate to see this issue as a direct parallel of the public sector versus private sector debate. Some public welfare services confer freedoms far greater than have ever before been enjoyed by ordinary people. And the marginalisation of welfare referred to above, restricting services to a selected group of needy people, carries with it far stronger implications for dependency, and for the subordination of claimants, than the collectively organised services they would replace. On the other hand, policy debates over the next ten years may be more concerned with the government ensuring that needs can be met, than with the direct provision of services. They may also be more concerned with the diffusion of responsibility and decision-making in public institutions, and with a stronger role for the 'customer' and the 'community'.

While it is easy enough to spend money to provide a service, governments have found it much harder to concert an ensemble of policy instruments to achieve an overall set of objectives: tax incentives or direct benefits; cash or care; provision of its own services or regulation of others'; central or local government. Generalisations about 'the role of the state' overlook the fact that The State is not a single body but consists of many agencies which are often in conflict. The state's influence pervades every aspect of our lives, but in so many different ways that it is often difficult to see a coherent pattern of action, promoting some desired overall objective. One member of the seminar wrote afterwards of the failure of government to 'get its act together'. Coordination of services at ground level is one of those obvious requirements that sensible people are always demanding and sometimes achieving. But coordination of policy so that the various activities of government might work with common objectives ought in principle to be far easier. Perhaps it is because each of the departments and agencies with an interest in social policy has to struggle so hard to defend its own ground that they appear to find it so difficult to take a view wide enough to create a consistent set of policies; if they all operated to the same end, they might achieve far more, and use fewer resources at the same time. Several examples of problems of this sort were mentioned over the three days. Alan Maynard (chapter 5) refers to the necessity for the NHS to spend millions of pounds on treating accidents and diseases which other policies could have prevented. John Kay (chapter 6) examines the messy and uncertain mix of state and private pension provisions. At the time of writing, we do not know if the recent reviews of the social security system have successfully addressed that problem, but there has been no indication that they will lead to a joint policy on income taxes and benefits, even though the overlapping effects of those two systems have been the subject of critical comment for years (see Tony Atkinson's analysis in chapter 4). Meanwhile, a major overhaul of the DHSS contribution to housing support has been launched within a couple of years of the implementation of the last set of changes; yet on neither occasion were arrangements made to consider what the government's financial role should be in the various sectors of the market.

One of the reasons for the failure of governments to develop coherent social policies is the immediacy of tasks within each programme compartment. With the departure of the Central Policy Review Staff there is now no public institution where medium term cross-departmental thinking can even be attempted. Hence the importance of the kind of policy research and development sometimes referred to as 'strategic' - longer-term and less obviously practical than the day-to-day monitoring of departmental activities, but more practical than an examination of the entrails of social relationships. Leeds Castle was one of the rare occasions when policy managers were brought into direct contact with that kind of research and analysis.

Priority issues

Here is one person's view of some of the challenges facing social policy over the next ten years.

The problem of **unemployment** was the spectre at the Leeds Castle feast. The agenda was structured to take a

DHSS's eye view of social policy and a direct analysis of unemployment was not included; but there was discussion of its importance to the policy fields which were explicitly under consideration. Not that we got very far. Lack of work is a social problem in its own right which today is at least as serious as the giants of want, ignorance, squalor and disease which were directly addressed by the welfare state. Current social programmes are partly able to ameliorate some of the consequences of unemployment, but the failure to deal with the problem itself is far more important than any of the short-comings of the public sector services which it is now fashionable to criticise. It is, of course, an organic problem which cannot be dealt with simply by providing a public service like the NHS - its origins lie in demographic and social changes as well as in technological development, international trade and economic management; while the expense is largely in the DHSS's budget, several other departments share responsibility for the various tasks which affect the prospects for employment - perhaps no one department bears a sufficient overall responsibility. It was clear, however, that the prognosis for unemployment was of considerable importance for the arithmetical constraints on social policy which underlay much of the discussion of individual programmes. The reduction in social security and other unemployment-related expenditure that would result from a solution to this problem, and the increase in tax revenue, would transform the budgetary picture and enable social policy planning to take place with far more room for manoeuvre.

Restraint of public expenditure is one of the key elements in the strategy by which it is said that the unemployment problem should be tackled. To people uninitiated to these mysteries, it seems a strange way for a government to enhance economic activity by running down its own considerable contribution to that activity; and odd to stimulate employment by laying off its own staff. The strategy requires confidence that the money spent on private transactions instead of through taxes would have a greater employment-boosting effect - a confidence that does not yet appear to have been vindicated. The aggregates of productivity, public expenditure, domestic product and so on, while convenient statistical indicators for certain purposes, are not necessarily the most appropriate way of measuring the impact of economic change on individual people and families. It is common for the need to restrict public expenditure in order to reduce the burden of taxation to be discussed as though the nation as a whole would thereby be saved money. In practice, of course, certain people will be directly worse off as a result of these changes, and others will be directly better off. It is therefore necessary to examine the distributive impact of economic and fiscal policies before it is possible to take any view as to whether they will improve the overall welfare of the nation - bearing in mind that the value of an extra pound must be considerably higher for a poor family than for a rich one.

One part of the attack on unemployment, with much wider implications, will therefore have to be a **policy for incomes.** This would involve much more than the arrangements for controlling the rise of earnings which were known as 'incomes policy' in the 1970s. It requires an empirical analysis of why certain types of task, and certain types of people, are well or poorly rewarded; simple perfect-market theories of supply and demand fail to explain the disparities between groups which appear to be governed by social and political relationships. This analysis could lead in the long run to an earnings structure that was more equitable and which stimulated more effort at the same time.

But an incomes policy would also consider the interactions between earnings, taxes and benefits, and between incomes and needs, in a way which cannot be attempted while each government department reviews its own activities without reference to the others. The possibility of the integrated administration of a unified tax/benefit system has been much discussed recently; some progress on administration is certainly to be expected, but integration of tax and benefit policies is the first priority.

There could be no clearer illustration of the confusion between alternative policy instruments than the currently wide-held belief that tax allowances add to incentives, reduce taxation and should be increased, while child benefits, which achieve the same objectives rather* more efficiently, are thought to be wasteful public expenditure and should be cut. It is becoming increasingly clear that while the most common problems of poverty are to be found among the elderly, the most serious cases are among families with children and the number of these cases has been increasing rapidly in recent years. Bob Pinker (chapter 3) adds his voice to those who have called for a **family policy.** While it is probably overambitious to expect a unified policy for so vague an entity as the family, covering so wide a range of economic and social activities, it is not too much to demand explicit consideration of families with children in all areas of public responsibility. All the main social policy headings are involved. While direct aid to families through social work and other personal social services is an essential last line of defence, it would be far better to solve the problems of unemployment, low pay, poor housing, urban decay and so on, rather than rely on personal services to deal with the stress caused by those problems to individuals.

The outstanding problem for social policy concerning the elderly may not be their pensions, so much as arrangements for their care. The steady increase in the numbers of **very elderly** people in the population is one of the factors which leads to the expected pressure on existing budgets, because such people make much more use of health and personal social services than others, as well as drawing pensions for a longer period than was common previously. But the need of many very elderly people for support and care is known to impose responsibilities on relatives and neighbours, most often on daughters, which are strenuous and may be particularly burdensome in an era when the majority of women are winning some emancipation from compulsory domestic   duties (see Alan Walker's discussion in chapter 7).   There was wide agreement at Leeds Castle about the seriousness of this issue - so much so that an enthusiastic academic commented at the end of the seminar that it looked as though any new money available might be committed to this field. He had to be reminded that less than 48 hours previously it had been rather clear that there was no new money likely to become available in the foreseeable future!

Even with unlimited money, however, it would have been by no means certain that the answer would have been simply for the state to take responsibility for elderly people. The needs of the elderly are various, and the relationships between them and their families vary too. Demographic change is leading to a social change, particularly affecting people in middle age. Public services have a role in moderating this change, and in influencing the allocation of the costs of care of the elderly between close relatives and other members of society. Defining this role may be the most important policy issue in the coming decade.

The capacity of health services and the personal social services to cope with this and other challenges may depend largely on their **management and efficiency**. Whatever the theoretical arguments, it is said that in practice our health service is one of the most efficient in the world in delivering high outputs at low cost. But like economic growth, efficiency is one of those things in which one can always aim for improvement, and in the absence of competitive markets or of easily measurable outputs, much reliance has to be placed on maintaining or improving efficiency and (to use a more positive term) effectiveness through vigorous management. This consists as much of increased output at fixed costs as of reducing costs for a given level of services, and the theme of Alan Maynard's analysis of health policy (chapter 5) might just as well have been applied to several public services.

Both those who aim to reduce public expenditure and those who hope to improve social services agree on the need for efficiency. However before too much comfort is drawn from this rare bipartisan accord, it has to be pointed out that the same improvements in efficiency cannot aid both a reduction in public expenditure, and improvements in service provision. There is a whole chain of 'who gains?' questions about the distribution of the yield of increased efficiency which have to be answered before its value can be assessed. Suppose, for example, the organiser of a home help service were to discover a way of rescheduling the workload so that ten elderly people could be helped where nine could be covered before. The organiser would expect to be able to add to the number of elderly people receiving home helps. However there might be other claims on the resources liberated by the improvement in efficiency: day care services for the elderly, or, perhaps, support for the parents of mentally handicapped children; or outside the social services department altogether, the same money might be spent on housing provision or, more likely, be returned to the tax payer. Clearly the gain from better productivity can fall anywhere. Where it falls is a matter of some importance, not least to the motivation of those who are directly involved in the productivity change. The manager and staff will have a strong motivation if they can see that improved output will directly help their own clients; they will be less eager if the only change is a reduction in their budget and a redundancy. The low morale in many areas of public employment may well be associated with the unceasing pressure to make savings and eliminate 'waste'; this pressure is easily interpreted as a criticism of the value of the service being provided. More widely, employees of social services required to cut down rather than to improve are unlikely to feel that social policy is being formulated in the interests of claimants, patients and clients. They are, therefore, less likely to participate enthusiastically in a drive for efficiency than they would if they perceived the motive to lie closer to the long-run objectives of their activity.

Morale may be particularly low among the employees of **local government,** which has generally been responsible for about a third of public spending on social programmes, but which has been especially affected by the squeeze. The efficiency and effectiveness of local government as an executive agency for social policy were frequently raised during the discussions at Leeds Castle, although none of the papers reproduced here directly addressed this issue. No representatives of local government had been invited to the seminar, and the organisers were criticised on this score. Some of the exchanges argued at an elementary level whether local authorities were good or bad. At a rather more analytical level, it was suggested that the standard of management in local authorities was highly variable: that some of them compared favourably with the very best in other fields, while others were of a worrying if not scandalous standard. Variation between local authorities is, indeed, one of the features of this approach to service delivery which is at once a strength and a weakness.

The quality of local government management may be an important issue, but it would be a mistake to see these discussions in terms of a slanging match between those for and against. Many observers who admire the roles played by local authorities express considerable concern about their ability to continue to fulfil them. Central and local government are now in a state of almost-formal war on the issues of rate-capping and abolition of the big-city authorities. Never mind who started it, there is a practical doubt, among those concerned with social policy, whether they can look to councils to deliver viable services during the conflict. Other important changes have been observed in local government in recent years. Where radical majorities of Left or Right have taken power, the quality and effectiveness of services have sometimes been subordinated to ideology. The relationship between elected members and officials has been changing, and this has led to new roles for professionals. You do not need to have taken sides about the desirability of each of these changes to lack confidence in the ability of local government to execute social policy during a period of flux. What is not yet clear is whether this upheaval will eventually lead to local services which are more effective and more responsive to need, or whether alternative means of delivering social services will be required.

When Michael O'Higgins was introducing his analysis of the prospects for public expenditure in the first session of the Leeds Castle seminar, he characterised social policy planning in the last decade in terms of a change from PPBS to PSBR. Confidence - perhaps excessive confidence - in the possibility of planning effective policy has given way to anxiety - perhaps also excessive - about the public accounts. There have been financial and political reasons for this change. But the strain on the economy has brought with it increasing social problems. There needs to be a fuller and deeper debate both about the concept of welfare and about the practical options; an analysis of the aims and resources for the country's social policy in the years ahead. It is hoped that these papers will widen the discussion among all concerned with social welfare in Britain and help to bring about further changes in the approach to social policy. The aim should be to programme all the resources available to meet growing needs more effectively.

References
H.M. Treasury (1984), The Next Ten Years: public expenditure and taxation into the 1990s, Cmnd 9189, HMSO.
Klein, R. and O'Higgins, M. (eds) (1985), The Future of Welfare, Basil Blackwell.
O'Higgins, M. and Patterson, A. (1985), 'The Prospects for Public Expenditure: A Disaggregate Analysis', in R. Klein and M. O'Higgins (1985).

1 Social policy needs and resources: the prospects for the 1990s *

MICHAEL O'HIGGINS

Introduction
For better or worse, the central issue in any debate about needs and resources for social policy in the 1990s is the level of public expenditure which will be available for social welfare, the services which this can purchase and the extent to which these services will be more or less adequate in meeting social needs than those we have at present. After a brief discussion of a wider framework within which this debate might ideally take place, this chapter returns to the narrower discussion of public expenditure and social services.

After summarising the results of some previous work projecting programme expenditure on different economic scenarios but using baseline assumptions about public policies, the chapter describes, quantifies and assesses the implications of three different stances on the overall level and particular details of programme expenditure. This examination provides the basis for an assessment of the extent to which resources are available either for the maintenance of current programmes or for new initiatives, and of the consequences for social policy planning.

---

* This chapter draws upon and extends the arguments of O'Higgins and Patterson (1985). Although elements of that paper are summarised here, its arguments are not repeated in detail. The chapter is the product of collaborative research with Alan Patterson. The research on which it is based was funded by the Economic and Social Research Council and the Joseph Rowntree Memorial Trust. It was revised while I was a Visiting Scholar in the Department of Sociology at Harvard University; I am grateful for their hospitality.

Assessing needs and resources in social policy

In a rational planner's ideal world, an assessment of needs and resources for a decade ahead would doubtless consist of a listing and quantification of needs, a costing of the services required to meet them and a discussion of the various resources from which these services might be financed or provided. In reality neither needs nor resources can be treated in such a comprehensive social audit.

Despite the interest aroused by Bradshaw's seminal article (1972) and work such as Culyer (1976), the concept of need in social policy remains elusive. Therefore, rather than seeking to quantify either levels of social need or of the need for social services (which two may not be the same), a second-best option would be to assess the impact of socio-economic changes on relative need. Thus, we might identify changes in the economic environment, demographic changes and changes in programme maturity, or there may be policy or technology changes which, with the benefit of increased knowledge, we believe will allow us to meet need better.

Such a listing is an indication of how an attempt, on a wide canvas, to project changing social need, or the changes in the need for resources, might proceed - it is also an indication of how far we are from such an attempt.

Any such comprehensive accounting would be implausible:

- because we often do not define the levels of service which we are willing - or will undertake - to provide in particular situations of need (for example kidney disease, social care);
- because we do not know the connections between wider social changes and particular manifestations of need (for examples the recent unexplained rises in the numbers receiving attendance allowance and other disability benefits; the connection between unemployment levels and the numbers receiving invalidity benefit); and
- because we do not understand the relationship between changing levels of social expenditure and programme effectiveness (for example lack of information about the impact on the level or quality of output of education or social service provision, of wide spending variations between the 108 local authority providers of these services in England).

Similar difficulties exist on the resources side. A full assessment of social resources would:

- detail the time, skills, and finances available throughout the community - public and private, voluntary and statutory, profit and non-profit;
- chart the ways in which their levels and availability might be affected by policy options such as tax relief, salary levels, cash benefits and regulatory strategies; and
- discuss the benefits and disadvantages of the alternative packages in which the various resource elements might be combined.

In practice, we tend to focus on public expenditure, discuss consumer charges as marginal sidelines and make benign references to the voluntary sector in a tone and volume which varies with the political flavour of the month.

Comprehensive assessments of prospects and options in particular policy areas may belie these sweeping generalisations. It remains, nonetheless, difficult to envisage a full-scale social audit of needs and resources, not just because of the technical limitations noted above, nor because of the size of the task, but also because such an exercise is not a matter of economic arithmetic - or even policy-analysis algebra - but of political preferences, judgement and decisions. This political context means there are no technically 'correct' levels of service, and may even dictate a preference for a relatively less explicit presentation of chosen service levels (in order to mask reductions).

All of this is fairly obvious and does not need elaboration here. Its particular relevance in this context is twofold:

- first, it is a reminder that a series of detailed micro-analyses of social need, however useful as longer-term education, may have little policy impact if their cost implications are inconsistent with political preferences about the level of public expenditure, however arbitrary this chosen level may be;
- second, it is a justification for the main sections of this chapter which take a narrow focus on public expenditure prospects and locate the debate about the resources available for social policy within a discussion of the implications of three alternative strategies on public expenditure.

Public expenditure prospects: the debate
The decision by the Treasury and Civil Service Select Committee to investigate the longer-term prospects for public spending is but the latest contribution to the growing debate on this issue. One major reason for the surge of interest in this topic is the realisation that despite a Conservative government with a strong commitment, at least initially, to cuts, real public spending has continued to rise in recent years. Table 1.1 shows that spending on public sector programmes has risen by an average of around $1\frac{1}{2}$ percent annually since Mrs Thatcher took office. These increases were initially accompanied by rises in the ratio of programme expenditure, and of total public expenditure to GDP, but the resumption of economic growth since 1981/82 has brought slight reductions in these ratios.

However, although the government has failed to cut public spending it has succeeded in changing the nature of the debate: instead of arguments about new initiatives in spending, discussion now focusses on whether we can afford both to maintain the quality and range of existing services and to meet the costs of demographic pressures and the maturing of past commitments.

The Treasury's official contribution to this debate was the Green Paper, The Next Ten Years: Public Expenditure and Taxation into the 1990s (Cmnd. 9189). The Green Paper assumes that public expenditure will be kept constant in real terms until 1988/89 and then examines the effect on the tax burden of two different public expenditure assumptions for the five years thereafter: unchanged real spending and spending growth of 1 per cent annually. On the economic growth assumption which the Green Paper adopts ($2\frac{1}{4}$ per cent growth annually until 1988/89, $1\frac{1}{2}$ per cent or 2 per cent thereafter) these levels of public expenditure would lead to a tax burden in 1993/94 which would be below 1978/79 levels. The Green Paper is, in other words, primarily concerned with how to achieve aggregate levels of public expenditure which would allow a reduction in the overall level of personal taxation. In this respect, it is a further stage of the government's argument that 'finance must determine expenditure, not expenditure finance'.

As a contribution to debate, the Green Paper has been criticised for its failure to examine a range of scenarios, for not setting out a broad range of options for spending changes and for the absence of any serious treatment of the scope for

Table 1.1 Expenditure by programme as a percentage of total programmes expenditure

Percentages

Year	1976/77	1978/79	1980/81	1982/83	1983/84
1 Defence	11.3	11.4	12.0	12.7	12.9
2 Overseas aid	1.9	2.8	1.7	1.9	1.9
3 Agriculture etc.	1.8	1.2	1.5	1.6	1.7
4 Trade, industry, energy and employment	5.7	6.1	5.5	5.1	5.0
5 Arts etc.	0.5	0.5	0.5	0.5	0.5
6 Transport	4.3	4.1	4.3	3.9	3.8
7 Housing	7.0	5.4	4.8	2.3	2.3
8 Other env. services	3.8	3.4	3.3	3.1	3.1
9 Law, order etc	3.1	3.1	3.4	3.7	3.9
10 Education & science	12.8	11.8	11.7	11.1	11.0
11 Health & PSS	10.9	11.3	12.2	12.1	12.1
12 Social security	21.2	25.0	25.2	28.5	29.0
13 & 14 Other public & common services	2.6	2.8	2.7	2.8	2.2
15 Scotland	5.6	5.7	5.8	5.5	5.6
16 Wales	2.3	2.3	2.3	2.1	2.1
17 N. Ireland	3.0	3.2	3.1	3.1	3.1
Programmes expend. (£m)	54,649	65,752	93,028	113,865	121,728
Index of expenditure on programmes in constant prices	-	100.0	102.0	106.6	108.0

Source: The Government's Expenditure Plans, 1984-85 to 1986-87, Cmnd. 9143, (HMSO), February 1984 and equivalent previous plans.

productivity gains in the public sector (Public Money, June 1984).

As a contribution to either policy debate or policy planning the Green Paper has a further major deficiency. Although it discusses the pressures for spending increases on particular programmes, it rarely quantifies or costs these pressures, and therefore provides no opportunity for an assessment of the aggregate cost or spending impact of individual spending programme changes. There is no indication of whether the immediate policy target of unchanged real spending is compatible with the pressure of particular programmes and no discussion of which programmes would or could be cut, and by how much, if such cuts proved necessary in order to attain the target. We are told the answer to the arithmetic of public expenditure, but given no clues as to how the answer is reached, how the arithmetic adds up.

In contrast to this aggregate-focussed approach, O'Higgins and Patterson (1985) presented a disaggregate model of public expenditure projection, which can examine the effect on the aggregate level of spending, of a wide range of assumptions about the cost pressures on particular spending programmes. The next section very briefly describes this model and summarises the results of a series of 'baseline policies' projections.

Public expenditure prospects: baseline policies

The projection model allows separate assumptions to be made in each of the 17 public expenditure programmes about: numbers employed; real wage rates; the relative price effect on and the volume of provision of other current expenditure (excluding social security transfers); and the relative price effect on and volume of capital expenditure. It also allows assumptions about changes in the real values of child benefit and retirement benefit and in the real values and number of recipients of other (non-employment) benefits. Changes in the numbers receiving child benefit and retirement pensions are endogenously calculated using the OPCS 1981 principal population projections; changes in the level of unemployment may be input directly, or (given assumptions about the rates of growth of GDP and productivity) may be calculated endogenously as the sum of the effects of changes in the size of the labour force and the GDP/productivity growth differential. The effects on social security spending are then produced using the Green Paper assumption that a variation of

100,000 in unemployment changes costs by £185 million. Specified changes in the level of efficiency of non-transfer expenditure may also be input.

The model operates in constant (1983/84) prices, allows assumptions to be varied in different years and focusses on total programme expenditure, rather than total public expenditure. This last feature reflects both the fact that the Public Expenditure White Paper definition of public expenditure includes as negative expenditure asset sales, which are essentially a form of financing, and the judgement that net debt interest (the other major component of the difference between public and programme expenditure) is spending which is largely outside the immediate control of government. Programme expenditure, therefore, seems preferable both as a policy focus and as a planning tool.

Baseline projections are simply calculations which measure the effects on spending of continuing over a number of years the programmes and standards required by current legislation. Since, as noted earlier, such standards are rarely specifically defined, some assumptions about political responses to factors such as demographic change are required.

The baseline projections of UK public spending nonetheless operate within assumptions which broadly reflect the apparent policies of the government with respect to particular programmes. For example, social security benefits are price-protected, health and social service spending is assumed to rise to match demographic changes, the NATO commitment to three per cent real growth in defence spending is allowed for and most public sector pay costs (defence and law and order excepted) are assumed to increase less rapidly than pay in the private sector. (See O'Higgins and Patterson, 1985, Tables 2 and 3 for full details.)

The baseline projections were calculated for six different economic scenarios in which annual GDP growth varied from 1 per cent to 3 per cent, whilst the growth of productivity per employee was between 1.5 and 2.2 per cent.

On all of the economic scenarios the results suggested that public spending would rise in real terms over the next decade. Depending upon the scenario the magnitude of the rise ranged from 6 per cent to 9 cent by 1988/89 and 11 per cent to 19 per cent by 1993/94. The ratio of programme expenditure to GDP, which was 40 per cent in 1983/84, had a range of 37 per cent to 40.5 per cent in 1988/89 and 34 per cent to 41 per cent by 1993/94. On assumptions designed to reflect current government policies - assumptions which many would, therefore, find restrictive - the central prospects for public expenditure suggest slow real growth, along with a decline in the share of GDP consumed. This suggests that it is unlikely that the Green Paper's stated objective of no real growth of public spending in the period up to 1988/89 can be met on current spending programme policies. It also suggests that this need not be a matter of undue concern for the government since with reasonable levels of economic growth, such increases in public spending are consistent with its having a declining share of national income.

O'Higgins and Patterson also examined the implications for the programme total of an assumption that given levels of programme outputs could be achieved with a 1 per cent annual reduction in the volume (and, therefore, cost) of inputs (excluding social security transfers) due to productivity and efficiency improvements. This proved to have a fairly large effect. Baseline spending increases of more than 5 per cent and 10 per cent over a five and ten year period, respectively, are reduced to 2 per cent and 4 per cent if these 'efficiency gains' are assumed.*

Having summarised the major features of a set of baseline - i.e. unchanged policies - projections it is now appropriate to examine the implications of alternative policy stances. This also allows the remedying of one inherent weakness of baseline projections: they may accurately show that the implications of the sum of individual policies is inconsistent with aggregate policy targets (CBO, 1982) - but it is not necessarily the case that the aggregate policy target will be relaxed in order to accommodate the projected disaggregate overspends. The next section of this paper presents analyses which examine the implications of assuming adherence to the target of no real growth in public expenditure, as well as of two other spending strategies.

Public expenditure prospects: three spending options
Whilst O'Higgins and Patterson (1985) assumed broadly constant baseline policies and examined their implications in

---

* This finding is consistent with the emphasis which Judge and Knapp (1985) place upon the improvement of efficiency as a means of increasing the volume of welfare outputs.

different economic scenarios, this section examines the effect of three different approaches to public spending within a common set of assumptions about economic growth (since to have attempted multiple political and economic assumptions simultaneously would have rendered unmanageable the presentation of the results). The analyses, therefore, assume 2 per cent annual growth in GDP over the next decade. The associated central assumptions about annual real earnings growth is 1.5 per cent, with unemployment constant at around 11 per cent. The sensitivity of these latter assumptions is tested by alternative assumptions of annual real earnings growth of 1.25 and 1.75 per cent with associated changes of -0.4 and 0.4 percentage points, respectively, in the rate of unemployment. (This places the unemployment rate in the range 7 per cent to 15 per cent in 1994/95.)

Given these economic assumptions, three spending scenarios, which for convenience are labelled **constant, constrained** and **carry-on** are created. The **constant** scenario assumes that the aggregate policy target of no real growth in public expenditure will be enforced until 1988/89 and may be enforced thereafter. This implies tight control of individual spending elements and a willingness to implement significant cuts in some programmes if this is necessary in order to contain overall spending.

By contrast, the **carry-on** scenario assumes that with economic growth extra resources will be devoted to service improvements and that benefit levels will be increased in line with real growth in earnings.

In between these two is the **constrained** position where, although there is no prohibition on spending growth, there is no expectation that service quality or benefit levels in general will increase in line with national income. Some services or benefits may be expected to fare better than others in the allocation of such extra funds as are made available.

Table 1.2 sets out the main features of a simple interpretation of the policies generated by each of these strategies. It will be seen that certain programmes are assumed to be treated similarly under each spending strategy. For example, defence and law and order real pay levels are always assumed to increase at the same rate as private sector pay; volume spending on defence in each case reflects the NATO commitment followed by continued slight growth; each assumes the volume of education expenditure will decline until 1988/89 in response to demographic shifts. (It may also be noted that all the analyses assume that health and social service spending increases to match demographic pressure in addition to the specific changes noted in Table 1.2; the numbers receiving child benefit and retirement pension change with the demographic structure and the numbers receiving unemployment benefits with the unemployment rate.) These assumptions which are common to each programme reduce the extent to which the three scenarios represent clearly separate political outlooks; however, since certain political threads appear likely to remain common until at least 1987/88 this loss is compensated by a gain in realism. The differences in the three scenarios may then perhaps be seen as reflecting different responses to pressures on the remainder of public expenditure rather than as wholly distinct political strategies.

The scenarios differ in respect of their assumptions about changes in the values of social security benefits, the numbers employed (as a measure of the volume of care) in the health and personal social services, and both the real wages and the volume of capital and non-pay current expenditure throughout public sector programmes.

The constant scenario assumes no increases in the value of any social security benefits or in public sector pay rates (defence and law and order excepted) throughout a period when private sector earnings are increasing by around 1.5 per cent annually. It also assumes a 1 per cent annual decline in the numbers working in the health and social services over the next few years (though the growth allowed to meet demographic pressure would offset much of this). No increases in the volume of other public sector provision are allowed. The constant scenario, in other words, allows only for the commitments on defence and law and order, and effectively cancels the protection from demographic pressure of the health and social services.

In the carry-on scenario all social security benefits and public sector pay rates increase in line with private sector earnings. Health and social services staff numbers and public sector volume provision increase only slightly less rapidly, at 1 per cent annually. Therefore, while this scenario would reduce the pressure on public services, and their clients and employees, it does not represent a return to halcyon days.

The constrained scenario offers more modest growth in health and social service staffing and public sector volume provision, and allows pensions and public sector pay to rise at two-thirds the rate of private sector earnings. The real value

Table 1.2 Projecting public expenditure: assumptions under three spending scenarios

Real annual % change from 1983/84 level

	SCENARIO		
	Constant	Constrained	Carry On
GDP	2	2	2
Private sector earnings	1.5 (±0.25)	1.5 (±0.25)	1.5 (±0.25)
Unemployment rate	0 (±0.4)	0 (±0.4)	0 (±0.4)
SOCIAL SECURITY			
Child Benefit - value	0	0.5 (±0.1)	1.5 (±0.25)
Retirement Pension - value	0	1.0 (±0.2)	1.5 (±0.25)
Unemployment Benefits - Value	0	0.5 (±0.1)	1.5 (±0.25)
Other Benefits - value	0	0.5 (±0.1)	1.5 (±0.25)
Other Benefits - volume	0	0	0
DEFENCE			
Number employed	0	0	0
Real pay rates	1.5 (±0.25)	1.5 (±0.25)	1.5 (±0.25)
RPE - other current spending			
(to 1987/88)	2	2	2
(after 1987/88)	1.5	1.5	1.5
Volume other current spending			
(to 1985/86)	3	3	3
(after 1985/86)	1.5	1.5	1.5
Volume of capital spending			
(to 1985/86)	3	3	3
(after 1985/86)	1	1	1
LAW AND ORDER			
Number employed			
(to 1987/88)	1	1	1
(after 1987/88)	0	0	0
Real pay rates	1.5 (±0.25)	1.5 (±0.25)	1.5 (±0.25)
Volume other current spending	1	1	1
HEALTH AND SOCIAL SERVICES			
Number employed			
(to 1987/88)	-1	0.5	1
(after 1987/88)	0	0.5	1
RPE - other current spending	0.5	0.5	0.5
RPE - capital spending	0.5	0.5	0.5

In addition, increases to match demographic pressures are assumed.

Table 1.2 (Cont'd)

Real annual % change from 1983/84 level

		SCENARIO	
	Constant	Constrained	Carry On
EDUCATION			
Volume - other current spending			
(to 1988/89)	-0.5	-0.5	-0.5
(after 1988/89)	0	0	0
Volume - capital spending			
(to 1988/89)	-2.0	-2.0	-2.0
(after 1988/89)	0	0	0
ALL OTHER PROGRAMME ELEMENTS			
Number employed			
(to 1987/88)	-1	-1	-1
(after 1987/88)	0	0	0
Real pay rates	0	0 (±0.2)	1.5 (±0.25)
RPE - other current spending	0	0	0
Volume of other current spending	0	0.5	1
RPE - capital spending	0	0	0
Volume of capital spending	0	0.5	1

Notes

1. Annual increases of 1 per cent until 1986/87 in the volume of other current expenditure on Northern Ireland, and of 9 percent to 1984/85 in the volume of other current expenditure and 50 per cent to 1984/85 in the volume of capital expenditure on the other public and common services are, following the 1984 public expenditure White Paper plans, assumed in each scenario. An annual decrease of 5 per cent until 1986/87 in the volume of other current expenditure on the trade and industry programme is also assumed.
2. The number (volume) of recipients of child benefit and retirement pensions is assumed to change in line with the demographic changes forecast for the relevant age groups. Similarly, health and social service spending is assumed to rise in line with demographic pressure, in addition to the specific changes noted in the table.
3. The RPE is the relative price effect.
4. As noted in the text, the central assumption about private sector annual real earnings growth is 1.5 per cent, with unemployment constant at 11 per cent. The sensitivity of these assumptions is tested by alternatives which allow annual real earnings growth to be 0.25 per cent higher and lower, with unemployment 0.4 percentage points higher and lower, respectively, and corresponding adjustments to the value of public sector pay rates and social security benefits. The bracketed elements in the table indicate the variables to which these sensitivity assumptions were applied.

of other social security benefits is increased less rapidly, by 0.5 per cent annually.

Results

The results of the analysis are set out in Table 1.3 in the form of an index of real total programme expenditures and the ratio of programme expenditures to GDP.

On the central assumptions about wage growth and unemployment rates, the data suggest that even on the constant scenario programme expenditure would grow by a total of $2\frac{1}{2}$ per cent by 1988/89 and almost 7 per cent by the middle of the 1990s. This rise would be accompanied by an annual fall of about half a percentage point in the programme expenditure/GDP ratio, leaving it around $34\frac{1}{2}$ by 1994/95.

The expenditure index grows rather more rapidly on the constrained scenario, being 6 per cent greater by 1988/89 and more than 15 per cent greater by 1994/95. These rises are still accompanied by a decline in the programme expenditure/GDP ratio, though of a lesser order than in the constant scenario.

In the carry-on scenario programme expenditure rises by more than 9 per cent in real terms by 1988/89 and by well over 20 per cent by the middle of the next decade. The programme expenditure/GDP ratio, on the central assumptions, declines slightly to just under 40 per cent.

The effects of the two alternative assumptions about wage rate rises and unemployment levels are symmetrical about the central assumptions so their impact can be discussed with reference only to the higher wage and unemployment assumption. In the period up to 1988/89, this increases the programme expenditure index by between 1 and 2 per cent of the various scenarios, the rise being greatest in the carry-on scenario. By 1994/95, the effect of this assumption is to add an additional 2 percentage points to the programme expenditure index on the constant scenario and over 4 percentage points on the carry-on scenario. This latter figure is equivalent to about £5 billion at 1983/84 prices.

Whilst the results are sensitive to the wage and unemployment assumption, they are clearly affected to a much greater extent by the choice of scenario. Although the differences between the assumptions governing each scenario appear to be slight, they make a difference, on the central assumptions, of over £8 billion by 1988/89 between the

Table 1.3 Projecting public expenditure - results of three spending scenarios

		SCENARIO		
		Constant	Constrained	Carry On
CENTRAL ASSUMPTIONS				
1988/89	I	102.50	106.23	109.28
	R(%)	37.16	38.51	39.62
1994/95	I	106.75	115.11	122.67
	R(%)	34.37	37.06	39.49
HIGHER WAGE/UNEMPLOYMENT ASSUMPTIONS				
1988/89	I	103.33	107.54	110.88
	R(%)	37.46	38.99	40.20
1994/95	I	108.77	118.35	126.83
	R(%)	35.02	38.10	40.83
LOWER WAGE/UNEMPLOYMENT ASSUMPTIONS				
1988/89	I	101.56	104.81	107.59
	R(%)	36.82	38.00	39.01
1994/95	I	104.83	112.03	118.79
	R(%)	33.75	36.07	38.24

1983/84 Programme Expenditure Index (I) = 100.00
1983/84 Programme Expenditure/GDP (R) = 40.03%

constant and the carry-on scenario; by 1994/95 this difference is almost £20 billion. The different scenarios also significantly affect the growth of expenditure on some of the social services programmes, as Table 1.4 shows. By 1988/89, for example, expenditure on the health and personal social services programme is 18 per cent greater in real terms under the carry-on scenario, 12 per cent greater under the contrained scenario but less than 3 per cent greater under the constant scenario. Similarly, while social security expenditure rises by more than 8 per cent on the carry-on scenario, it is basically flat on the constant scenario. Therefore, relatively slight annual differences in the cost of particular elements of programme expenditure can make significant differences to the aggregate level of expenditure after a few years.

The need for spending cuts?
Table 1.3 demonstrated that even with the quite restrictive assumptions underpinning the constant scenario, real levels of public expenditure continued to rise, so that they were $2\frac{1}{2}$ per cent higher by 1988/89 and almost 7 per cent higher by 1994/95. The government's declared commitment is to hold public expenditure constant until 1988/89 and the Green Paper envisaged either continued constancy or 1 per cent annual growth thereafter. The results of the constant scenario would suggest that whilst holding public expenditure growth to 1 per cent annually may be feasible - on very restrictive assumptions - it cannot be kept constant without explicit cuts in the levels of some services. The government has as yet given no indication of where such cuts might take place, if they are to be enforced. It is in this sense that the aggregate policy target of the Green Paper is inconsistent with the currently declared set of particular programme policies.

In order to give some indication of the nature of the policy changes which might be necessary if the government were to hold to its commitment, Table 1.5 sets out the impact of a range of possible cuts. It focusses in particular on a number of social security benefits, not least because of the current set of Social Security Reviews. Obviously this listing is not an agenda, and many other combinations would be possible. The list is merely intended to indicate the magnitude of the changes which might be necessary.

The table indicates that a once and for all cut of 10 per cent in the real value of unemployment benefits would eliminate less than one fifth of the 2.5 per cent expenditure

Table 1.4 Impact of scenarios on particular programmes (using central assumptions)

Programme		Constant	SCENARIO Con-strained	Carry on
Social security				
1983/4	P	29.0	29.0	29.0
1988/9	N	100.7	104.5	108.5
	P	28.5	28.5	28.8
1994/5	N	101.5	110.0	119.7
	P	27.6	27.7	28.3
Health and personal social services				
1983/4	P	12.1	12.1	12.1
1988/9	N	102.7	112.2	118.4
	P	12.1	12.7	13.1
1994/5	N	105.9	125.5	141.4
	P	12.0	13.2	13.9
Education				
1983/4	P	11.0	11.0	11.0
1988/9	N	94.8	97.8	99.3
	P	10.2	10.1	10.0
1994/5	N	94.8	101.5	105.1
	P	9.7	9.7	9.4
Housing				
1983/4	P	2.3	2.3	2.3
1988/9	N	99.8	102.6	105.3
	P	2.2	2.2	2.2
1994/5	N	99.8	106.0	112.3
	P	2.1	2.1	2.1
Defence				
1983/4	P	12.9	12.9	12.9
1988/9	N	120.9	120.9	120.9
	P	15.2	14.7	14.3
1994/5	N	144.4	144.4	144.4
	P	17.5	16.2	15.2
Law and order				
1983/4	P	3.9	3.9	3.9
1988/9	N	114.1	114.3	114.4
	P	4.3	4.1	4.0
1994/5	N	129.4	129.7	130.0
	P	4.7	4.3	4.1

N = Specific programme expenditure index (1983/4=100)
P = Specific programme expenditure as a % of total programme spending.

Table 1.5 Impact of selected cuts on spending on the constant scenario

		Programme Expenditure Index	
Option		1988/89	1994/95
	Constant Scenario - Central Assumptions	102.50	106.75
A.	10% cut in value of unemployment related benefits in 1984/85	102.05	106.30
B.	50% cut in value of child benefit in 1984/85	100.92	105.05
C.	10% annual cut in value of unemployment related benefits	100.65	103.65
D.	10% annual cut in the value of retirement pensions	97.43	98.26
E.	10% annual cut in real public sector wage rates (excluding defence and law & order)	92.96	90.68

Change required to maintain expenditure index equal to 100 in 1988/89:

A.	Unemployment related benefits	55%	cut in 1984/85
B.	Child benefit	79%	cut in 1984/85
C.	Unemployment related benefits	13.5%	annual cut
D.	Retirement pensions	4.9%	annual cut
E.	Real public sector wage rates (excluding defence and law and order)	2.6%	annual cut
F.	Value of all social security benefits	2.1%	annual cut
G.	Value of all social security benefits and real public sector wage rates (excluding defence and law and order)	1.1%-1.2%	annual cut

excess which the constant scenario predicts for 1988/89. A much larger cut of 50 per cent in child benefit eliminates about three fifths of this 'excess'. The table also indicates that a 10 per cent cut each year in the real value of unemployment benefits would remove most of the excess by 1988/89, whilst a similar annual cut in the value of retirement pensions would remove double the amount required. Finally the table examines the impact of a 10 per cent annual cut in real public sector wage rates, excluding wages in the defence and law and order programmes which, it is assumed, the government is committed to protecting. As might be expected, such a large annual cut in the public sector wage budget would eliminate the over-run four times over.

The exact magnitude of the cuts required under each of these options in order to hold the programme expenditure index at precisely one hundred in 1988/89 - in other words, to fulfil the government's commitment, given the other assumptions in the constant scenario - are given at the bottom of Table 1.5. This demonstrates that if unemployment benefit were to pay for the entire over-run, the required cut would be 55 per cent if it were done once and for all, or $13\frac{1}{2}$ per cent annually if were to take place in sections. Alternatively, child benefit would have to be cut by just about four-fifths, or retirement pensions by around 5 per cent each year. None of these options - apart perhaps from some change in child benefit - appears particularly likely; this is not so obviously the case with the next option, annual cuts of around $2\frac{1}{2}$ per cent in the real pay of the public sector. This would be equivalent to nominal wage rises of about $3\frac{1}{2}$ per cent a year at a time when inflation was 6 per cent. Readers may judge for themselves how likely this is, but it seems clear that if the government does attempt to keep public expenditure constant, public sector pay rates are likely to be a target for some part of the required saving.

It may be argued that small cuts on an 'across-the-board' basis are more likely than large cuts to particular benefits. The final options in Table 1.5, therefore, indicate that if the government sought to keep spending constant by cutting the real value of all social security benefits, annual cuts of about 2.1 per cent would be required, whilst if the savings were to be made by cutting the real value of both social security benefits and public sector wages (excluding defence and law and order), annual reductions of just over 1 per cent would be necessary.

The scope for increased expenditure

The discussion of the results so far has emphasised the extent to which there is likely to be real growth in public expenditure, whatever the scenario. Given the government's policy intentions, this has been interpreted in terms of the difficulty it would pose for the government, and the consequent search for spending cuts which might take place. However, the government's desire to hold spending constant, even if this means service cuts, does not appear to be widely shared by voters. As Peter Taylor-Gooby (1985) has concluded from studies of public attitudes to social welfare, 'support for high spending irrespective of judgements on the state of the economy suggests that people are unlikely to be convinced by arguments that claim that low growth must lead to welfare cutbacks'. Therefore, since the results also indicate clearly that on almost all the scenario outturns the ratio of programme expenditure to GDP will decline, it is worth examining the resources which would be available under each of these scenarios if the policy target were not constant public expenditure but a constant ratio of public expenditure to GDP. Table 1.6 gives the results of such an analysis.

The data in Table 1.6 indicate the amounts of money which would be available in 1988/89 and in 1994/95 for new initiatives, new policy developments, or a more generous meeting of existing needs. Although the data are interpreted here in terms of the scope they allow for increased expenditure, it should be noted that they also measure the amounts which would be available for tax cuts as compared to a situation where the programme expenditure/GDP ratio is maintained. There are obviously areas where tax cuts could be used to further social policy aims.

Two points stand out from the results in the table. First, the level of resources available is surprisingly large: on the constrained scenario, for example, £5 billion are available in 1988/89 and more than £11 billion in 1994/95 on the central assumptions. Obviously, resources are also available in the in-between years, but insofar as they produce spending commitments which continue beyond one year they will reduce what is available thereafter. The second point which emerges from the table is the very great differences in the amounts which would be available on the different scenarios. In 1988/89, the difference between the constant and the carry-on scenarios is more than £8 billion on the central assumptions, and by 1994/95 this difference has grown to £19 billion.

Table 1.6   Scope for expenditure increases assuming a
                     constant programme expenditure/GDP ratio

Wage/Unemployment Rate Assumptions	SCENARIO		
	Constant	Constrained	Carry On
Central			
1988/89	9,636	5,103	1,377
1994/95	21,401	11,232	2,042
Higher			
1988/89	8,629	3,492	-571
1994/95	18,943	6,298	-3,025
Lower			
1988/89	10,778	6,816	3,425
1994/95	23,745	14,973	6,768

Note: The data represent the difference in £ millions 1983/84
        between the outturn programme expenditure GDP ratio on
        the various scenarios and the actual 1983/84 ratio of
        40.03%. Positive figures indicate that the scenario ratio is
        lower than in 1983/84, and may be interpreted as
        measuring the spending - additional to that included in the
        scenario - which would be possible if the ratio were
        restored to its 1983/84 level.

These data give some indication of the orders of
magnitude of the finance which might be available for new
policy initiatives during the early 1990s, and raise the question
of the extent to which the forces of creeping incremental
growth across all programmes need to be resisted if we are to
have the scope for significant policy changes in particular
areas (Klein and O'Higgins, 1985). Even if the constant
scenario is left aside, as being unduly restrictive, the
differences between the constrained and the carry-on
scenarios are sufficiently large to allow major policy develop-

ments. However, the resources available, without increasing the programme expenditure/GDP ratio above its 1983/84 level, if the carry-on scenario were implemented would not so allow.

Conclusions

The analysis has suggested that on each of three different spending scenarios, programme expenditure is likely to rise in real terms over the next decade by amounts which vary between 2½ and 10 per cent by 1988/89 and 6½ and 23 per cent by 1994/95. Almost all these changes would, however, allow the ratio of programme expenditure to GDP to decline. If the government is to maintain its commitment to keeping public expenditure constant until 1988/89, the analysis suggests that clear cuts will be required in some programmes, or in real public sector wages, which may appear to be a more likely target.

The results of the modelling also indicate that if the policy target was simply to maintain programme expenditure at its 1983/84 level relative to GDP, a policy target more in line with the evidence on public attitudes to welfare provisions, this would leave significant scope for extra spending, particularly on the constant and constrained scenarios. However, the extent of this scope is strongly influenced by the degree to which incremental additions are made to the resources available for existing programmes. To the extent that existing priorities are simply continued unaltered, as exemplified by the carry-on scenario, these extra resources are reduced. This suggests that in considering social policy needs and resources over the next decade, two inter-linked questions need to be prominent.

- first, which of the existing services, benefits or policies are priorities for incremental growth when resources are available;
- second, which new initiatives should have priority claims on the resources released by any restraint of incrementalism which is possible?

These two questions are inter-linked not simply in an arithmetic sense but also in a policy planning sense. If it is known that resources which are saved by the exercise of incremental restraint are available for new initiatives, then the likelihood of that restraint is correspondingly greater. Similarly, if the price of incremental growth is explicitly seen to be the reduction of the scope for new initiatives, we may then at least make decisions to support incremental growth explicitly rather than through institutional or policy inertia. Social policy has adapted to surviving within cash limits; the results of this analysis suggest that the challenge for the 1990s may be that of achieving creativity within constraints.

References

Bradshaw, J. (1972), 'A Taxonomy of Social Need', in G. McLachlan (ed), <u>Problems and Progress in Medical Care</u>, Oxford University Press.

CBO (1982), <u>Baseline Budget Projections for Fiscal Years 1983-87</u>, Congressional Budget Office.

Culyer, A.J. (1976), <u>Need and the National Health Service</u>, Martin Robertson.

Judge, K. and Knapp, M. (1985), 'Efficiency in the Production of Welfare: The Public and the Private Sectors Compared', in R.Klein and M.O'Higgins (eds), <u>The Future of Welfare</u>, Basil Blackwell.

Klein, R. and O'Higgins, M. (1985), 'Social Policy After Incrementalism', in R. Klein and M. O'Higgins (eds), <u>The Future of Welfare</u>, Basil Blackwell.

O'Higgins, M. and Patterson, A. (1985), 'The Prospects for Public Expenditure: A Disaggregate Analysis', in R. Klein and M O'Higgins (eds), <u>The Future of Welfare</u>, Basil Blackwell.

Taylor-Gooby, P. (1985), 'The Politics of Welfare: Public Attitudes and Behaviour', in R.Klein and M. O'Higgins (eds), <u>The Future of Welfare</u>, Basil Blackwell.

GOSHEN COLLEGE LIBRARY
GOSHEN, INDIANA

2 Alternative futures for social policy and state welfare

ADRIAN WEBB

The purpose of this chapter is to provide one starting point for a discussion of alternative futures in the 1990s. Consequently, an attempt has been made to avoid short-term preoccupations without losing sight of the political and economic constraints within which social policy is likely to have to operate. The aim has been to provide a framework rather than to offer blue-prints.

The scope of the topic

To discuss alternatives to present policies and trends is to raise at least three inter-related sets of issues which can be expressed in the form of three questions:

(i)   What should be the future of statutory and non-statutory ways of meeting social needs and of resolving social problems?

(ii) What ways of meeting social need are likely in practice to be adopted in the foreseeable future and what social, economic and political constraints will most significantly shape the choices to be made?

(iii) What are the likely implications of the different ways of meeting social need for the social structure and political stability of our society, for its economic performance, and for the patterns of values and relationships in society?

These questions raise quite different and yet equally fundamental considerations and justice cannot be done to any one of them in a short chapter. Nevertheless, at least some consideration must be given to each when discussing the various alternative futures which are noted below.

The welfare state and contemporary social policy

To discuss alternatives implies an analysis of what is to be, or may need to be, changed. Such an analysis ought, logically, to begin by clarifying the nature of contemporary social policy.

It would be a valuable exercise, but our social policy inheritance is so complex as to defy easy characterisation. A very basic starting point will therefore have to suffice.

Although the idea of a 'welfare state' has dominated thinking about social policy throughout most of the post-war period, that idea has itself been a complex one. State social services have been crucial, but they have not constituted the whole story. Our inheritance has consisted of at least three core elements:

(i)   An overall commitment to collective action to prevent, reduce or to meet social needs, combined with public accountability in meeting those needs.

(ii)   An acceptance of a mixed economy of welfare involving state, voluntary, private and family/informal responses to need - the precise mix has always been contentious, not only with respect to private provision.

(iii)   A set of state services and expenditures.

The post-war idea of a welfare state set these basic components within a broader set of commitments. One of the most fundamental was that to the maintenance of full employment. Another, which was more controversial and the meaning of which has been more hotly debated, was the commitment to redistribute incomes and command over resources. The most fundamental, however, was the bi-partisan commitment to promote social objectives, and specifically to reduce social injustice. While there was ample room for disagreement about specific objectives, there was broad agreement on the legitimacy and feasibility of a considerable degree of state intervention.

The role of the state within the social policy heartland has itself been far from simple. At least four primary roles have been to the fore.

(i)   <u>Strategic policy making</u>: the analysis of social issues and problems and the development and monitoring of responses/solutions.

(ii)   <u>Financing the meeting of need</u>: providing subsidies and transfer payments and funding service provision in order, in principle, to increase the capacity of the needy to meet their needs.

(iii)   <u>Service production</u>: the direct provision of publicly produced services.

(iv)   <u>Safeguarding rights</u>: the policing of individual and collective rights, including consumer rights to a specific quality and level of service.

Despite the wealth of detailed changes and developments, the basic inheritance of the post-war 'welfare state' remained surprisingly unchanged until comparatively recently. The changes which have occurred in recent years have taken two forms: an increasingly voluble criticism -from most points on the political compass - of the role of the state in theory and/or in practice; and a growth - in some fields very rapid - of non-statutory ways of responding to social needs. It is tempting to see these two as directly and simply related, but there have also been other forces at work. For example, increasing levels of real disposable income have had an impact, as have long-standing shortfalls and inadequacies in state services. However, the primary change has been in the theory of the state.

The dimensions of discontent
The arguments for a change of direction are diverse, as are their implications for action. Three broad categories of discontent can usefully be distinguished:
- pragmatic arguments which rest on the implications of current trends or of changing circumstances;
- analyses of the 'failure' of state welfare to achieve its presumed objectives and concern about its unintended consequences;
- principled critiques of the objectives and/or outcomes of state welfare.

The most conspicuous amd most pragmatic of all arguments for a change of direction would appear to be that of financial feasibility: the edifice of state welfare is becoming too expensive to sustain. It is the subject of Michael O'Higgins's contribution to the book. However, I would argue that it is not particularly strong as a purely pragmatic argument. While there is room for fierce debate around the margins, the costs of simply 'maintaining' the principal state social services are not necessarily horrendous and what is horrendous is necessarily a political and not a purely pragmatic decision. It is also a decision which takes us firmly into the principled arguments about state welfare. Other examples of pragmatically rooted arguments for change arise from the increased levels of real disposable income among some groups on the one hand and the impact of mass unemployment on the other.

The challenge posed by changing circumstances is well illustrated by the latter. While central to the production process, paid employment has traditionally fulfilled a number of other essential roles: the distribution of income; the assignment of status; the production of that sense of social and personal worth which comes from worthwhile work; the fostering of social engagement and networks of social relationships; the promotion of social stability. Long-term mass unemployment has highlighted the need to re-examine income maintenance policies, but existing programmes did at least facilitate an immediate response to the partial breakdown of paid employment as a means of distributing income. Most of the other needs arising from mass unemployment have yet to be faced in a systematic way. Voluntary work and the voluntary sector have been pressed into action alongside the various MSC programmes, but these are limited and ad hoc responses.

If voluntary work, for example, is to be used as a major means of attempting to instil a sense of personal and social worth, the implications for social policy are considerable. Present experience of involving unemployed people in the voluntary sector already indicates that staff-volunteer ratios need to rise in order to place people carefully and support them fully; alternatives to paid employment will not be generated on an appropriate scale without significant investment. Similarly most organisers and agencies are now proceeding cautiously in negotiating the increasingly sensitive boundaries between paid and unpaid work.

If, on the other hand, the generation of paid employment is re-asserted as a primary social goal, the underlying task of welfare - as a labour intensive field of activity - may need to be redefined in order to place job creation on a par with the meeting of social need. A central question then becomes: what levels and patterns of paid work are generated by different patterns of financing and producing social provision? Bosanquet's brief examination of employment opportunities in the personal social services does not suggest that a deus ex machina is waiting in the wings (Bosanquet, 1985), but the issue has barely been addressed to date.

To argue - with the second approach - that the welfare state has 'failed' is to presume that there are clear objectives against which to measure it. One cluster of objectives can be summarised as the promotion of equality and social rights. Not only has the welfare state failed to generate a more equal society, it is argued (Field, 1981; Le Grand, 1982), it has even failed to contain poverty. To correct this failure while also preserving and expanding social rights to universal services -as opposed to (stigmatised) access to selective and charitable services - implies the protection and expansion of universal services as well as further measures of positive discrimination. However, there is a conceptual problem: much confusion surrounds the term equality. It is frequently used to mean equality between income groups and social classes as well as to mean equity - a fair distribution of resources by geographical area, client group, and by need (Weale, 1978a; Jones et al, 1978). Universal services are now seen to be a blunt instrument for effecting vertical redistribution (equality between classes) precisely because they are designed primarily to effect contingency redistribution (distribution according to need).

To preserve the social rights generated by universal services while also pursuing equality necessarily implies high levels of public expenditure and a radical pursuit of progressive taxation. It might also imply more employment in the state social services. As an approach it is definitely on the contemporary ideological map, but it requires rapid economic growth. Alternatively, it requires an ability to protect the least advantaged in the face of continued economic stagnation or decline. In either case it would demand a high order of political leadership and a reversal of present objectives and power relationships.

A different, though related, view of the 'failure' of the welfare state rests on the assumption that it was intended, in part, to promote social stability and economic efficiency. Given the plethora of arguments against state welfare which highlight its presumed contribution to economic inefficiency, it is salutory to remember that debate in the inter-war and war years did place great store on the contribution of state welfare to the enhancement of skills in the workforce, to the fostering of high morale and national identity, and to the reduction of class antagonism - with consequential benefits in the field of economic performance (Webb, 1983). These objectives remain valid, as does Titmuss's view that the costs of technological, economic and social change cannot necessarily be allowed with impunity to lie where they fall (Titmuss, 1976). What this amounts to, of course, is a highly unfashionable argument - whether one talks of social contracts, the use of the social wage in an incomes policy, or the pursuit of a 'one nation' philosophy. Nevertheless, both social adaptability and political stability are problematic in the face of rapid technological change (especially when combined with comparative economic decline). To see the welfare state as having had no stabilising effect in the past is to move beyond the evidence available to us; to assert that it could in fact have an important stabilising role in a more corporatist political system is to raise interesting questions (Mishra, 1983).

A third argument about 'failures' takes a more humanistic tone. Whatever else it was intended to be, the welfare state was certainly meant to be a liberating force - a means of enabling ordinary people to have greater freedom in and control over their own lives. However, it was also designed around professional - not amateur or lay - workers and the commitment to equity entailed bureaucratic and publicly accountable ways of proceeding in large scale organisations. The end product, far from being a source of liberation, it is argued (Gladstone, 1979; Hadley and Hatch, 1981), has been a frustrating and disabling experience for the citizen/consumer. Professional dominance has grown (Wilding, 1982) and has increased the dependence of lay people on esoteric knowledge and expertise. State welfare has also figured prominently in the centralisation of public administration (Hadley and Hatch, 1981). The end product is seen to have been unresponsiveness and low levels of innovation. Each of these critiques is easily overdrawn, but the unintended consequences of state welfare are real and the appeal of alternative philosophies, modes of working and styles of organisation and management are strong.

However, beyond these arguments about specific 'failures' there are principled critiques of state welfare and contemporary social policy arising from feminism, from the resurgence of fundamentalist forms of socialist thought and from neo-liberalism. This last approach - which is profoundly anti-statist in principle, though not necessarily in practice - will be briefly discussed below as one prime example of these principled critiques.

The dimensions of choice
The basic options for the future are comparatively few, although detailed variants and the interaction between them generate complexity. The primary choices seem to be:

- to effect a radical shift away from - or towards greater - state involvement;
- to effect more modest and reformative changes in the existing balance between statutory and non-statutory involvement;
- to adopt new philosophies, objectives, operational goals, or approaches to management which might - in principle - apply to both statutory and non-statutory sectors and/or have implications for the balance to be struck between these sectors.

Each will be considered in turn.

A radical transformation in the role of the state

The case for a radical reduction in the role of the state can be defended from two perspectives which are closely related but which can usefully be separated: political liberalism and economic liberalism (Room, 1979).

Political liberalism focuses attention upon the role of the state per se. The essence is that state intervention cannot legitimately or successfully promote social justice and that no such attempt should be made. These arguments fundamentally challenge the broad agreement about the legitimacy of state intervention to promote social objectives which was the real core of the post-war 'welfare state' (Bosanquet, 1983). For Hayek (1976) the problem is that the state lacks an agreed standard of social justice and its intervention provokes political instability by raising expectations which cannot be fulfilled, and - more generally - that the market is an inherently amoral system on which it would be inappropriate to impose a moral framework (whether that be the pursuit of equality or the rewarding of merit) (Plant, 1984). For Nozick (1974) the role of the state must be minimal because the state cannot legitimately curtail individual freedom by raising taxes to assist those in need. The end result is that charity and voluntary action are the only legitimate responses to need. This trenchantly minimalist view of the state can be modified if a goodly slice of state paternalism is seen as in fact defensible (Weale, 1978b). But the centre-piece of the argument is the endlessly contestable notion of liberty and of the threat posed by state intervention.

However, a radical displacement of the state can also be advanced on other grounds. The essence for the economic liberal is that scarce resources will be used most efficiently if the role of the state is pared down and that of the market is expanded: the most fundamental source of inefficiency arises from the absence of preferences expressed through the price mechanism in a competitive market. Such a transformation is also seen to favour economic growth, consumer choice, innovation and responsiveness.

Although Minford's (1984) recent formulation of this case is one of the most compressed, it has the merit of focussing solely on the issue of efficiency: inefficiency is seen to arise from state consumption (state purchasing of services to be distributed free or at a subsidised price), from monopolistic state production, and from the impact of taxation. The case against public consumption rests on the very limited range of genuine public goods which require state intervention. Problems of excess demand, of rationing and of over-provision are emphasised. Consequently, one of the frequently cited arguments against state production - that it can result, especially in the fields of health and education, in under-production (and consequent job losses) - is ignored. The possibility of externalities is also ignored in the process of minimising the role of the state.

The case against public production is reasonably typical of much polemical writing in the field. Public monopoly and the absence of the competitive spur are the nub. However, while the defects of state monopoly are treated with great theoretical seriousness, it is assumed that privatised services would be competitive - except in the case of natural monopolies. The solution where natural monopolies exist (District General Hospitals?) is the creation of potential competition, or contestability, by selling franchises. However, past experience with franchises does not instil confidence; and monopolies, cartels and muscular multi-nationals need to be taken seriously, not ignored.

The fundamental weakness of the argument, however, is that an analysis of the deadweight welfare loss arising from profit maximizing monopolists operating in priced markets is simply transferred without hesitation to state monopolies which do not trade in priced goods and which are not profit maximizing. Moreover, even if this leap could be made, the conclusion must be that state monopolies under-produce, not that they are inefficient in any other sense. At the end of Minford's article, however, the theoretical argument that state social service monopolies result in social inefficiencies is simply transformed into an assertion that they are also technically inefficient.

The perceived inefficiencies of taxation are also instructive. Minford argues that lower marginal tax rates are crucial to incentives and therefore to economic growth. He also identifies the reduction of the poverty trap as a route to growth; the benefits of reducing taxation are therefore assumed to be concentrated on the low paid. Not only is this contrary to recent past practice, it ignores the scale of political leadership needed to so direct tax savings in advance of economic growth.

To achieve major tax reductions requires a highly residualist view of the redistributive role of the state: the efficient relief of poverty is seen as the sole social objective. A radical transfer of responsibility to the family is also necessary: 'The logical action to take is therefore for such responsibilities (for example for elderly relatives and handicapped children) to be made legally mandatory, just as child battering or child neglect are penalised by the law. Neglect of these family responsibilities would be actionable by the state' (Minford, 1984). One is left to assume that state intervention is presently necessary because able-bodied kin avoid caring responsibilities and that the frail, elderly parents of handicapped 'children' will henceforth suffer the full weight of the law if they fail to cope.

To accept the notion of contingency redistribution (for example state provision for people with non-insurable health risks and not merely for the 'genuinely poor') immediately removes the possibility of a truly radical reduction of public social expenditure and leads us to consider more modest adjustments to the role of the state. However, available evidence on public attitudes towards social policy issues clearly suggests that the politically feasible room for overt change is limited: the bastions of state welfare are difficult to abandon altogether, but a radical redistribution of income and wealth to presently stigmatised, low-status groups is also difficult to achieve (Taylor-Gooby, 1985). The line of least political resistance is to protect the heartlands of middle-class consumption and production, while fostering the truly radical possibilities at a primarily rhetorical level.

One of the most significant features of the ideological polarisation of the past decade and a half is that it has dramatically underlined the need seriously to contemplate change while also increasing the purely political costs and benefits of many of the alternatives. One of the major past defects of social policy has been the tendency to treat state welfare as an end in itself and therefore to concentrate on resource inputs as symbols of progress and commitment - to the neglect of outputs. The polarisation of debate has ensured that alternatives to the state have also become ends in themselves for many, while state welfare has become even more unquestionably an end in itself for others. In addition, what is easily sacrificed in public debate is analysis of precisely how options are to be implemented and of their likely implications once implemented. These defects of analysis permeate many of the more reformative, as well as the more radical, proposals.

A shift from state welfare to competitive markets
The balance between state and private/market systems has obviously become open to further adjustment in both the financing and the production of social provision. Although they can only be mentioned in passing, all the traditional objections to such moves need to be set against the arguments which were outlined above. The classical arguments for state intervention are that externalities can be recognised, equity can be promoted, the social costs of change can be pooled, the liberty of the less advantaged can be extended, and equality can be sought. While these arguments are not redundant - and the issue is how much and what kinds of state expenditure they should imply - they do not necessarily constitute a defence of state service production.
        The most fundamental defence of state production was Titmuss's assertion that certain goods and services are not 'economic goods' at all because they involve unduly high levels of uncertainty, of risk, or of vulnerability on the part of the consumer (Titmuss, 1976). As a case it is easily demolished precisely because it accepts the economists' tenets as a starting point and then seeks to detect a 'natural break' in what is a continuum of uncertainty, vulnerability etc. The argument which has been central to social policy is stronger when expressed directly: removing the price mechanism allows service providers to place their clients' interests to the fore, maximises trust in the service relationship (and, inter alia, reduces malpractice suits etc), enhances social solidarity by attaching tangible social rights to citizenship, and reinforces other-regarding behaviour rather than individualistic materialism. The associated fear is that private production (whether or not for profit) entails - at best - a residual and stigmatised state service for the poor and for marginal groups.

This case implies a series of hypotheses about individual and group behaviour, only some of which have been partly tested, but it fundamentally rests upon the argument that social objectives are as valid as more narrowly perceived economic objectives.

Despite their importance, these considerations can easily be swept aside by the harsh realities of the moment. Let me, therefore, highlight a few of the severely practical issues which are raised by a partial shift away from the state, but which are easily lost to view in the heat of partisan advocacy. First, the protection of the most vulnerable from the effects of cuts has been espoused in public policy since the mid-seventies (Webb and Wistow, 1982), but to implement such an approach is to resist the order of priorities reflected in public support for social services and benefits (Taylor-Gooby, 1985). To accept public support as the arbiter of what is the core role of the state is to concentrate resources more firmly on the key universal services and on some of the least vulnerable groups in the population (Le Grand, 1984).

Second, publicly provided services are ideally rationed according to need, not supplied on demand. However, to combine state financial support (subsidies, vouchers, grants) with private production can pose a serious potential loss of financial control. It is a dilemma which has been highlighted by the growth of publicly financed places in private residential care (Challis et al, 1984) and it is one which poses major headaches in some other developed countries. There are antidotes (for example, the development of rationing by social and not merely financial need within the state income maintenance services) but they are not necessarily cheap or without problems.

Third, private production (whether profit motivated or not) implies that the producers can choose their clients. A residual state service will therefore be necessary unless there is a buyers' market or the state contracts out production and stipulates that a comprehensive and universal service must be provided.

Fourth, the combination of state financial support and private production also poses a problem of lack of control over the type of provision funded. For example, professional opinion has long supported a move away from institutional care which private production can rapidly undermine unless specific incentives/sanctions are deployed to promote private alternatives to residential care. A related contradiction arises if the weight attached to family and informal care is counter-acted by the growth of publicly financed residential provision available on demand (Wistow, 1984).

Fifth, 'privatisation' can be permitted in the production of services directly available to the consumer, in 'support services', or in both. The most readily privatised direct services are those (least professionalised) forms of care needed by the most vulnerable client groups. The need for safeguarding consumer rights is acknowledged in principle, but it is far from easy to guarantee in practice. For example, the staff (in SSDs) responsible for the registration of homes are under great pressure: the potential for public concern is very high.

Sixth, the general issue which arises is that public control of private production depends on the avoidance of cartels and monopolies and the preservation of convincing sanctions. Much private residential care, for example, remains a cottage industry at present, but the rate of change is rapid. (Johnson, 1983; Challis, 1982; Klein, 1982). Whether the public sector can hope to be on equal bargaining terms with the private producer is a moot point. It ultimately depends on the maintenance of a buyers' market, or significant public sector capacity which could be used to withdraw recognition from recalcitrant producers. It is not only quality control and public protection of consumer rights which depends on this sanction; the entire assumption of greater productive efficiency also rests on it.

Reforming the mixed economy: the case for welfare pluralism

Welfare pluralism - as the name implies - involves a deliberate creation of diversity. One potential strand in the argument has been covered in discussing 'privatisation'. However, some proponents of welfare pluralism place the emphasis on substantial and rapid expansion of voluntary provision as a means of breaking up state monopoly services. The case does not assume a minimalist attitude towards the state; in fact, it tends to presume the maintenance or expansion of state expenditure. It also endorses the traditional welfare state objectives of meeting a wide range of needs through universal services.

Nevertheless, many of the criticisms of state welfare, and the reasons for change which are given prominence, are similar to those advanced earlier. Advocates of voluntarism seek to offer a radical transformation without recourse to the cash nexus of the market place. The problems which arise from the position of the state as a monopolistic supplier of services could be partly offset by an expansion of the voluntary sector, it is argued, as follows.

(a) Choice and preference: state monopoly tends to result in standardised services whereas voluntary provision is more diverse and could offer a degree of choice, alongside the state, which would permit a real expression of preferences.

(b) Paternalism: the very act of collectively purchasing or providing services for others is paternalistic, but this is exacerbated within the public sector by the demands of public accountability. The voluntary sector can take greater risks and give consumers greater freedom to reject advice and help.

(c) Competition, efficiency and innovation: state monopoly, it is argued, may be countered by competition from the voluntary sector. In the case of natural monopolies there is certainly no reason to assume that such potential competition would be inferior to that generated in the market place. More generally, however, the interesting question is whether voluntary organisations dependent - at least in part - on public funds would be allowed to compete with the state or with one another. The public sector tends to abhor 'duplication', which is seen as a source of waste rather than of competition. Purposive duplication may have much to recommend it in principle, but it is difficult to see it as a practical possibility. Nevertheless, the very presence of voluntary provision within the jurisdiction of a public authority may provide an element of contestability - even if direct competition for the same consumers is not a possibility. In the case of local authority services, voluntary organisations may most usefully sharpen thinking and policy making if they have independent access to public funds (e.g. to central government funds). However, such access raises the question of equity and co-ordination. Its merits have to be weighed against two other possibilities: local statutory funding which strengthens the strategic planning role of the local authority, and central funding which is conditional on statutory-voluntary collaboration and joint planning.

An additional argument, and one which characterises the case for welfare pluralism, is that state welfare currently involves a 'political monopoly' and undue concentrations of power. The state is seen to be virtually the sole arbiter of values and the sole channel of participation in public affairs. A greatly expanded voluntary sector would provide - is already providing - diverse opportunities for participation.

The problem with welfare pluralism as an argument for a radical transfer of responsibility for service provision from the state is that it emphasises the demerits of 'bureaucratic' state services as they presently exist and contrasts them with the presumed, but little researched, merits of voluntary provision - without considering the impact of large-scale expansion on voluntarism. As I have argued elsewhere (Webb, 1981), this is to confuse auspice and role. If voluntary organisations took responsibility for large areas of basic service provision, it is at least arguable that they would be forced to accept the same preoccupation with equity which currently produces many of the 'bureaucratic' characteristics of statutory services. They could well become enmeshed in much closer public accountability which would inhibit risk taking and responsiveness. Moreover, scale itself is a crucial factor and there is no good reason to assume that its impact can be ignored.

That the welfare pluralist case tends to dwell on the supposed defects of contemporary social policies and of the role of the state is not surprising: it is an argument for growth in voluntary organisations. However, a more disinterested observer might usefully proceed by noting that the state and the voluntary and informal care systems are delicately and closely entwined and that the starting point for a discussion of change ought to be an analysis of the most pressing contemporary needs. Let me note three:

(i)   The level of present, and future, unmet need underlines the importance of expanding the sum total of provision - not least by using public expenditure to underpin and harness 'community resources'.

(ii)   The level of need may be less challenging than the changing nature of need and of available care. Parker (1981) has given particular emphasis to the growing need for what he calls 'tending' - simple domestic and personal care of the kind which has traditionally been undertaken by women. Alternative sources of tending are: the family and informal care system; paid, non-professional workers; and volunteers. All three make significant contributions at present but public expenditure constraint has reduced the tending capacity of statutory services since the mid seventies (home helps, meals on wheels - see Webb and Wistow, 1983).

(iii)   The issue underlined by Parker's work and pursued by others is that of the <u>caring capacity of the community</u>. The extent to which the state does, and can, influence the volume and pattern of informal care is open to debate, but the impact of offsetting some of the costs of caring, of interweaving formal services and informal care, of offering incentives to care, and of providing financial support for new patterns of service could be considerable.

The evidence suggests, for example, that families caring for handicapped dependants experience higher costs of living and lower incomes than do other families: families, therefore, finance, as well as produce, care for their handicapped members (Social Policy Research Unit, 1981). Considerations of equity, and the pragmatic concern to maintain this pattern of care, have begun to focus attention on these costs of informal care. The income and career opportunities foregone by women and the non-financial costs of caring have begun to be explored in some detail (Equal Opportunities Commission, 1982; Finch and Groves, 1980; Nissel and Bonnerjea, 1982; Glendinning, 1983).

The importance of the interaction between the state and informal care is highlighted by the fact that the proportion of elderly people - particularly men - in institutional accommodation fell steadily from 1911 to 1961 (Donnison and Ungerson, 1968). The enhancement of purchasing power in old age and housing policies appear to have had a direct and measurable impact on the viability of informal care. By way of contrast, the hasty movement of mentally ill people from hospitals into poorly prepared and supported local communities in Italy may well have had the effect of increasing the prison population (Jones and Poletti, 1984).

Perhaps surprisingly, state financing of non-statutory provision is also beginning to become an important issue in relation to the two other components of the mixed economy to which I would draw attention: self help, or mutual aid; and volunteering. Mutual aid is essentially a philosophy of helping rather than a separate provision system; it emphasises the merits of mutual support by fellow sufferers. As such it could potentially thrive within state, private or voluntary services and at an informal level it probably does. At the more formal level, specialist mutual aid groups tend to operate as voluntary organisations (Richardson and Goodman, 1982). Despite the apparently rapid growth in the number of mutual aid groups they remain fragile and patchy in their distribution. The energy and skills which can be deployed through mutual aid groups may depend to a significant degree on the level of public subsidy, or pump-priming, which is made available. The importance of public finance as a catalyst has already begun to be recognised (DHSS, 1984).

Voluntary work is a major feature of our culture and of many other developed countries: volunteers are deployed in the statutory, voluntary and private sectors. Estimates of the proportion of the population involved vary considerably - depending, in part, on the way in which voluntary work is defined (Humble, 1983). At minimum, however, at least 15 per cent of the population seems to be actively involved. The stereotype of the volunteer (a middle aged, middle class woman) is not totally inaccurate, but it is totally misleading (Humble, 1982) - not least because the stereotypical volunteer may be expected to be self-financing, while the majority of contemporary volunteers are not, and cannot be expected to be. 'Volunteers' in the informal sector (e.g. the neighbour who gives a helping hand) are presumably self financing, but attempts to expand voluntary work increasingly depend on the payment of expenses. What evidence there is suggests that voluntary work remains a 'good buy' even when one allows for the waste involved in drop-out and turnover. Nonetheless, it is not a free resource.

The potential for change is clearly considerable, but public expenditure looks to be central to growth in all these areas of provision. The alternatives to state production are far more numerous and are somewhat more convincing than are those to state funding. Moreover, the present rate of expansion of local voluntary action is far greater than is likely to be funded in the future by local authorities. Present policies involve the creation - with central government financial support - of many projects and organisations which have no long-term financial future. While nature can afford to be profligate, enabling a thousand flowers to bloom is not necessarily an efficient way of organising public policy.

Alternative themes and philosophies

The emergence of alternative themes and the re-weighting of philosophies is inevitably subject to fashion; identifying current preoccupations which are likely to exert an enduring influence is a risky business. Nevertheless it may be useful to comment on three themes which cut across the various systems of statutory and non-statutory provision: value for money; decentralisation; and prevention.

The first is almost certainly destined to remain at the centre of the stage in one form or another. It is variously expressed as 'value for money', cost-effectiveness, or the efficient use of resources. A wide range of meanings and objectives is compressed within these phrases. The crucial differences revolve around:

- the time-scale envisaged (e.g. long, medium or short);
- the scope of the system within which 'value for money' is sought (e.g. a particular public expenditure programme, the public sector as a whole, the utilisation of real resources throughout the economy, the social as well as economic costs and benefits pertaining to all relevant actors in the society);
- the precise objectives of a concern for 'value for money' (e.g. cost compression in the public sector as an element in an economic strategy, the creation of 'room' within a programme in order to innovate or meet new demands, or the avoidance of long-term costs arising from short-term decision making).

The danger of short-term cost compression is that 'value for money' can become synonymous with the preoccupations of public expenditure restraint; it can also conceal long-term issues or involve the sacrifice of long-term goals. For example, the nature of a long-term, cost-effective strategy towards high dependency groups (e.g. the frail elderly, mentally handicapped) is highly debatable, but short-term expenditure decisions can determine the pattern of provision for many years ahead. Similarly, the <u>targeting</u> of services - whether provided publicly, privately or by voluntary organisations - is an especially crucial issue for the future. Effective targeting of services requires close co-ordination of packages of intervention and not merely a more cost-conscious approach towards the production or allocation of any <u>one</u> type of service. However, this approach to the cost-effective use of resources necessitates a significant input of research/analytical skills, managerial time, political backing and inter-agency co-ordination. Each of these is jeopardised by the shorter-term preoccupation of achieving immediate savings within a particular programme or sector.

The fundamental problem of 'value for money' is very deeply engrained; it requires a long-term and widely supported response. The development of the 'welfare state' involved a minimalisation, even a denial, of scarcity (Heald, 1983; Webb and Wistow, forthcoming). It was reinforced by the values of the public social service professions, by their impact on decision-making, and by real - albeit slow - economic growth. Meanwhile, the role of some services - especially the NHS (Klein, 1983; Vaizey, 1984) - was transformed by rapid technological change, but the idea of 'value of money' was seen, to a significant degree, as a euphemism for expenditure cuts or incursions into professional. autonomy. While a decade of expenditure restraint has undoubtedly changed the agenda and transformed the debate, this view of 'value for money' as merely an ideological preoccupation, or weapon, has also been strengthened. My personal goal for the 1990s in this field, therefore, would be to establish a broadly based, rather than a narrow and hotly contested, commitment to 'value for money' in which the cost-effective use of scarce resources was seen to be both a matter of social justice and also congruent with many professional objectives. While the issue will not cease to be important, there is a danger that a drive for value for money which fails to appeal to professional values and which appears to be rooted in short-term needs will fail to achieve a productive long-term transformation in the use of resources.

Prevention is a perennial issue precisely because it tends to be most attractive when ill-defined and because it is continuously vulnerable to short-term pressures. It is certain to be important in the future as a pious hope, but for it to be more than that demands a clear specification of a particular notion of prevention in respect of particular conditions, needs or social problems. Primary prevention was obviously and spectacularly successful in the case of communicable diseases, but secondary prevention has been more characteristic in recent decades. The goal has typically been to facilitate early intervention, or to avoid particular forms of intervention (such as care in institutions), rather than to prevent needs arising in the first place. However, all patterns of preventive action pose the problems noted in relation to 'value for money'; they tend to require medium to long-term time horizons, co-ordinated and well targeted service delivery, and the support of professional and other field-level decision-makers. Primary prevention also tends to demand substantial change at the individual or societal level.

A key feature of an emphasis on prevention, however, is that it can challenge conventional assumptions about what are the central and peripheral areas of concern for the state. The school meals service is a good example of an area of state intervention which has come to be seen as peripheral, but which could well be seen as central given a long-term, dietary view of health care. It certainly illustrates the need to define the core and peripheral roles of the state with care. Moreover, prevention necessarily implies, I would argue, a sophisticated form of policy analysis and strategic planning and a capacity for collective control over economic and social structures, processes and trends. It does not necessarily imply a particular role for the state in the production of services, but it does assume that the state has at its disposal effective means of influencing change.

Decentralisation may prove to be one of the issues which rapidly fades away, but past experience suggests that it is also a perennial, if episodic, concern. The central purposes of de-centralisation need to be specified clearly since different patterns and styles of organisation and management maximise different objectives; they also have different implications for the types of decision which may have to be centralised as a precondition of decentralising others. But multiple objectives may be pursued simultaneously if decentralised systems are appropriately designed. Shadow pricing can be used, for example, to enhance cost consciousness in professional decision-making while also creating known limits within which consumers and professionals can negotiate and agree authoritative service 'contracts'. As with 'value for money', the merits and demerits of particular alternatives depend on precise delineation of the proposal and of objectives.

An interesting contemporary example of the dilemmas alluded to above, and of the need for careful analysis, is to be found in the 'patch' debate. ('Patch' is a proposal to devolve social services responsibilities to small generalist teams serving highly localised areas.) It is a very particular issue, but it reveals many of the problems of evaluating alternative futures. In essence, the 'patch' argument is that a highly decentralised organisation and delivery of state personal social services can transform both the role and output of statutory services while also stimulating alternative ways of meeting social need.

As an approach to change in the statutory services, patch claims to offer a route to greater worker satisfaction and participation, reduced 'bureaucracy' and rigidity, decentralised and more rapid decision-making, improved team work and a move from crisis to preventive work. The perceived benefits to clients are those of better and earlier access to services, increased participation and control over the services received, and reduction of professional 'distance' and power (Hadley and McGrath, 1980). The perceived benefit to the Exchequer is that of 'value for money': community resources (informal care by family and neighbourhood) are released. The only contemporary desideratum which 'patch' does not seem to offer to fulfil is that of entirely removing the need for state provision and/or finance. It has received attention and support across the political spectrum.

Scepticism can slide into cynicism as easily as advocacy into punditry. Patch may well prove to be a multi-faceted boon. There is, for example, some initial supportive evidence for one of its most apparently optimistic claims: increased accessibility resulting in a larger total volume of referrals may well, in some circumstances, be accompanied by shorter waiting times and a cost-effective prevention of larger, more time-consuming and crisis-ridden problems (Bayley, 1983/84).

However, patch does raise problems and criticisms, and the precise details of implementation can be seen to be crucial to the broad principles and objectives served. Does decentralisation mean, in practice, greater decentralisation of some decisions at the patch level, combined with greater centralisation of others at the directorate level and a growing vacuum in between (Beresford, 1983)? (The same question may be asked of other examples, such as the restructuring of the NHS.) What do teamwork , role flexibility and 'deprofessionalisation' really mean? Is it likely to result in deskilling and a reduced capacity to handle the difficult crises which no amount of preventive work will head off (Pinker, 1982)? What does increased participation really mean?

Identical questions surround a far more fundamental attempt to transform the role of state social services by a process of decentralisation, democratisation and mobilisation of community resources. The Italian experiment arising from Law 180, 1978 - and known as Psychiatrica Democratica - has involved a rapid move away from institutional provision, the destigmatising of mental illness, the location of responsibility at sub-municipal level (services for the mentally ill in Rome are now the responsibility of nine separate authorities, for example) and the mushrooming of voluntary and private provision. Comment in Britain has ranged across the spectrum from distinctly positive to eulogistic. The exception is a highly critical and concerned account of a study visit (Jones and Poletti, 1984). The picture painted is a gloomy one of very low levels and standards of provision and in some cases of clear exploitation. The rush to an ill-developed and patchily implemented alternative may have been a far from resounding success in many of the less prestigious localities in Italy. The outcomes noted are the very reverse of those intended.

Conclusion

The support for, and feasibility of, a truly radical shift away from all public expenditure on social needs are so weak that I have largely discounted it as an option. I have rather assumed that the costs of simply 'maintaining' existing social expenditure commitments in the future are not necessarily too daunting, especially if international comparisons within Europe provide the yardstick. However, simply 'to maintain' commitments is almost meaningless: the pressures of technological change, and of changes in 'the caring capacity of the community', all point to pressures for increased public social expenditure. Some potential developments in non-statutory production could also add to these pressures.

Moreover, even given realistic optimism about economic growth and assuming a political desire merely to contain social expenditure as a proportion of GDP, there needs to be a prolonged concern with 'value for money' and a strategic view of priorities designed to maintain some room for manoeuvre. My personal argument is that the historic lack of interest in 'value for money' and the preoccupation with inputs not outputs will only be reversed if a concern for cost-effectiveness is deeply rooted, which means that it has to emphasise effective as well as economical service provision. Widespread support for an efficient use of resources cannot be secured unless the commitment to meet social need is seen to be unequivocal and equally deeply rooted. As I have noted, however, a real alternative possibility is that continued economic decline will simply underpin a scramble for immunity from its consequences - to the detriment of the social services and their clients.

Although this chapter is an attempt to provide a framework, I have also tried to develop a theme which can finally be summarized. Circumstances have made it increasingly necessary to re-examine the interaction of economic and social policies rather than to treat them as semi-autonomous fields of endeavour, and also to re-assess the role of the state. One response is to treat social policy as the residuum and to allow economic 'needs' to determine social objectives. The price of doing so, however, is to subordinate social objectives and to imply that they are irrelevant to economic goals except insofar as they represent a barrier to attaining those goals.

Since the weighting of these considerations will be determined by the outcome of ideological conflict and power struggles, my concern may seem to be irrelevant to the Civil Service. In fact, however, it highlights the crucial nature of one of the traditional roles of the Civil Service: the consideration of how to evaluate and implement potential policies. Quite different objectives and values may be served depending upon the precise manner in which an idea is implemented. Herein lies the most challenging feature of any attempt seriously to discuss alternatives to the present pattern of welfare provision: macro and micro considerations have to be handled simultaneously. There is little point in contemplating significant change without going back to first principles and assessing the objectives which should be given priority, but it is equally self defeating to ignore the details of how change is to be implemented since those details will determine what is achieved in reality. One of the prominent features of the debates which have been reviewed in this paper is that existing state services - with all their known defects and limitations - have been contrasted with hypothetical alternatives operating within less exacting constraints. Like has typically not been compared with like. This is true of advocacy of 'market' alternatives, of voluntary sector alternatives, and of such themes as decentralisation. The prime task of policy analysis must be to explore alternatives in sufficient detail, and within sufficiently exacting requirements, that the likely defects as well as advantages are revealed and the implications for political, social and economic objectives can be duly weighed.

Put differently, at the core of contemporary debate about the future of social policy there is deep-seated conflict about social objectives, but also a profound unwillingness to distinguish between assertion and evidence and between theoretical models and practical realities. The former is not directly a matter for the Civil Service, but the latter is. For example, it is presently asserted that different approaches to welfare provision exhibit different 'system properties': flexibility or rigidity, competitive efficiency or wastefulness, responsiveness or bureaucratic inertia. These assertions need to be challenged as assertions, the preconditions of actually realising desired system properties need thoroughly to be assessed and evidence needs to be sought on the implications in practice of instituting changes in policy.

The necessity for such policy analysis is heightened by the robust nature of contemporary political debate, by the range of options open to us, by the complexity of the costs and benefits surrounding alternatives, and by the costs attendant upon simply ignoring problems and avoiding choices.

References

Bayley, M. (1983/84), The Dinnington Project Reports, mimeo, University of Sheffield.

Beresford, P. (1983), 'Power to the People', Community Care, 24 November.

Bosanquet, N. (1983), After the New Right, Heinemann.

Bosanquet, N. (1985), 'Welfare Needs, Welfare Jobs and Efficiency', in R. Klein and M. O'Higgins (eds), The Future of Welfare, Basil Blackwell.

Challis, L. (1982), Private and Voluntary Provision for the Elderly, mimeo, Centre for the Analysis of Social Policy.

Challis, L., Day, P. and Klein, R. (1984), 'Residential Care on Demand', New Society, 5 April.

DHSS (1984), Helping the Community to Care, Press Release, 5 July.

Donnison, D.V. and Ungerson, C. (1968), 'Trends in Residential Care 1911-61', Social and Economic Administration, Vol. 22, pp.75-91.

Equal Opportunities Commission (1982), Who Cares for the Carers?, EOC.

Field, F. (1981), Inequality in Britain: Freedom, Welfare and the State, Fontana.

Finch, J. and Groves, D. (1980), 'Community Care and Care in the family: a case for equal opportunities', Journal of Social Policy, Vol. 9, No. 4, pp.487-511.

Gladstone, F.J. (1979), Voluntary Action in a Changing World, Bedford Square Press.

Glendinning, C. (1983), Unshared Care: Parents and their Disabled Children, Routledge & Kegan Paul.

Hadley, R. and Hatch, S. (1981), Social Welfare and the Failure of the State, Allen & Unwin.

Hadley, R. and McGrath, M. (1980), Going Local, Bedford Square Press.

Hayek, F.A. (1976), Law, Legislation & Liberty, Vol. 2: The Mirage of Social Justice, Routledge & Kegan Paul.

Heald, D. (1983), Public Expenditure, Martin Robertson.

Humble, S. (1982), Voluntary Action in the 1980s, The Volunteer Centre.

Humble, S. (1983), 'Alive and Kicking - But How Much of it?', Involve, No. 27, October (The Volunteer Centre).

Johnson, M. (1983), 'A Sharp Eye on Private Homes' and 'Controlling the Cottage Industry', Community Care, 4 and 25 August.

Jones, K., Brown, J. and Bradshaw, J. (1978), Issues in Social Policy, Routledge & Kegan Paul.

Jones, K. and Poletti, A. (1984), Transformation of the Asylum: The Italian Experience, mimeo, University of York.

Klein, R. (1982), 'Private Practice and Public Policy', in G. McLachlan and A. Maynard (eds), The Public/Private Mix for Health, Nuffield Provincial Hospitals Trust.

Klein, R. (1983), The Politics of the National Health Service, Longman.

Le Grand, J. (1982), The Strategy of Equality, Allen & Unwin.

Le Grand, J. (1984), 'The Future of the Welfare State', New Society, 7 June.

Minford, P. (1984), 'State Expenditure: A Study in Waste', Economic Affairs Vol. 4, No.3 pp.i-xix. Quotation from p.xiii.

Mishra, R. (1983), Welfare State in Crisis, Harvester Press.

Nissel, M. and Bonnerjea, L. (1982), Family Care of the Handicapped Elderly, Policy Studies Institute.

Nozick, R. (1974), Anarchy, State and Utopia, Basil Blackwell.

Parker, R.A. (1981), 'Tending and Social Policy', in E.M. Goldberg and S. Hatch (eds), A New Look at the Personal Social Services, Policy Studies Institute.

Pinker, R. (1982), 'An Alternative View', Appendix B in P. Barclay (Chairman), Social Workers: Their Role and Tasks, The report of a Working Party under the chairmanship of Peter M. Barclay, Bedford Square Press for NISW.

Plant, R. (1984), Equality, Markets and the State, Fabian Tract 494.

Richardson, A. and Goodman, M. (1982), Self Help and Social Care: Mutual Aid Organisations in Practice, Policy Studies Institute.

Room, G. (1979), The Sociology of Welfare, Basil Blackwell.

Social Policy Research Unit (1981), The Financial Consequences of Disablement in Children, Research Report to DHSS, No. 77, 6/81, SPRU, University of York.

Taylor-Gooby, P. (1985), 'The Politics of Welfare: Public Attitudes and Behaviour', in R. Klein and M. O'Higgins (eds), The Future of Welfare, Basil Blackwell.

Titmuss, R.M. (1976), Commitment to Welfare, Allen & Unwin.

Vaizey, J. (1984), National Health, Martin Robertson.

Weale, A. (1978a), Equality and Social Policy, Routledge & Kegan Paul.

Weale, A. (1978b), 'Paternalism and Social Policy', Journal of Social Policy, Vol. 6, No. 2, pp.157-173.

Webb, A.L. (1981), Collective Action and Welfare Pluralism, ARVAC, Occasional Paper No. 3.

Webb, A.L. (1983), 'Policy-Making: a case of intellectual progress?', in P. Bean and S. MacPherson (eds), Approaches to Welfare, Routledge & Kegan Paul.

Webb, A.L. and Wistow, G. (1982), Whither State Welfare?, Royal Institute of Public Administration.

Webb, A.L. and Wistow, G. (1983), 'Public Expenditure and Policy Implementation: The case of Community Care', Public Administration, Vol. 61, Spring, pp.21-44.

Webb, A.L. and Wistow, G. (forthcoming), Planning and Scarcity: Essays on the Personal Social Services, Allen & Unwin.

Wilding, P. (1982), Professional Power and Social Policy, Routledge & Kegan Paul.
Wistow, G. (1984), 'Cuts in the personal social services: definition and trends', BASW/Local Government Campaign Unit conference, 25 October.

3 Family services

ROBERT PINKER

Introduction

The purpose of this chapter is to examine the implications of medium- and longer-term social and economic trends for the provision of social services to families with children, including those living under 'normal' circumstances and those living in disadvantaged conditions, with some reference to associated patterns of deviance from social conventions. Taking the family as its main institutional concern, the chapter will be focussed for policy purposes on the personal social services and their interaction with employment, education and housing services.

Other contributors will be discussing aspects of family life in relation to the care of the elderly and the sick, and the associated service aspects of income and health care provision. In principle, however, the central concern of this chapter is common to all fields of social policy; while the family is a relatively integrated and unitary institution whose members may require a wide range of social services over time, the services themselves are for a variety of political and administrative reasons departmentally separated and provided by different levels of government as well as by voluntary and private agencies operating under different auspices.

The search for a more efficient and flexible relationship between the actual contexts in which people live and the whole range of administratively separate social services has been a long-standing preoccupation of policy-makers. Such a relationship is hard to achieve, for various reasons. Both the structure and functions of family life and the declared ends and means of social policy change over time. The family is not a homogeneous institution, and some people do not live in families. The interests of families and their individual members do not always coincide. In addition the family as a social institution sometimes evokes very sharply differing political and philosophical judgements. It is both defended as the fountainhead of social stability, welfare and morality and attacked as a major cause of social and sexual inequality and oppression. Writing in 1979, I suggested that:

'The family has always been an object of suspicion amongst social reformers. In recent times psycho-analytic theory has sought to explain the pathologies of family life, while the main thrust of Marxist sociology has indicted the family as a repressive institution, inextricably associated with the source of all repression - private property. The family is of course the most subversive of all social institutions since it accommodates both its apologists and its antagonists with equanimity. There is an implicit conflict in collectivist social welfare, given that one of the primary aims of social policy is to preserve and restore families and hence the emotional foundations of the institution of private property, while it seeks at the same time to achieve a more equitable distribution of property in general terms' (Pinker, 1979, p.38).

The basic value assumptions of this chapter are that policy and family interests are sometimes complementary and sometimes contradictory, but that in a free society an element of conflict is both unavoidable and desirable. It is unavoidable because familial loyalties can never be described in either unconditionally egoistic or altruistic terms. They are par excellence expressions of conditional altruism - conditional in the sense that individuals often feel morally obliged to place the interest of their own families before those of others, but altruistic in the sense that familial loyalties evoke intense and enduring forms of affection, devotion and dutifulness between members. The same complex network of sentiments can give rise to equally intense forms of conflict and animosity. One of the perennial problems of social policy is how best to encourage and support the more conditional forms of familial altruism and reconcile them with the broader considerations of social welfare.

Nevertheless these conflicts are desirable in a society insofar as they provide evidence that neither the more conditional and exclusive forms of familial altruism nor the more unconditional and inclusive forms of redistributive collectivist welfare are clearly dominant. Unless some kind of precarious compromise exists, the notion of a 'mixed economy of welfare' has no substantive meaning.

Recent attempts to shift the focus of social policy from the family to something called 'the community' are inspired by two basically incompatible ideologies. From a collectivist perspective the idea of community appears to offer a broader and more generous institutional framework for welfare altruism. In discovering a more authentic sense of local community, citizens will become more politically conscious and better equipped to campaign for more statutory services. From an individualist perspective the same idea of community offers an alternative institutional basis within which informal groupings of neighbours will assume more responsibility for their own welfare, until it becomes possible to reduce the statutory sector to residual status. Neither of these approaches, if successfully implemented, would be likely to provide a rational basis for social policies in a complex society which is still characterised by marked inequalities. The essence of rational policy is that it is designed to take the broader view, and to strike the best possible balance between local claims on scarce resources. These are bound to conflict with each other at times if they are concerned with interests primarily affecting particular communities or families.

During the 1960s and 1970s one of the main reasons why the notion of community increasingly dominated the debate about the future role of the personal social services was the belief of many social reformers that community could provide a better institutional framework for universalist welfare provision than the family. Joan Cooper reminds us that the Seebohm enquiry was originally established as a family service committee and that its terms of reference were formally limited to local authority social services. National assistance, probation and the questions about the extent to which welfare 'was to be provided by central and local government were excluded by implication since the emphasis was on appropriate machinery' (Cooper, 1983, pp.64-65). Nevertheless, although the Committee formally continued its enquiries on this basis, it always described itself as a 'personal social services committee' and it considerably broadened its de facto terms of reference. In doing so, the Committee was trying to ensure that due consideration was given to the needs of both households of parents with children and households of adults without children, as well as individuals without any family attachments. It also wanted to press the case for a universally accessible service in which hitherto neglected groups like the elderly, the mentally ill or handicapped would receive equitable treatment.

In addition to these issues there was the problem of defining the family for policy purposes - a consideration which led the Committee to argue that 'We could only make sense of our task by considering also childless couples and individuals without any close relatives, in other words, everybody' (Cooper, 1983, p.66). In one sense this approach was misguided because it drew the Committee away from a relatively modest definitional problem into the intrinsically open-ended and endless debate about 'community'. Although the structure of families is highly variable, it remains true that the majority of people belong to families, and their authentic sense of membership can serve as a sensible basis for service provision. This is not the case with the notion of community, which defies definition and cannot serve as a basis for equitable and rational social policies. The intellectual confusions into which the Barclay Report was led in its concern with 'community social work', 'communities' and 'communities of interest' illustrate my point (Barclay, 1982, pp.xii-xiii; Pinker, 1982, pp.242-2 and 244-5).

Social change, social policy and the family

There is no such thing as 'the normal family' but for policy purposes there are different kinds of 'normal' family, taking as a rough index of normality an evident ability to manage its own affairs and to discharge its responsibilities to dependent members within the terms of its own resources and those of the social services which its members are legally required or entitled to use. Disagreements occur about what constitutes 'normal' or reasonable use of existing social services and also about the range and level of services which ought to be provided by the state.

Not all high-level users of social services incur social disapproval. Families whose members make intensive use of educational services are generally admired, in contrast with the 40 per cent of one-parent families for whom supplementary benefit is the primary source of income. In this respect it is unmarried parents who tend to be singled out for censure. Generally speaking, governments show most concern about the morality of their subjects with regard to activities which lead to increases in public expenditure. Illegitimacy, for example, was a not infrequent occurrence amongst aristocratic and wealthy families throughout the history of the English poor law, but rich bastards never attracted much censure. It is the indiscretions of the poor which give rise to indignation among rate-payers. Opinions about what constitutes 'normal' usage of social services tend to vary according to the status of the services and needs in question; the key determinant of status is whether or not the service is seen as an 'investment' which will make future claims on social services less likely.

Families and households can be categorised by reference to various characteristics, including the composition of their membership, their income in relation to their household size and composition and their type of housing tenure. These basic features are usefully summarised in the Central Policy Review Staff and Central Statistical Office report on People and Their Families (1980) and more recently in the publications of the Study Commission on the Family (Craven et al, 1982; Wicks et al, 1983).

We see from Table 3.1 that in 1980 married couples with one or more dependent children accounted for 32 per cent, and lone parents with at least one dependent child accounted for a further 4 per cent of all households in Great Britain. The Central Policy Review Staff study emphasises the extent to which 'the structure of the population and the habits of people are altering in important ways'. First, there are now fewer young children than there were twenty years ago, but it is 'too soon to assess whether the slight rise in numbers of births since 1978 indicates that the fall in the birthrate of the previous 14 years has at last levelled off' (CPRS and CSO, 1980, p.6). The total number of children under 16 declined from almost 13 million in 1978 to just over 12 million. The size of the 0-4 age group is expected to rise by about 23 per cent during the coming ten years, while that of the 5-15 age group will fall by about 16 per cent to the end of the decade.

Secondly, the size and structure of the family unit is changing, with fewer large families but with a significant increase in the number of one-parent families. The Study Commission on the Family points out that over the last twenty years 'There has been a 500 per cent increase in the divorce rate', that one in three marriages is likely to end in divorce, but that a high proportion (about 80 per cent) of divorcees will marry again. Nevertheless the high divorce rate means that more children in one-parent families will experience periods in which they are at high risk of poverty, and there are currently about 900,000 one-parent families, including 1.5 million dependent children (CPRS and CSO, 1980, p.12). A breakdown of the total number of children aged under 16 shows that in

1977 roughly 37 per cent were members of families consisting of two dependent children, 22 per cent were members of families consisting of four or more dependent children, while 14 per cent were only children. A further 11 per cent were in lone parent families and another 1 per cent were children in care (CPRS and CSO, 1980, p.17).

Table 3.1   Households by type: Great Britain

Percentages

	1961	1980
One person		
- under retirement age	4	8
- over retirement age	7	14
Two or more single people		
- one or more over retirement age	3	1
- all under retirement age	2	1
Married couple		
- without children	26	27
- with 1 or 2 dependent children	30	26
- with 3 or more dependent children	8	6
- with independent child(ren) only	10	8
Lone-parent		
- with at least one dependent child	2	4
- with independent child(ren) only	4	4
Two or more families	3	1

Source: Social Trends, 12, HMSO, 1981, Table 2.2.
Taken from Wicks et al, 1983, p.9.

Thirdly, there have been striking changes since the end of the Second World War in the number of wives employed outside the home. Married women now account for about a quarter of the workforce and roughly 50 per cent of married working women are also caring for a dependent child. About 70 per cent of all working mothers are employed part time; a further analysis shows that 28 per cent of the women whose youngest child is under 5 years of age go out to work and that three-quarters of these do so on a part-time basis. Only a very small minority - about 6 per cent - work full time, although almost a quarter of all mothers appear to resume outside work of some kind by the time their babies are eight months old (Wicks et al, 1983, pp.17-18).

Fourthly, the economic recession and the growth of unemployment have adversely affected the life chances of some families. Approximately 1.3 million children are members of families in which the male head of household is unemployed, and it appears that the risk of unemployment is greatest among men with large families. A third of all unemployed men have dependent children; in addition a quarter of the 16-18 year old age group are currently unemployed (Wicks et al, 1983, p.18). These trends in unemployment have exacerbated the problem of family poverty.

Fifthly, the growth in the number of one-parent families has increased the number of dependent children at risk of poverty. The major cause of this increase has been the growth in the incidence of divorce and separation. Approximately 325,000 one-parent families are dependent on supplementary benefit for their subsistence. There is therefore a heavy concentration of low-income families in this group. In 1977, 44 per cent of the $1\frac{1}{4}$ million children in one-parent families were 'found in the bottom 20 per cent of all households ranked by their income (after taking into account the effects of different household size and compositions)' (CPRS and CSO, 1980, p.21). A more recent study concludes that nearly a half of all one-parent families had incomes below 120 per cent of the long-term supplementary benefit level, compared with 6 per cent of married couples with childen (Popay et al, 1982).

The Study Commission on the Family summarises the position as one in which 800,000 children 'are in families with incomes at the supplementary benefit level and, altogether, there are some 2,360,000 children in families with incomes below 140 per cent of the supplementary benefit level' (Wicks et al, 1983, pp.36-7). The Central Policy Review Staff studies point out that:

'In 1975 some four times as many families with the husband in work would have had incomes below the equivalent of the supplementary benefit entitlement level if the wives had not been working' (CPRS and CSO, 1980, p.112).

Sixthly, members of ethnic minorities are disproportionately represented amongst the poorest families. They are at highest risk of unemployment, poverty and educational disadvantage, and occupy much of the worst housing (Berthoud et al, 1981). The very modest amount of data available on the household income of ethnic minority groups provides some evidence of their relative income disadvantage, although the differences are more marked among male than female workers. Brown and Madge conclude that:

'Low earnings, large households and high housing costs of minorities mean that they are far more likely than the indigenous population to experience poverty' (Brown and Madge, 1982, pp.58-60).

There is much more substantial evidence confirming the relative educational disadvantages and underperformance experienced by the children of ethnic minorities (Finch, 1984a, pp.37-8; Tomlinson, 1980; Little, 1978). Perhaps the most dramatic commentary on the incidence and consequences of racial disadvantage is given in the Scarman Report (1981), which stresses the close links between high unemployment and social disorder.

The most radical changes in social policy since 1979 have occurred in the field of housing, which is a major determinant of the material quality of family life. Since 1980 nearly half a million council dwellings have been sold, and the proportion of the population living in public sector housing has fallen below 30 per cent. The generous incentives to house purchase under this scheme have been complemented by a new system of housing benefits which has sharply increased the rents of better-off tenants. Malpass suggests that the new scheme has brought about a 'very substantial switch of assistance from general to rebate subsidies. The result is that in most parts of the country the only way that a council tenant can receive assistance with housing costs is to qualify for means-tested benefits' (Malpass, 1984, pp.98-9).

Malpass goes on to argue that, so far as low-income families are concerned, the new scheme has changed 'what is essentially a housing activity to what is essentially a social security activity'. The cost of housing benefit is now counted as a part of social security and not of housing expenditure, with local authorities acting as administrative agents for a central government department. The overall effect of these policy changes has been to increase the number of owner-occupier families and to reduce the number of families in public housing with the shift of some better-off families into the private market. The problem of housing debt in the public sector remains a serious one.

Families in trouble and the social services

Statutory social services have emerged over time in response to a variety of human needs which could not be adequately met by the unaided efforts of individuals, families, neighbours or the other informal community networks of mutual aid. Four major factors account in large part for the expansion of these services. The first is the growth in the scale and complexity of industrial societies, which has significantly changed the quality of the relationship between individual citizens and their social environments. Secondly, the wealth and productivity of industrial societies has contributed both to rising levels of expectation in terms of personal living standards and social justice and to our material capacity to meet these expectations. Thirdly, the processes of social and economic change occur on such a scale and at such levels that the effective capacity of individuals to anticipate and cope with the adverse consequences of change has been significantly reduced.

Fourthly, there is a whole range of needs and human crises which are not necessarily the outcome of 'socially generated disservices'. They are needs of a more personal and idiosyncratic nature which may arise from crises in family life due to the breakdown of marriage, for example, or physical or mental illness, illegitimacy, death and bereavement, or the social isolation and natural infirmities that sometimes attend old age. Some human needs have evidently social causes, and others evidently personal ones, and many needs arise from an interaction of social and personal factors which is often difficult and sometimes impossible to disentangle. It is, however, at the individual level that we more frequently encounter the personal crises and tragedies which defy solution or which can respond - at best - only partially to support or containment.

The great majority of nuclear and extended families manage their own affairs successfully. They do so partly by drawing on the resources of their own members, partly through reciprocal forms of aid between friends and neighbours and partly through an intelligent and responsible use of statutory social services. It is, however, as misleading to draw a hard and fast line between 'normal' and 'deviant' families as it is to group all 'normal' families into a single homogeneous category. Any family can be adversely affected by an exceptional crisis beyond its capacities or control. These contingencies include sudden loss of income caused by unemployment or ill health; family breakdown with its attendant financial and emotional costs; severe and prolonged problems of caring for a dependent relative; and serious housing problems.

There are also minorities of families which live permanently on the margins of subsistence and survival in conditions of relative poverty, lacking the social skills and resources to cope without more or less continuous help from most of the statutory services. Closely but not exclusively associated with these problems are patterns of deviant behaviour including family violence and child abuse; child neglect; non-school attendance; and crime and delinquency, including various forms of addiction. Not all poor families make heavy demands on statutory social services, and some are poorer than they need to be because they do not make sufficient use of these services.

A small minority of families experience problems of such complexity and intractability that they need the help of local authority social services departments, to which they may be referred by other agencies. Part of the rationale for having social workers at all is that social workers have acquired over time a special responsibility for people whom no other agency or profession will accept as a primary obligation (Pinker, 1981, pp.5-7).

Many social work tasks involve statutory responsibilities and the exercise of social control as well as the provision of social care, and they all involve the provision of a personal service, within a professional framework. Other social services deal with needs which fit into a general category - the need for money, housing, health care, and so on and, while these services are not unresponsive to the idiosyncrasies of personal need, their response is limited to provision of the service in question. In contrast, as I have said before:

'One of the central aims of social work is to ensure that, somewhere in the vast bureaucratic apparatus of the welfare state, there will be someone to whom an individual in need can turn, as a person rather than a supplementary benefits claimant, a tenant, a patient, an old-age pensioner - or any of the other roles that men and women, as social creatures, are heir to' (Pinker, 1981, pp.12-13).

Local authority personal social services also meet a wide spectrum of needs ranging from what might be called the 'normal' risks and contingencies of living to the needs of individuals and families with very serious and often long-term social and emotional problems. Family failure of one kind or another and having no family are major causes of the demand for personal social services - which would be overwhelmed if the majority of families ceased to cope as well as they do.

Research carried out for the Barclay Report suggested that a team of three social workers, a social work assistant and a team leader, serving a population of about 10,000, would see something like 500 to 600 people a year, and spend an average of about three hours with each client. In practice, however, 'They would concentrate their time most heavily on a small number of clients, particularly those at risk of coming into care' (Barclay, 1982, chapter 2 and p.32). Other evidence on the work of these teams suggests that about 25 per cent of cases were closed on the first day; 50 per cent after the first week; 80 per cent after three months; and 90 per cent within the year. There is a hard core of about 10 per cent who stay on the books (Goldberg and Warburton, 1979, pp.59 & 67).

About one-third of all social work clients are physically frail, elderly and disabled, nearly one-third are young families with financial and housing problems, and another 16 per cent are highly disturbed families with histories of violence, mental illness, family conflict and breakdown, and neglect and delinquency. Goldberg and Warburton point out that the majority of social work clients simply require material assistance and advice. A minority of cases, including:

'children coming into care, families at serious risk of neglecting a child and most seriously disturbed families, remain open and (tend) to consume large amounts of social work and other resources over years, with few visible results' (Goldberg, 1978, p.7).

It should be noted that a relatively small population in various types of residential care accounts for nearly half of the local authority social service budgets, that the costs of residential care are high, and that they are likely to go on rising (DHSS, 1981; Bosanquet, 1985). Nearly half of all local authority residential care expenditure goes to the elderly, with children the next most important group. Of the total number of nearly 90,000 children in care, 'around 35,000' were in residential care of some sort on 31 March 1982, 'Broadly the same numbers as are boarded out with foster-parents' (House of Commons, 1984). The total number of children in residential care is falling, as local authorities are making less use of Community Homes with Education and voluntary homes. Since the early 1960s various non-custodial alternatives have been developed to meet the needs of children at risk or in trouble. Nevertheless official and public concern about the incidence of child abuse, delinquency and vandalism continues to grow.

It is not possible to provide comprehensive data on juvenile offenders because information is limited to apprehended offenders over the age of criminal responsibility. Few cases of vandalism are ever reported. The 14-16 age group continues to have the highest rate of reported offending for any age group, with the most dramatic increase among girls. Various explanations of the causes of juvenile delinquency have been offered, including broken homes, poor parenting, poverty, youth unemployment, and the mass media. The Central Policy Review Staff study suggests that there is 'no evidence of a direct link between working mothers and delinquency' (CPRS and CSO, 1980, p.36). Meanwhile the search for more positive and credible explanations continues. The incidence of crime and delinquency, like the incidence of poverty, is not amenable to exact measurement.

The controversial Children and Young Persons Act of 1969, with its emphasis on welfare rather than judicial procedure, was never fully implemented and it failed to achieve its aim of diverting young offenders as far as possible from custodial sentences. Detention centres for the under-17s were retained, and the age of criminal responsibility was not raised to 14. Throughout the 1970s more juvenile offenders received custodial sentences, partly because juveniles in breach of care orders were often sent to a detention centre or Borstal (Downes, 1983, p.27). It is too early to assess the effectiveness of new provisions under the 1982 Criminal Justice Act such as youth custody and shorter, more punitive detention centre orders, although it should be noted that the past failure rate of detention centres in terms of recidivism has been over 70 per cent. Among the various non-custodial alternatives, provision remains for intermediate treatment, community service orders, probation orders and care orders while the child is living at home or in a foster-home. Nevertheless the potential scope is likely to be curtailed in future because of cuts in the community service section of the Home Office budget for 1983/84 which reduced its share of the total from 0.68 per cent to 0.60 per cent.

When families encounter serious troubles or break down altogether, nearly all the major social services are directly or indirectly involved. Nevertheless a major responsibility falls on the local authority social services departments, whose budgets are very small in relation to the range and complexity of the work undertaken. The personal social services account for about 8 per cent of all local government expenditure, or 2 per cent of total public expenditure. Despite these responsibilities it is frequently argued that much of their work could be transferred to voluntary and private agencies and volunteers.

Some indication of the consequences which follow the cessation of local authority services is given in Howard and Briers's Department of Health and Social Security report (1979) on the effects of the social workers' strike in Tower Hamlets between August 1978 and June 1979. During the strike an emergency desk was staffed by senior personnel. Despite the application of stringent 'genuine emergency' criteria, there were 12 to 14 urgent referrals every day, concerned with children and old people at risk, fostering problems and fuel disconnections. Over a period of 10 months, 182 children and 194 old people had to be admitted to residential care. All other service agency workers, including health visitors, medical and nursing teams in hospitals, general practitioners and teachers, were pushed 'well beyond their limits' (Howard and Briers, 1979, p.9). The incidence of rent arrears and fuel debts rose steadily. It was found that:

> 'Those people who formed the bulk of the clientele of social workers, as distinct from the more practical services, are those for whom the resources of relatives, neighbours and friends had already been exhausted and do not attract help because of the nature of their problems' (Howard and Briers, 1979, p.10).

Howard and Briers describe the overall effects as 'a catastrophe' for vulnerable families, with suffering caused to children who were detained in care and to other children who could not be admitted into care. Carefully planned fostering arrangements broke down, intermediate treatment groups stopped operating, supervision orders were not implemented, the incidence of child abuse rose, and the work of the Juvenile Bureaux increased. Ironically it seems much easier to identify the essential duties of professional social workers when they are not at work than when they are.

Some of this statutory work is focussed on a small minority of seriously disturbed and damaged individuals and families - those who made up some of the 8 to 10 per cent who 'stay on the books'. Failure to achieve 'success' with these clients is not necessarily an adverse reflection on the effectiveness of social work intervention, although skilled social work support can help to maintain these clients over time, and even to prevent further deterioration and break-up. The ability to manage one's own life and to provide adequately for one's dependants constitutes a set of social skills which - in common with other human attributes like intelligence - follows a normal distribution in a total population. Some localities, however, are characterised by a disproportionately large number of relatively incapable people, and this concentration reinforces the general sense of deprivation which is a feature of such localities. No amount of high-flown rhetoric, whether it comes from moralising individualists who believe in the virtues of self-help or from ideologising collectivists who blame an unjust and oppressive political system, makes much impact on this problem.

The case for a family perspective in social policy

Although the great majority of families with dependent children neither use nor need the personal social services, other major statutory provisions like health care, education and social security are universally available and utilised, and just over 1 in 4 families live in local authority housing. For future planning purposes it may be helpful to distinguish between the majority of families which at any one point in time manage quite effectively without requiring social services of a personal nature and the small minority which do not. With regard to the majority the problem of inter-departmental service co-ordination is largely one of ensuring as far as possible that policies take adequate account of both common and constant needs and the variations which occur as a result of differences in family functions, roles and relationships. Families, however, are not static units, and a second consideration is the need to monitor the effects of new policies on different kinds of families as well as the changes in family life which have other social and economic causes.

In recent years there has been a revival of informed interest in the development of integrated family-focussed policies which bridge departmental boundaries. In their fourteen-nation comparative study, Kamerman and Kahn distinguish between the 'five European countries that have explicit and comprehensive family policies, five with more narrowly focussed but specific policies and four without explicit family policies. These four are the United States, the United Kingdom, Canada and Israel' (Howard and Briers, 1979, p.159; Kamerman and Kahn, 1978). Cooper draws attention to our 'lack of emphasis on, at least, the assumed economies of integrated service provision, and a minimal desire to measure costs and benefits' (Cooper, 1983, p.162). Much of the work of the Study Commission on the Family also points to the need for a more clearly articulated 'family perspective' in British social policy which will ensure that the changing relationship between social policy and family life is continuously monitored and evaluated (Wicks et al, 1983, pp.47-9).

The Central Policy Review Staff report on a <u>Joint Framework for Social Policy</u> (1975) explored the same issue nearly ten years ago and came to similar conclusions. The Study Commission on the Family argues the case for 'family impact' studies which would evaluate actual outcomes against intended policy effects, utilising data already available in the Family Expenditure Survey and the General Household Survey as well as in the Census. There would be a problem in deciding which part of the government should have responsibility for such an initiative, which has implications for so many departments. The idea of a Minister for the Family has understandably won little support, but other possibilities include the setting up of a Family Policy Review Board, either within government or on an independent basis, or including it in the agenda of the new House of Commons Select Committees (Wicks et al, 1983, pp.46-9).

Brown and Madge (1982) reach similar conclusions about the need for a more integrated approach to family policy in their review of the Transmitted Deprivation Programme. They suggest that the causes of family deprivation and failure are both personal and structural and that only joint planning across service departments at central and local government levels can provide an effective response. They also argue that:

> 'The development of a selective service to help the most deprived, while superficially an attractive idea, is neither appropriate nor desirable as a policy option ... While there is indeed some concentration and overlapping of deprivations it is not really possible to isolate or identify "the deprived" ' (Brown and Madge, 1982, p.291).

In a period of radical economic change it is wrong to assume that there is a clear and unbridgeable distinction between the two populations. Many more families are now at risk of falling into poverty because of unemployment than has previously been the case. Recent studies have drawn attention, for example, to possible links between unemployment and clinical depression and its adverse effects on family life and eventual return to work (Warr, 1983; Warr and Parry, 1982). They favour a more comprehensive approach which is addressed to both the special needs of seriously deprived families (with positive discrimination programmes where appropriate) and the contingencies and risks which affect ordinary families and better-off localities.

Consideration of the special needs of families in trouble or at risk shifts the debate about policy co-ordination from the level of strategic planning to the more tactical issues which arise in day-to-day administration and liaison between particular services and agencies. Dependence on social security is an obvious main cause of relative poverty, and this problem, as Beltram's recent study (1984) shows, involves not only low levels of provision but uneven take-up and the much debated 'poverty trap'. Social security reform is beyond the scope of this paper, but so long as the present anomalies and complexities continue, serious liaison problems will persist between social security and the personal social services.

This issue was discussed in the Joint DHSS/Local Authorities Association report in 1980 (DHSS/LAA, 1980). Tester's more recent report to the DHSS explores the problem in greater detail. She concludes that 'The Department's welfare responsibility is clearly not being completely fulfilled at present' and that there is a reluctance on the part of the DHSS to become involved in 'welfare' (Tester, forthcoming, p.9). She recommends that the discretionary powers of the Special Case Officer should be strengthened, that supplementary benefit officers should receive better training, that social work students should undertake practice placements in local offices, that DHSS officers should become more actively involved in local community associations and that a system of executive grade liaison officers should be introduced. If these proposals were complemented by a local authority area team system in which a few staff specialised with families experiencing 'material and financial difficulties' and had a prime responsibility for co-operating with social security, public utilities and housing services, we might begin to move away from the adversarial relationships which too frequently characterise 'liaison' between these services at present.

Nevertheless social work services 'can achieve only minimal relief for those who have conditions of gross and material deficiency' (Fuller and Stevenson, 1983, p.86). In the service sector of job creation and training the evidence suggests that there are inter-generational continuities of disadvantage. As Atkinson and others have pointed out, it is 'the structure of jobs and earnings which should be the direct focus of policy' (Atkinson et al, 1983). Consequently there are limits to what can be achieved through better co-operation between local training schemes, schools and welfare agencies.

In housing policy, however, there is evidence that much can be done to improve the quality of life in run-down and hard-to-let estates by well planned schemes of tenant participation and self-management. Anne Power's (1984) Department of the Environment-sponsored project on local housing management shows what can be achieved when a co-ordinated and adequately resourced attempt is made to improve the quality of life on deprived, hard-to-let council estates. Projects were set up in 20 estates characterised by high incidence of poverty, unemployment, vandalism, rent arrears and unlettable dwellings. The centralised systems of estate management were replaced by estate offices open all day, with their own resident caretakers, repair men and rent collectors. 19 of the 20 projects had local beat policemen and 16 of the estates developed active tenant associations. Dramatic improvements were achieved in the productivity of repair staff, in the reduction of vandalism and in the letting of empty properties. Less impact was made on the serious problem of rent arrears, although reductions were achieved in four of the estates, and in another four estates the arrears increased at a slower rate than elsewhere in the authority. The greatest success was achieved with new tenants in the prevention of rent arrears. The problem of rent arrears is difficult to eradicate once it becomes endemic in an estate, and the project was carried out during a period of high rent increases. Power comments that:

'The projects which had reduced rent arrears had achieved this through swift personal visits ... Bad debts and threats of eviction were carried through with Court action, but with a good personal system this was almost never necessary' (Power, 1984, p.25).

What this initiative shows is how much can be achieved when there is good inter-agency liaison, in this instance between housing, social services, the police and the tenants themselves.

In the fields of education and pre-school provision one of the most evident and long-standing deficiencies is the lack of adequate day care for the under-fives and after-school provision for older children. Progress here is not helped by the lack of adequate co-ordination between the various agencies involved. Day care is provided by local authority social services departments, registered voluntary and private agencies, child-minders and play groups. Various types of nursery school and class are provided by education authorities. Available provision falls far short of demand. A Central Policy Review Staff study found that only about 120,000 day nursery and child-minding places were available for the 900,000 children under five whose mothers go out to work (CPRS, 1980; Johnson and Cooper, forthcoming). Day care in Britain has been treated as 'essentially an emergency service for mothers who have special needs or who cannot cope' (Hodgkin et al, 1983; Finch, 1984b).

There are at least three ways in which adequate day care services could contribute to an integrated family policy. First, a substantial minority of families are kept above the poverty line because both spouses work. Secondly, day care itself creates employment and opportunities for paid volunteer work. Thirdly, day care can make a positive contribution to better child-rearing and development and the prevention and redress of social inequalities. With regard to all the main service sectors - statutory, voluntary and occupational - the UK has dropped behind many other industrial nations in its neglect of day care. Then, there is the future role of local authority personal social services, which are concerned with both the personal and the structural causes of need, and are directly and continuously involved with individuals and families at greatest risk of breakdown. It is therefore essential that their own organisation should positively contribute to better liaison with other statutory, voluntary and private sector services and with the informal sectors of care.

There is a current vogue among some of the local authorities for decentralised services and 'patch' systems of social work, with minimal specialisation. The case for highly generalist social workers has been strongly supported by the Barclay (1982) and Parsloe (1983) reports. Nevertheless the success of schemes like the Kent Community Care project has been based on the assumption that the more contracting agencies with which a local authority is involved, the more essential it becomes for the authority to have clearly specified objectives, a carefully designed system of financial incentives and a continuous programme of evaluation. As Judge (1983) suggests, the achievement of equity and efficiency in the distribution of resources requires 'the most careful assessment of relative needs' as well as 'comprehensive cost information about the resources at their disposal, together with incentives to guide their effective deployment'. Other key features of the Kent Community Care Project are its reliance on systematic case management at the level of individual worker and client, and the development of specialist expertise in social work practice. All the available evidence shows that informal networks of social care serviced by volunteers do not run themselves and often do not survive for long, without continuous support and case management from the local authority. Where needs are complex, the tasks of co-ordination and co-operation extend from the social services. Whatever the manifest deficiencies of the current patterns of social work organisation in area teams, it seems improbable that any alternative system which is more geographically dispersed than present ones will improve levels of co-operation and efficiency in both the formal and the informal contexts of social care.

Stevenson has outlined an organisational model for the personal social services which, in my view, strikes the right balance in meeting both of these requirements. Her proposal (see Figure 3.1) is based on area teams of specialist social workers, each of whom is responsible for a particular client group and for liaison with the other main public and social services involved, including a worker with special responsibility for making the best use of community resources (Stevenson, 1981, pp.131-6; Pinker, 1982).

Unless inter-service and agency links are strengthened, initiatives in other policy sectors will always leave a steadily

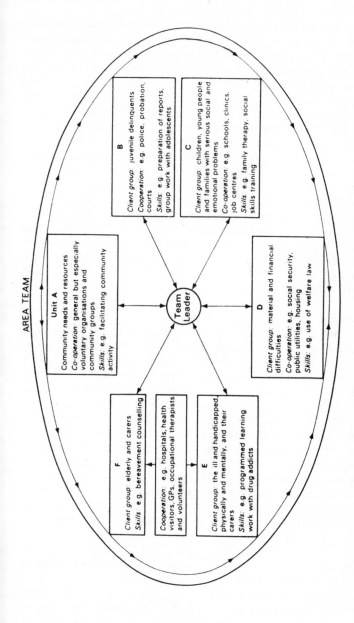

AREA TEAM

Unit A
Community needs and resources
Co-operation: general but especially voluntary organisations and community groups
Skills: e.g. facilitating community activity

B
Client group: juvenile delinquents
Cooperation: e.g. police, probation, courts
Skills: e.g. preparation of reports, group work with adolescents

C
Client group: children, young people and families with serious social and emotional problems
Co-operation: e.g. schools, clinics, job centres
Skills: e.g. family therapy, social skills training

Team Leader

D
Client group: material and financial difficulties
Co-operation: e.g. social security, public utilities, housing
Skills: e.g. use of welfare law

F
Client group: elderly and carers
Skills: e.g. bereavement counselling

Cooperation: e.g. hospitals, health visitors, GPs, occupational therapists and volunteers

E
Client group: the ill and handicapped, physically and mentally, and their carers
Skills: e.g. programmed learning work with drug addicts

Figure 3.1:   A model for team organisation

Source: Olive Stevenson, *Specialisation in Social Service Teams*, Allen and Unwin, 1981, p.132.

91

accumulating residue of 'failures' on the books of local authority social services departments. A greater degree of social work specialisation by client and by age group will also improve the effectiveness of interventive work with the minority of families which are afflicted with serious social and emotional problems. The lamentable record of child abuse scandals and enquiries over the past fifteen years must in part at least be attributed to deficiencies in currently popular versions of generic social work education and practice*.

Social workers, however, account for only about one in ten of all local authority social service staff, and successful care depends on teamwork and a sensible division of labour throughout the departments. This is unlikely to be achieved by breaking up area teams and scattering their members in penny packets, or 'patches', across the catchments of local authorities in pursuance of under-resourced 'preventive' work. It is signally irresponsible for social workers to spend their time looking for 'unmet need' when they are not coping adequately with manifest need.

Non-statutory services and the family

Is it possible to maintain - or even to increase - the quality and quantity of care provided in the total 'mixed economy of welfare' at a time when demand is rising and local authority social services departments are subject to strict spending restraints? The 'mixed' economy consists of formal statutory, voluntary and private sector services and a whole range of informal care arrangements based on self-help and mutual aid which lie largely outside the terms of financial exchange.

The belief that a large, untapped reserve army of volunteers still exists in modern British society provides the incentive for improving links between the formal and the informal sectors of social care. One of the key features of seriously deprived communities, however, is their lack of community spirit, and policies based on the belief that local

---

* The recent DHSS study of child abuse inquiry reports refers to 'much good work interspersed with numerous omissions, mistakes and misjudgements by different workers at different times', to the need for 'special training on child abuse matters', and to the lack of 'adequate supervision' and regular and objective reviews of cases (DHSS, 1982, pp.68-71).

volunteers can make up for the lack of statutory resources in these areas treat the cause of the problem as if it were the remedy. The bulk of the evidence suggests that volunteers are most numerous in well-integrated and affluent communities and scarcest in the relatively deprived ones. Nevertheless there are many supportive or tending tasks which can usefully be undertaken by volunteers working on an informal basis, under certain circumstances.

The subject of informal care and the personal social services has recently been reviewed by Johnson and Cooper (forthcoming), and some useful pointers for future policy emerge from the available evidence. First, there are about $1\frac{1}{4}$ million 'carers' for dependent people in Britain at the present time. The majority of them are women, usually daughters-in-law or spouses, and elderly relatives are the main beneficiaries. Secondly, the psychological and physical costs of caring can be severe, and the provision of a modicum of statutory support is an essential element in good community care.

Thirdly, there is a growing volume of criticism, largely but by no means exclusively from feminists, directed at the main assumption underlying all community care policies which are designed to enlist more volunteer help - namely, that community care exploits and perpetuates sexual inequality and 'the traditional unequal division of labour as between men in the workplace and women in the home' (Finch and Groves, 1983, p.10). On balance it would be unwise to expect volunteers to fill major gaps in statutory provision. Much depends on the balance which is held between altruism and prudential self-interest. A century ago the largest occupational group of women workers were underpaid and exploited domestic servants. There is a danger that in the pursuit of cheap community care we will recreate a new under-class of female skivvies composed of 'paid' and unpaid volunteers.

Fourthly, there are disagreements about the extent to which it is possible or desirable to integrate and 'interweave' the formal and the informal systems of social care. Some researchers believe that this is possible and desirable, but that decentralisation of the local authority and other social services is a precondition of success (Bayley, 1973, 1980; Ball, 1982; Hadley, 1981; Hadley et al, 1982). Others take a different view, arguing that formal and informal care systems are based on 'entirely discrete sets of paradigms' and that the gaps between them cannot for practical purposes be assumed to be bridgeable (Abrams, 1978, 1980; Pinker, 1982). In a forthcoming study on Neighbours Abrams appears to have qualified his earlier view about this relationship.

Fifthly, there is evidence which challenges the conventional belief that volunteering and mutual aid are largely inspired by spontaneous feelings of public service and unconditional altruism. Abrams found that a sense of duty or social obligation, tempered by a prudential eye on the prospect of reciprocity in the future, was a more important motive than simple altruism. In one of his last published papers he identified the phenomenon of a 'new neighbourhoodism', defining it in highly instrumental terms. He argued that most people live in 'new' neighbourhoods and that 'attempts to revive traditional local social networks are largely misguided'. People contribute to neighbourly activities like mutual aid after prudent consideration of the possible gains and losses involved (Abrams, 1980; Johnson and Cooper, forthcoming). In summary, although Titmuss's notion of the gift relationship may be admired as a paradigm of the welfare ethic, unconditional altruism can never be a sufficient basis for either equitable social policies or effective informal community care. These research findings suggest that one way of extending and strengthening supportive caring networks is to treat altruistic and pecuniary motives as complementary rather than antagonistic factors. The Community Care Scheme in Kent has developed successfully on this principle (Judge, 1983, p.16; Davies and Challis, 1981).

Judge recommends that estimates of local voluntary resources should be built into the calculation of Grant Related Expenditure Assessments and that instead of viewing this approach as 'a tax on altruism' we should treat it as entirely consistent with the Layfield principles on which the GREA methodology was originally based*. An alternative view would be that incentives rather than disincentives are more likely to encourage local authorities to seek out volunteer support.

There are other possible trade-offs which might increase the number of available volunteers. In the Kent study the typical 'paid volunteers' are 'relatively young, middle-class women, often with fairly minimal family commitments, or

---

*   For the relevant work on needs indicators see Bebbington and Davies (1980).

where there are children, the resources to purchase child care facilities'. It is difficult to estimate whether more 'paid volunteers' would be forthcoming if better care facilities were provided for their own children. Day care itself might be used more widely as a context for 'paid volunteer' employment.

Lastly, there is the role of formal voluntary agencies like the Family Welfare Association and the Family Service Units, which receive grant aid from local authorities and undertake contracted work on their behalf. Without statutory funding, the role of the voluntary sector would be very severely curtailed, and there is recent evidence that some local authorities are having to reduce grant aid to voluntary agencies as part of their general policies of retrenchment. In a free society voluntary agencies have a vital contribution to make in extending choice in welfare and in sponsoring new initiatives. Voluntary social services have an essential role to play in future policy but, short of an ideological revolution in social welfare, they cannot become either an effective or an efficient substitute for the statutory sector and they cannot be used to reduce overall public expenditure on the social services. To a considerable degree, voluntary social services are another way of spending public money, and the ad hoc proliferation of short-term voluntary initiatives is not the most efficient way of doing this.

Conclusion

There is a strong case to be made in favour of an integrated family policy involving either directly or indirectly all the relevant social services. Such a proposal has implications for planning at central and local government levels and for creating more structured methods of liaison at the level of service provision.

Twenty years ago the proposals of the Longford Study Group (Longford, 1964) in favour of establishing a family service were sharply challenged by Richard Titmuss, who thought that a family service would be too narrowly focussed on families with young children at risk, and would overlook the needs of people without families. Titmuss rejected the idea of basing personal social services on any kind of biological or sociological criteria, and went on to press the case for a unified and universalist set of services (Younghusband, 1978, pp.229-33). In retrospect we may well come to the conclusion that although the proposals of the Longford Report were too narrowly focussed they were pointing in the right direction, in contrast with those of the Seebohm Report which, by pointing in every direction, lacked any focus at all.

The problem we face today is a problem of focus in service provision. There is nothing incompatible in serving both families and their communities. Nevertheless it would be more sensible to treat the family as the initial focus for policies affecting the majority of people and thereafter to work outwards, utilising extra-familial systems of mutual aid and support on an ad hoc and pragmatic basis. Some social scientists need to be reminded that the family has not ceased to exist because it is subject to so much change. Indeed its ability to change and adapt is a main reason why it endures.

The available research evidence suggests that the family is a far more important source of informal care than the community. Outside the network of familial relationships there is a lack of geographical fit and functional complementarity between the potential providers and recipients of informal care. Put very bluntly, the providers and recipients tend to live in different localities, and high levels of mobility are not likely to result in more 'neighbourly' services. It is also frequently the case that volunteers are least likely to provide the most appropriate services for the people who are in greatest need. Furthermore advocates of enlightened self-interest and competitive individualism should not be surprised if research evidence shows that there is no clear-cut division between altruism and egoism in human motivation when the focus of interest is shifted from workplace to family and neighbourhood.

More attractive financial incentives are likely to improve the supply of informal care providers. Adequate day care services have a vitally important place in an integrated family policy. Better liaison between social services at local levels is a pre-condition for improving the quality of life in very deprived neighbourhoods where informal care networks tend to be least well developed. Formal voluntary agencies and the informal volunteer sector cannot assume more welfare responsibilities than they currently discharge, without more financial support from the state. Finally, more specialisation in the personal social services is likely to increase efficiency and effectiveness in the provision of services, in the prevention of family breakdown and in improving co-operation within the formal sector and between the statutory services and informal carers.

References

Abrams, P. (1978), 'Community Care: Some Research Problems and Priorities', in J.A. Barnes and N. Connelly (eds), Social Care Research, Bedford Square Press for the Policy Studies Institute.

Abrams, P. (1980), 'Social Change, Social Networks and Neighbourhood Care', Social Work Service, No. 22, February.

Atkinson, A.B., Maynard, A.D. and Trinder, C.G. (1983), Parents and Children: incomes in two generations, Heinemann Educational Books.

Ball, Colin and Meg (1982), What the Neighbours Say, Volunteer Centre (forthcoming for Penguin).

Barclay, P. (Chairman) (1982), Social Workers: Their Role and Tasks, The report of a Working Party under the chairmanship of Peter M. Barclay, Bedford Square Press for NISW.

Bayley, M. (1973), Mental Handicap and Community Care, Routledge & Kegan Paul.

Bayley, M. (1980), 'Neighbourhood Care and Community Care: A Response to Philip Abrams', Social Work Service, February.

Bebbington, A.C. and Davies, B. (1980), 'Territorial Needs Indicators: A New Approach', Journal of Social Policy, Vol. 9, part 2, and Vol. 9, part 4.

Beltram, G. (1984), Testing the Safety Net, Occasional Papers on Social Administration, Bedford Square Press/NCVO.

Berthoud, R. and Brown, J.C. with Cooper, S. (1981), Poverty and the Development of Anti-Poverty Policy in the United Kingdom, Heinemann Educational Books.

Bosanquet, N. (1985), 'Welfare Needs, Welfare Jobs and Efficiency', in R. Klein and M.O'Higgins (eds), The Future of Welfare, Basil Blackwell.

Brown, M. and Madge, N. (1982), Despite the Welfare State: A Report on the DHSS/SSRC Programme of Research into Transmitted Deprivation, Heinemann Educational Books.

Central Policy Review Staff (1975), A Joint Framework for Social Policy, HMSO.

Central Policy Review Staff (1980), Child Care Facilities in Britain, HMSO.

Central Policy Review Staff and Central Statistical Office (1980), People and their Families, HMSO.

Cooper, J. (1983), The Creation of the British Personal Social Services, 1962-74, Heinemann Educational Books.

Craven, E., Rimmer, L. and Wicks, M. (1982), Family Issues and Public Policy, Study Commission on the Family.

Davies, B. and Challis, D. (1981), The Thanet Community Care Project: Some Interim Results, PSSRU Discussion Paper, 194/3, mimeo.

DHSS (1981), Health and Personal Social Service Statistics for England, HMSO.

DHSS (1982), Child Abuse; A Study of Inquiry Reports, 1973-81, HMSO.

DHSS/Local Authority Association Joint Working Party on Relations with the Social Services (1980), Liaison in Practice. Guidance on liaison between local authority social services and social work departments and the supplementary benefit organisations of the Department of Health and Social Security, DHSS.

Downes, D. (1983), Law and Order: Theft of an Issue, Fabian Tract 490.

Finch, J. (1984a), Education as Social Policy, Longmans.

Finch, J. (1984b), 'The Deceit of Self-Help: Pre-School Play Groups and Working-Class Mothers', Journal of Social Policy, Vol. 13, part 1, pp.1-20.

Finch, J. and Groves, D. (1983), A Labour of Love: Women, Work and Caring, Routledge & Kegan Paul.

Fuller, R. and Stevenson, O. (1983), Policies, Programmes and Disadvantage: A Review of the Literature, Heinemann Educational Books.

Goldberg, E.M. (1978), Social Work Since Seebohm: All Things to All Men?, NISW.

Goldberg, E.M. and Warburton, W. (1979), Ends and Means in Social Work, Allen & Unwin.

Hadley, R. (1981), 'Social Services Departments and the Community', in E.M. Goldberg and S. Hatch (eds), A New Look at the Personal Social Services, Policy Studies Institute.

Hadley, R. et al (1982), 'A Case for Neighbourhood-Based Social Work and Social Services', Appendix A in P. Barclay (1982).

Hodgkin, R., Streather, J. and Tunstill, J. (1983), 'The Case for Prevention', Community Care, 13 October, No. 483, pp.31-32.

House of Commons (1984), Second Report from the Social Services Committee, Session 1983-84, Children in Care, Vol. 1, House of Commons Paper 360-1, para. 202, HMSO.

Howard, A. and Briers, J. (1979), An Investigation into the Effect on Clients of Industrial Action by Social Workers in the London Borough of Tower Hamlets, report by the Social Work Service of the Department of Health and Social Security, DHSS.

Johnson, M. and Cooper, S. (forthcoming), Informal Care and the Personal Social Services, Policy Studies Institute.

Judge, K. (1983), 'From the Tyranny of the Case to the Myth of the Community: Reflections on the Barclay Report', in The Barclay Report: Papers from a Consultation Day, National Institute for Social Work Paper 15, NISW.

Kamerman, S.B. and Kahn, A.J. (eds) (1978), Family Policy: Government and Families in Fourteen Countries, Columbia University Press.

Little, A.N. (1978), Educational Policies for Multi-Racial Areas, Inaugural lecture, Goldsmiths College.

Longford, Lord (Chairman) (1964), Crime: A Challenge to Us All: Report of the Labour Party's Study Group, Transport House.

Malpass, P. (1984), 'Housing Benefits in Perspective', in C. Jones and J. Stevenson (eds), The Year Book of Social Policy in Britain, 1983, Routledge & Kegan Paul.

Parsloe, P. (Chairman) (1983), Report of Council Working Group: Review of Qualifying Training Policies, Paper 20.1, CCETSW.

Pinker, R. (1979), The Idea of Welfare, Heinemann Educational Books.

Pinker, R. (1981), The Enterprise of Social Work, Inaugural lecture, London School of Economics & Political Science.

Pinker, R. (1982), 'An Alternative View', Appendix B in P. Barclay (1982).

Popay, J., Rimmer, L. and Rossiter, C. (1982), One Parent Families: Parents, Children and Public Policy, Study Commission on the Family.

Power, A. (1984), Local Housing Management: A Priority Estates Project Survey, Department of the Environment.

Scarman, Lord (Chairman) (1981), The Brixton Disorders, 10-12 April 1981, Report of an Inquiry, Cmnd. 8427, HMSO.

Stevenson, O. (1981), Specialisation in Social Service Teams, Allen & Unwin.

Tester, S. (forthcoming), Local Liaison with DHSS Social Security Officers: Final Report of a Study Commissioned by the DHSS on Liaison Arrangements between DHSS Local Officers and Other Statutory and Voluntary Agencies.

Tomlinson, S. (1980), 'The Educational Performance of Ethnic Minority Children', New Community, Vol. 8, No. 3, pp.213-34.

Warr, P. (1983), 'Job Loss, Unemployment and Psychological Well-Being', in E. van de Vliert and V. Allen (eds), Role Transitions, Plenum Press.

Warr, P. and Parry, G. (1982), 'Depressed Mood in Working-Class Mothers with and without Paid Employment', Social Psychiatry, Vol. 171, pp.161-165.

Wicks, M., Popay, J. and Rimmer, L. (1983), Final Report of the Study Commission: Families in the Future, Study Commission on the Family.

Younghusband, E. (1978), Social Work in Britain: 1950-1975: A Follow-up Study, Vol. 1, Allen & Unwin.

4 Social security, taxation and the working population over the next ten years *

A.B. ATKINSON

Summary

Public expenditure on social security has grown so that it now represents 12.0 per cent of GDP. The recent Treasury Green Paper's determination to hold the total of public expenditure constant in real terms for at least the next five years implies a reduction in this ratio at least to 10.5 per cent, perhaps even to 9.7 per cent over the next ten years. The government presents this as a straight choice between higher benefits and lower taxes. This is, however, an oversimplification, and this chapter examines in detail some of the various options for incremental changes in tax and benefit policy for working families.

Policy for social security spending has to be related to that for individual benefits and programmes, and may have different implications depending on demographic, behavioural and other changes. In the second section of the chapter we examine the spending picture in more detail in light of a range of assumptions about benefit uprating policy and about unemployment trends. While a policy to uprate benefits in line with earnings would maintain the ratio of social security expenditure to GDP at 12.0 per cent, a policy to uprate in line with prices only would allow it to fall to 10.5 per cent. Even this, however, involves a 7 per cent increase in real expenditure over the ten year period.

In the third section, a broad indication is given of the impact of these policies on individual families, using for this purpose a micro-computer model which allows a range of policies to be examined rapidly and flexibly. The choice

---

*   This paper is based on research which forms part of the ESRC Programme on Taxation, Incentives and the Distribution of Income, directed by M.A. King, N.H. Stern and myself. I alone am responsible for the views expressed.

between full earnings uprating and price only uprating implies a difference of 2.2 percentage points in the average tax burden in 1994-95. The decision to go for a reduction in tax rates rather than earnings indexation would have a small but clear adverse affect on the distribution of income among working families - the poorer half would share 34.2 per cent of equivalent income under the maintain-benefits policy, compared with 33.9 per cent under the cut-taxes policy. The loss of child benefits involved in the latter policy has particularly adverse effects (obviously) on families with children, and on the wife's share of couples' income. But preferring an income tax cut to maintaining the relative value of benefits would reduce replacement and marginal tax rates.

These calculations assumed that potential savings accruing through price indexation of benefits would be devoted to a cut in the basic rate of tax. In the fourth section, we examine other policy options which yield the same gross totals, but which affect individual families differently. One supposes an increase in personal tax allowances in preference to a cut in the basic rate. A second devotes the same resources to a significant increase in child benefit, partially clawed back by taxing it as wife's income. A third is directed at the equalisation of husbands' and wives' tax treatment, and a fourth integrates the National Insurance Contributions with income tax.

Each of these policies has advantages and disadvantages compared with alternatives, within an identical budget. By extension, other, more radically different, policies or sets of policies could be proposed, still within the same budget. One of the purposes of the analysis has been to ask questions about the precise objectives of the government. Different policies can be proposed, to achieve different ends.

Introduction
This chapter is concerned with the implications for those in work of likely developments in social security over the next ten years, notably those arising for demographic reasons or because of existing policy commitments, and of different options for policy change over that period. The scope is limited in that it is concerned with the position of those in work, and it should be borne in mind that the changes in policy would have major implications for those not in work, notably the sick, disabled, unemployed, and single parent families where the parent is not in work. By focussing on social

security, the analysis is also limited in that it does not consider the relation between cash benefits and the provision of care.

The determination of long-term policy towards social security is often seen in terms of a trade-off between the generosity of benefits and the 'burden' imposed on the working population in terms of taxes and contributions. The present government has given priority to reducing the tax burden and this - on the trade-off view - implies that a move must be made towards reducing benefits relative to the general level of incomes. An alternative government more concerned with raising benefits, or extending their scope, would choose a different policy, but its room for manoeuvre may be limited by the willingness of taxpayers to finance such improvements. The trade-off is like that which consumers in economics textbooks are supposed to face, except that it is benefit increases versus tax reductions, rather than apples versus pears.

This kind of trade-off may be illustrated by reference to the Green Paper The Next Ten Years: Public Expenditure and Taxation into the 1990s (Cmnd. 9189). The Green Paper deals with the totality of public spending, but its analysis may be developed to bring out the significance for social security. In Figures 4.1 and 4.2, the information supplied in the Green Paper has been supplemented by that specifically relevant here.

First, the present government is concerned with the ratio of public expenditure to Gross Domestic Product (GDP). As is shown in Figure 4.1, where the ratio is represented by the height of the bars, there has been a general tendency for this to rise over the last twenty years. The figures for social security alone are given for alternate years at the top of each of the bars in Figure 4.1. They show that, since 1963, social security spending has increased much faster than GDP. In 1983-84, the planning total for social security spending in the UK (The Government's Expenditure Plans 1984-85 to 1986-87, Cmnd. 9143-II, Tables 2.12 and 2.17) amounted to some 12 per cent of GDP.

The Green Paper considers the implications of different policies with regard to government spending into the 1990s. These assume that there would be no real increase for five years up to 1988-89, during which period GDP is forecast to grow in real terms at $2\frac{1}{4}$ per cent per annum, and then two alternative rates of real growth in public expenditure - either

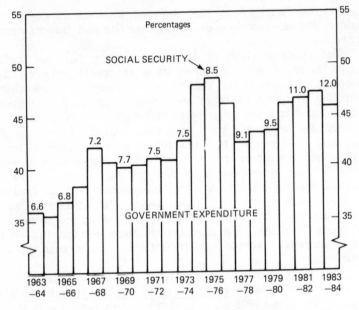

Sources: General government expenditure from Cmnd. 9189, Chart 2; social
security spending (figures for calendar years) from *National Income
and Expenditure 1983,* Tables 1.1 and 9.4, and comparable tables in
earlier years.

Figure 4.1: General government expenditure and social
security spending in relation to GDP (market
prices) 1963-64 to 1983-84

zero or 1 per cent per annum - for the five years up to 1993-94, with real GDP growing at either $1\frac{1}{2}$ or 2 per cent per annum. If the same assumptions are appled to social security spending alone, taking the 1983-84 figure of 12.0 per cent as a base, then the implied percentages of social security spending to GDP in 1993-94 are:

	Assumed GDP growth (1988-93) per annum:	
Assumed spending growth (1988-93) per annum:	$1\frac{1}{2}$ per cent	2 per cent
zero	10.0	9.7
1 per cent	10.5	10.2

The implications for the tax burden on the working population may be represented in a number of ways. The Green Paper gives prominence to the percentage of income paid in income tax by a married man with no children at average earnings, and the chart published there is reproduced as Figure 4.2. This brings out the general increase over the period up to the mid-1970s, with a decline thereafter, although the decline is less marked when account is taken of National Insurance contributions (employee contributions have been added in Figure 4.2 and are shown by the shaded area). The Green Paper indicates the effect of the different policies to restrict total government expenditure on the tax burden measured in this way, on the assumption that all of the tax reduction would be concentrated on income tax personal allowances. With 1 per cent growth in total spending in the latter half of the period, and the slower rate of GDP increase, the proportion taken in income tax from the married man on average earnings would fall from 20 per cent in 1983-84 to 17 per cent in 1993-94. With zero growth in public spending and the faster rate of GDP increase, the reduction would be 7 percentage points.

The Green Paper may therefore be interpreted as presenting us with a trade-off between increasing real expenditure on benefits and reducing the tax burden on the working population, and this is the way in which the issue is often viewed. Such a representation serves to bring home the important fact that choices have to be made. It is however an over-simplification and it would be misleading to leave the

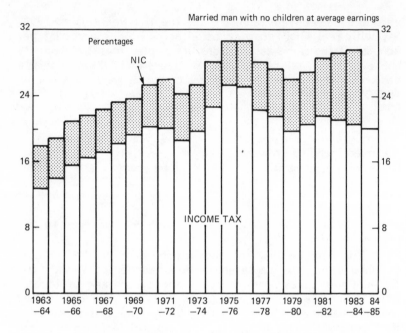

Figure 4.2 caption area

Married man with no children at average earnings

Percentages

NIC

INCOME TAX

Sources: Income tax from Cmnd. 9189, Chart 7. NIC calculated applying rates
ruling at 31 October and assuming man not contracted out, based on
average earnings of full-time men, all occupations, Great Britain,
excluding those whose pay is affected by absence, linked prior to 1970
to the series for average adult male earnings in production industries
and some services.

Figure 4.2: Income tax, and employee national insurance
contributions (NIC) as per cent of gross earnings

analysis at this juncture. First, policy for total social security spending has to be related to that for individual benefits and programmes, an aspect stressed by O'Higgins and Patterson (1985). Zero real growth in total spending may have quite different implications for the level of benefits depending on demographic, behavioural and other changes which affect the number of beneficiaries. In the second section, we examine the spending picture in more detail, working from three different assumptions about the level of individual benefits to the implications for financing. This approach may appear to run counter to the general tenor of the Green Paper, which is 'to decide first what can and should be afforded, then to set expenditure plans for individual programmes consistently with that decision' (Cmnd. 9189, p.3), but in the case of social security it is the parameters of the programme, such as the benefit rates, rather than total spending, which the government directly controls. The outcome will depend on economic and social developments, such as changes in the level of unemployment (where we consider a range of assumptions).

The second respect in which the simple trade-off view is misleading is that it only deals with the aggregate cost to the working population, whereas it is the impact on individual families which is of ultimate concern. The married man on average earnings cannot necessarily be assumed to be representative; and we need to take account of the full diversity of family circumstances. In the third section we present the results of such an analysis based on an extrapolation of the 1980 Family Expenditure Survey. This shows the predicted effect of the different spending policies on the distribution of net incomes and tax burdens. It considers how the impact varies by income groups and between family types. It considers what can be said about the distribution within the family. The analysis is concerned not only with tax burdens but also shows the implications for marginal tax rates and the incentives faced by individual workers.

The picture which emerges from this more detailed investigation is inevitably more complex than that with which we began, and readers may conclude that this is yet another example of the propensity of academics to render arcane a subject which is essentially simple. There is however an important lesson, since the detailed analysis brings out that the range of options is wider than is suggested by the simple trade-off view. There is a fuller menu of policy possibilities. A given average tax burden on the working population is consistent with the development of policy in several directions, and in the fourth section we consider four alternatives, each constructed on a revenue-neutral basis.

When one contemplates this wider menu, it becomes clear that more consideration needs to be given to the basic objectives of policy. Why is it that the government wishes to cut taxes? What are the aims of the social security system? We return to these issues in the concluding section.

In this paper, projections are made over the ten year period to the mid-1990s commencing with 1984-85. Projection even ten years forward involved heroic assumptions about the development of the economy. Here it is assumed throughout that real GDP grows on average by 2 per cent per annum, which lies between the two Green Paper assumptions described above. It is assumed that real earnings per worker rise at $1\frac{1}{2}$ per cent per annum, with a range of assumptions about unemployment:

Uo   no change in unemployment rate between 1984-85 and 1994-95;

U-   3 percentage point fall in unemployment rate;

U+   3 percentage point rise in unemployment rate;

The assumptions about policy towards benefits are:

P1   All benefit scales, including post-award increases in earnings-related pensions, increased in line with earnings,

P2   All benefit scales, and post-award amounts, constant in real terms for 5 years and then rise at 1 per cent per annum for the next 5 years,

P3   All benefit scales, and post-award amounts, constant in real terms.

The first of these assumptions may be seen as maintaining the 'status quo', as it has generally been interpreted in recent decades. The second and third may be seen as corresponding, at the level of benefit scales, to the Green Paper assumptions about total spending*.

---

*   Note that policies P1 and P3 are identical to the social security uprating assumptions in O'Higgins's 'Carry-on' and 'Constant' policy packages, (see chapter 1).

Overall picture

The overall picture in terms of total social security spending has been examined by O'Higgins and Patterson (1985), whose forecasts of social security spending for 1993-94 take account of demographic developments affecting the number of pensioners and child benefit recipients and of the changing levels of unemployment induced by different rates of GDP and productivity growth. In general, they assume that there would be no real increases in social security benefits - assumption P3 above - although they consider variants where there is a real increase in pensions.

Table 4.1   Social security spending 1984-85 and 1994-95
(United Kingdom, projected)

1984-85 £ billion

	1984-85	P1	1994-95 P2	P3
National Insurance	20.7	26.2	24.1	23.2
Child benefit	4.3	5.3	4.8	4.6
Supplementary benefit	6.2	7.0	6.3	6.0
Rent rebates	2.5	2.8	2.0	1.9
Other benefits	1.9	2.2	2.0	1.9
TOTAL	38.4	46.9	42.8	41.1

Notes: Total includes administration expenses a d spending in Northern Ireland not shown above.
All projections based on the central unemployment assumptions (Uo).

These estimates provide a valuable reference point, but they do not go into sufficient detail for the present purpose and they do not allow us to see the effect of the alternative assumptions P1 and P2. Nor do they relate the expenditure to the changes in taxation and contribution rates which are what directly affect the working population. In view of this, we present below a set of estimates built up from the individual programmes, taking as the starting point the planning totals in 1984-85. These are shown in the first column of Table 4.1, where expenditure in Northern Ireland is treated as a separate category, as in the Public Expenditure White Paper which is the source of the figures.

(a) National Insurance

The expenditure on National Insurance (NI) benefits, and especially that on pensions, has received considerable attention. The long-term projection of benefits, and the contributions required to finance them, has been the subject of the Government Actuary's First Quinquennial Review (House of Commons, 19 July 1982), as well as a number of academic articles, such as Hemming and Kay (1982).

The estimates here are based on those in the Government Actuary's Review. The calculations by the Government Actuary are not directly applicable, since they cover the period 1985-86 to 1995-96 (as well as later years), and assume in the central estimates an unemployment rate of 6 per cent. It is assumed here that the changes over the ten year period can be displaced by one year, and can be taken as corresponding to the assumption Uo of constant unemployment. This should be sufficient to give at least a broad order of magnitude. The estimates for the increase in NI benefits for our three assumptions P1 - P3 may be obtained by the appropriate combination of those made by the Government Actuary. These are expressed first in terms of constant earnings levels. On assumption P1, there is an increase of some 9 per cent. This is largely attributable to the rise in earnings-related pensions; the cost of flat-rate pensions being expected to remain more or less unchanged. With assumption P2, there would be essentially no change relative to earnings levels; and with assumption P3 there would be a $3\frac{1}{2}$ per cent reduction. With our assumed growth of real earnings over the ten years, the overall level of earnings would rise by 16 per cent, so that all three assumptions would imply a rise in real expenditure on NI benefits. This is summarised below:

Assumption	Per cent growth over 10 years at constant earnings	in real terms
P1	9.0	26.5
P2	0.4	16.4
P3	-3.5	11.9

The changes in real terms are used to arrive at the estimates in £1984-85 shown in the first line of Table 4.1.

Adopting the same assumptions as the Government Actuary, we may relate the changes in spending to the sources of financing. On assumption P1, the £1.6 billion increase, at the 1981-82 earnings levels used in the Review, is assumed to be financed by an increase of £0.9 billion in contributions, of £0.1 billion in the Treasury Supplement and £0.6 billion via a decrease in the reduction for contracted out members. As a result, the increase in the percentage contribution rate (Class 1) is 0.3 percentage points. This relatively modest rise, given the increase in total spending relative to earnings, is achieved because of the increased payments by those contracted out and because of the fall· in the number of married women benefiting from the option of paying reduced contributions. By the same token, the assumption P2 would allow a reduction of 0.7 percentage points, and assumption P3 1.2 percentage points, in the Class 1 contribution rate. (This rate applies to the total of employee and employer contributions; for the purpose of our analysis we assume that the changes are all in the employee rate.)

The Government Actuary's calculations relate only to the National Insurance fund, but the implications for the government budget do not stop at this point. The Treasury Supplement has to be financed; and the changes in benefit levels will affect income tax receipts. The income tax liability on the state earnings related pension is likely to be of increasing importance, even when account is taken of the age allowance (see Altmann and Atkinson, 1982), and we assume here that a third of the increase would be taxable at a rate of 30 per cent. On assumption P1, this more or less counterbalances the increased Treasury Supplement. With P2, the extra tax would permit a reduction in the basic rate of 0.2 percentage points; with P3 the reduction would be 0.3 percentage points.

The Government Actuary provides estimates of the effect of unemployment being higher or lower by 3 percentage points, where this takes account of the change in NI benefits and in contribution revenue. On this basis, we can draw the tentative conclusion that the required Class 1 contribution rate would be 1 percentage point lower on assumption U- and 1 percentage point higher on assumption U+. These calculations may understate the sensitivity to variations in the unemployment rate if receipt of a wider range of benefits is taken into account, including for example invalidity benefit.

(b) Other benefits

The prediction of spending on NI benefits involves strong assumptions; this is true to an even greater extent when we turn to the non-contributory benefits. The estimates shown in Table 4.1 for child benefit take account of the expected increase in the number of qualifying children, assumed to be 6.4 per cent on the basis of the increase in the UK population aged under 15 shown in the Green Paper (Table 3). The estimates for supplementary benefit and rent rebates make allowance for the increase in earnings-related pension, which may be expected to reduce the dependence of pensioners on these means-tested benefits. These factors tend to cancel. The effect of variations in unemployment is taken into account in calculating expenditure on supplementary benefit. Total predicted spending shows no change in real terms on assumption P3 (with no change in unemployment), whereas on policy P1 the total rises by the same percentage as earnings.

The financing of this expenditure is assumed here to be derived from income tax. If personal allowances and tax brackets increase with earnings levels, then unchanged policy would lead to a rise in revenue at the same rate (this assumes that deductions from the tax base would also rise proportionately). On assumption P1, there would therefore be no adjustment in tax rates. With assumptions P2 and P3, tax could be reduced, and this is assumed to take the form of a reduction in the basic rate of tax of 1.5 percentage points (assumption P2) or 2.0 percentage points (assumption P3). With assumption U-, the reduced cost of supplementary benefit would allow a further 0.5 percentage point reduction; with assumption U+, the tax rate would be 0.5 percentage points higher.

(c) Total

The predictions for total spending under the three policies P1-P3 are brought together in Table 4.1. What do they imply for the overall prospects? If it is the government's intention to hold the total constant in real terms, then it does not appear that this would be achieved even on Policy P3, where there would be a 7 per cent real increase. This would be less if unemployment were to fall, although with assumption U- the increase would still be 4 per cent in real terms. If unemployment were to rise as supposed under assumption U+, then real spending would increase, under P3, by 10 per cent. This latter calculation appears to be broadly in line with those of O'Higgins and Patterson: for example, their scenarios A and B, which involve rising unemployment, show real increases of 10.5 per cent and 8.2 per cent. In order to hold total real spending constant, it appears that it would be necessary to reduce benefit levels in real terms, or to restrict the scope of benefits.

If the aim of the government is to contain the rise in social security spending relative to GDP, then this appears much more easily attained. With policy P1, and constant unemployment, the ratio would exhibit little change, remaining around 12 per cent, but with P2 it would fall to 11 per cent and with P3 to 10.5 per cent. Seen in this way, the aggregate picture seems much more manageable; and continuation of a 'status quo' policy, maintaining benefits in line with earnings, appears quite feasible into the mid-1990s.

Impact on individual families

The implications of the different policies for income tax and National Insurance Contributions (NIC) are summarised in Table 4.2. For the married taxpayer on average earnings who features in the Green Paper, the impact of these changes is readily calculated. On the assumption that tax allowances and brackets rise in line with earnings, and that the man is not contracted out for NIC, policy P1 would mean a slight increase in the proportion deducted for income tax and NIC, from 29.0 per cent to 29.3 per cent. (In these calculations, 'average' earnings have been taken as £182, which generates an income tax burden of 20 per cent as quoted in the Green Paper.) In contrast, the policy P3 would allow a reduction in both NIC and income tax, with the average rate falling from 29.0 per cent to 26.3 per cent. So the difference between policies P1 and P3, on which we concentrate here, amounts to trading off the lower benefits, relative to earnings, under P3 against a tax cut of 3 percentage points.

Table 4.2 Predicted tax and National Insurance contribution (NIC) rates 1994-95

Percentage rates

| | Assumption | | | Variation with | |
	P1	P2	P3	U-	U+
NIC (Class 1)	9.3	8.3	7.8	-1.0	+1.0
Reduction for contracting out	0.9	0.9	0.9	unchanged	
Income tax basic rate	30.0	28.3	27.7	-0.5	+0.5

It is however clear that the circumstances of individual taxpayers may differ considerably from those assumed in these hypothetical calculations:
- the man may be contracted out for NIC purposes, in which case the amount paid would rise more or fall less,
- there may be deductions against taxable income, for items such as mortgage interest, which would reduce the benefit from tax rate reductions,
- his wife may be in paid employment and also be affected by changes in income tax and NIC,
- if there are dependent children, then the family may be affected by changes in child benefit,
- the family may be entitled to means-tested benefits, such as housing benefit.

These different circumstances could be taken into account by extending the range of hypothetical calculations, but this is not sufficient, since we also need to know how frequently they are found in real life. We do not want to devote a great deal of attention to combinations of circumstances which are never found in practice. For this reason, any analysis of the impact of the policy changes, and alternatives to them, must be based on evidence from a representative sample of actual families, and this is what is presented below, based on the Family Expenditure Survey (FES).

The use of evidence from surveys such as the FES is not without difficulty. First, the FES, while a very high quality survey, suffers from a significant degree of non-response and there are reasons to believe that certain types of income, such as that from self-employment, are understated. In our work, we have attempted to adjust for these shortcomings, in the grossing up to the whole population, and in multiplying up the amounts of income to bring them into line with external evidence. Nevertheless, such adjustments are only approximate. Secondly, we are interested in predicting the effect of changes in policy. This has involved assumptions both about how they would actually work and about the responses of families to such changes. In the latter case, we at present assume that there is no alteration in gross incomes, but our current research is directed at refining this assumption. For the present, the assumption may be regarded as equivalent to that made in the official estimates of the effect of direct tax changes.

The third problem with the use of survey data is that it involves substantial computation, and it is not typically easily accessible to the user. Being able to carry out the analysis quickly and flexibly is particularly important when one wishes to consider a number of policy options and where there is room for a range of opinion about the parameters which should be entered (for example, those forecasting demographic changes).

These practical considerations led to the calculations reported here being based on a sub-sample of families in the FES small enough to be analysed on a BBC micro-computer in a reasonably short time (around 30 minutes). The use of a sub-sample (1 in 5 of the families in the relevant population) means that the results are surrounded by a greater margin of error. (One way of looking at it is to say that the sampling errors are enlarged by a factor of $\sqrt{5}$.) The results from the sub-sample cannot therefore be regarded as a perfect substitute for analysis based on the full FES sample. They should be regarded as providing only a broad first look at the implications of the range of policies. (More detail of the program is provided in the Appendix.)

The results are based on families in the 1980 FES where the head, either male or female, is in full-time paid employment, so that those families are excluded where the head is unemployed, sick, self-employed or retired. The analysis is intended therefore to illuminate the effects on families with a head in employment, referred to for convenience as 'working families'. It should also be stressed that the picture based on the FES is a 'snapshot', and that it does not take account of changing circumstances.

In adjusting the figures for our purposes, two steps are necessary. First, we increase the 1980 gross incomes to put them on a 1984-85 basis, adjusting in line with aggregate indicators. It should be emphasised that this does not attempt to 'predict' the 1984-85 situation; for example, no allowance is made for increased unemployment. What the calculation represents is a 'thought experiment' as to the effect of the 1984-85 policy on families in the employment circumstances of 1980. The second stage is the projection forward to 1994-95. This again involves adjustment of gross incomes, which are assumed to rise at the same rate as earnings, and for convenience we express all amounts at 1984-85 levels (so that a policy decision to increase a benefit less than earnings will be shown as a reduction in the benefit). In the case of 1994-95, adjustments are also made for the changing number and composition of families. These are built up from projections of the number of children, of the number of single parent families, and of the number of employees in different categories (see Appendix). These adjustments are only approximate, and the program is written in such a way that users may enter alternative assumptions. The 1994-95 projections make no allowance for changing unemployment, so that they should be regarded as equivalent to assumption Uo. It should also be noted that no allowance is made for changes in household formation (for example, more young people living at home), which would affect housing costs and benefits.

Our results take account of several important factors missing from the hypothetical calculation for the married man on average earnings. These include working wives, income from sources other than earnings, and deductions from taxable income for mortgage interest. There is contracting out for NIC purposes and some of the wives retain the right to pay reduced contributions. Family net income is calculated allowing for child benefit, Family Income Supplement (FIS), passport benefits and housing rebates. Several of these factors work in the direction of reducing the average tax rate, for example the inclusion of benefits received, although some work in the opposite direction (for example, single people pay more tax than married at any given income). As may be seen from Table 4.3, the average tax rate for the sample of working families is in fact estimated to be 25.4 per cent in 1984-85.

Table 4.3   Projected average tax burden 1984-85 and 1994-95

Percentage rates

	1984-85 policy	Policy options 1994-95		
		P1	P2	P3
1984-85 demographic structure	25.4	26.3	24.7	24.0
1994-95 demographic structure	25.2	26.1	24.5	23.9

Note: Average tax rate = (Income tax + NIC - benefits)/Gross income

The projected changes in the average tax rate to 1994-95 depend on two elements. First, there is the changing demographic composition, which may be seen from Table 4.3 to be predicted on unchanged policy to lead to a reduction in the average tax rate (for example, because more children lead to more child benefit) of some 0.2 per cent. The demographic factors appear therefore to be of rather limited significance, although it is possible that our assumptions about the magnitude of demographic change over the next ten years have been too conservative.

The second element in the projections to 1994-95 is the choice of policy option. Under Policy P1, which involves an increase in the NIC rate, the average tax rate is predicted to be higher by 0.9 percentage points than if present policy were maintained. (The same difference is found if Policy P1 is introduced with the 1984-85 demographic structure.) This is greater than the apparent rise in the standard NIC rate, and reflects the fall in the reduction for contracting out and the smaller number of married women retaining the right to pay reduced contributions. The same considerations also apply to Policies P2 and P3. Whereas the reduction in the average tax rate calculated at average earnings was 2.7 percentage points under Policy P3, the fall shown in Table 4.3 is 1.3-1.4 percentage points. The difference between policies P1 and P3 is also less: 2.3 percentage points, compared with 3.0 percentage points in the illustrative calculation. The reduction in the average tax rate is moderated by the existence of deductions against income tax and the reduced value of benefits. If, for example, the married man on average earnings paid £2,000 mortgage interest, then his present average income tax rate would be 13.7 per cent rather than 20 per cent, and he would benefit correspondingly less from the reduced basic rate.

The estimates shown in Table 4.3 assume that unemployment would remain constant (assumption Uo), and this is the basis used in the subsequent analysis. The effect of the changes in tax rates and NIC which would be associated with variation in the level of unemployment is illustrated below for Policy P1, where it should be noted that this assumes that the unemployed are drawn randomly from the working population (which is not of course likely to be true in reality):

	Average tax rate P1
Assumption U-	24.9
Assumption Uo	26.1
Assumption U+	27.3

A fall in unemployment of 3 percentage points would allow the average tax rate on working families to be reduced by 1.2 percentage points, so that on a status quo policy the tax burden would fall, rather than rise. This is in addition to the benefit to the unemployed.

As far as the working population is concerned, the choice between Policy P1 and Policy P3 is one between higher child benefit, FIS and housing benefit, on the one hand, and lower rates of income tax and NIC contribution, on the other hand. The latter may be expected to provide more benefit to those with higher incomes; the former is either flat-rate (child benefit) or declining with income. It seems likely therefore that in distributional terms Policy P1 will favour lower income groups, and this is borne out by the results shown in Table 4.4. For each family, we calculate income per 'equivalent adult', a couple counting for 1.6 single persons, and a child for 0.4. (The choice of such an equivalence scale is open to question; one of the advantages of the micro-computer program is that it allows the scale to be chosen by the user.) The figures in the table provide the ingredients for drawing Lorenz curves, showing the cumulative shares of the bottom 10 per cent, 20 per cent, and so on. It should be stressed that the distributions relate to the population of working families, not to the entire population, so that they cannot be used to draw conclusions about overall inequality, and that, in view of the sample size, only limited weight should be placed on the findings for the smaller sub-groups.

The differences shown in Table 4.4 are clearly small and should be taken only as an indication of the general direction of the changes. Under Policy P1, the shares of the bottom income groups would be slightly increased, since the rise in National Insurance contributions, particularly for those contracted out and for married women, would bear less heavily. In contrast, under P3, the shares of the bottom 10 per cent, 20 per cent, up to the bottom 70 per cent would all be lower. The Lorenz curve would lie outside, implying for example that the Gini coefficient would be higher (more inequality). The same would be true, to a lesser extent, under Policy P2. How far this could be offset by concentrating the tax reductions on raising thresholds, rather than rate changes, is considered in the next section.

The results in Table 4.4 show the distribution between families with different incomes, and the effects in part reflect the differential treatment of families with different numbers of dependants of varying composition. Policy P3, by reducing child benefit relative to earnings, will naturally bear more heavily on families containing children. (By the same token, the results will be sensitive to the choice of equivalence scale.) In order to bring this out, we show in Figure 4.3 the differences in average incomes of different family types, cumulating (from the right) from those with the highest number of dependants. (The theoretical rationale for this procedure, the analogue of the Lorenz curve when there are differences in family size, is explained in Atkinson and

Bourguignon, 1984.) For families with two or more children, the advantage under Policy P3 compared with the present policy is an increase in average net income of £1.21, but this is smaller than for families with one or more children, for whom it is £1.81. For all couples (with or without children) and single parents, it is £2.64. There is a distinct gradient. In contrast, under Policy P1, the difference (in this case a loss) is much more similar across family types.

Table 4.4   Distributional impact of policy change

Cumulative shares in total equivalent income

	1984-85 policy	Policy options 1994-95 P1	P2	P3
Bottom:				
10 per cent	4.7	4.7	4.7	4.6
20 per cent	10.8	10.8	10.7	10.6
30 per cent	17.7	17.8	17.6	17.5
40 per cent	25.5	25.6	25.3	25.2
50 per cent	34.1	34.2	34.0	33.9
60 per cent	43.6	43.8	43.6	43.5
70 per cent	54.3	54.5	54.3	54.2
80 per cent	66.5	66.6	66.5	66.5
90 per cent	80.6	80.7	80.6	80.6

Notes: (i)   equivalent income calculated counting a couple as 1.6 single persons and children as 0.4 single persons, but with each unit receiving a weight of unity.
(ii)   distributions calculated with 1994-95 demographic structure.

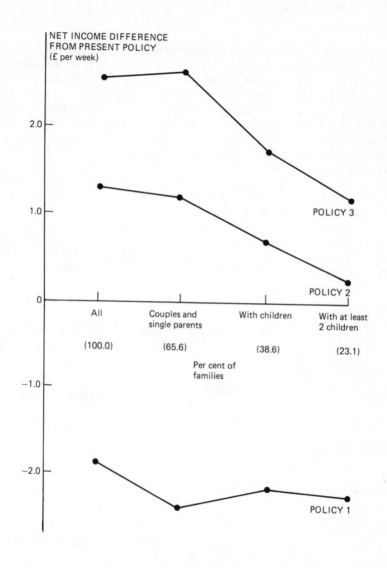

Figure 4.3: Average income of different family types with policies P1-P3

Much less commonly studied than the distribution between families is that <u>within</u> families. It is less frequently studied for the obvious reason that our knowledge about the division of resources between husband and wife is naturally very limited. It is however possible to say something about the distribution of income received. Table 4.5 shows the wife's 'share', defined as her earnings net of income tax and NIC plus child benefit, under the different policies. For few married couples, only about 1 in 20, does this share exceed 50 per cent, and for more than half it is less than 25 per cent. Under all three policy options there will be a tendency for the share to fall because of the smaller proportion retaining the right to pay reduced contributions. The fall is however more marked with Policies P2 and P3 on account of the decline in child benefit relative to earnings. By reducing child benefit, the government would be influencing the intra-family distribution of income received.

Table 4.5   Wife's net income as per cent of net family income

	1984-85 policy	Policy options 1994-95 P1	P2	P3
Cumulative per cent less than:				
10 per cent	32.5	32.1	34.2	35.6
15 per cent	39.2	39.3	40.7	41.4
20 per cent	45.4	45.4	46.5	47.1
25 per cent	52.7	52.7	53.3	54.3
30 per cent	64.1	64.4	65.2	65.8
40 per cent	80.5	81.4	81.8	81.8
50 per cent	94.5	95.3	95.3	95.3

One of the motives for cutting the tax burden on the working population is that of reducing any adverse effect on the incentive to work. This is, however, a more complex matter than at first sight appears, and we need to look carefully at the different types of decision that may be affected. In some cases, it may be the average rate of tax which is relevant. If a person is comparing the net income from working throughout the year with the benefit received if unemployed for the whole year, than a cut in the average rate of tax will raise the attractiveness of working. Turned the other way round, the 'replacement rate', or ratio of benefit to work income, will be reduced. Under Policies P2 and P3, the replacement rate does indeed fall, although most of this is attributable to the reduction in benefits relative to earnings, rather than to the tax changes.

The relevant decision may however be rather different. A person may compare the income from an extra week of work in a year with the benefit received if that week is not worked. In this situation, it may be the <u>marginal</u> rather than <u>average</u> rate of tax that is applicable. The marginal rate of tax is also likely to be relevant to decisions by those in work: for example, about overtime, intensity of effort, or seeking promotion. The impact of the different policies on the marginal rate of tax paid by the family head on an extra £1 of earnings is shown in Table 4.6.

For the person paying basic rate income tax, and below the NIC ceiling, Policy P3 would offer a reduction in the marginal tax rate, compared with Policy P1, of 3.8 percentage points. From the upper part of Table 4.6, it may be seen that the average reduction for the head of the tax unit is in fact 4.0 percentage points. For some people, those above the NIC ceiling, the reduction in the marginal rate will be less than 3.8 percentage points, but this is more than offset by the reduction in the number with very high rates arising from the withdrawal of means-tested benefits, commonly referred to as the 'poverty trap'.

In considering the poverty trap, it must be borne in mind that the absolute numbers in the survey are small, and the estimates are subject to considerable sampling error. Our analysis considers therefore as a group all those in the range 60 per cent and higher, rather than the smaller number with rates in the 80s plus. In any case it seems quite reasonable to treat as 'high' any marginal tax rate in excess of the top income tax rate. Table 4.6 shows about 3 per cent of the

Table 4.6 Marginal tax rates of family head and wife

	1984-85 Policy	Policy options 1994-95 P1	P2	P3
(a) On extra £ earnings by family head				
Marginal tax rate: Up to 10 per cent	1.2	1.2	1.2	1.2
11-20 per cent	-	-	-	-
21-30 per cent	2.4	2.6	5.2	5.2
31-40 per cent	87.5	87.4	86.3	86.7
41-50 per cent	4.8	4.8	3.9	4.0
51-60 per cent	1.0	1.2	1.2	1.0
61 per cent plus	3.1	3.0	2.3	1.9
Average marginal rate	38.7	39.6	36.8	35.6
(b) On extra £ earnings by wife (per cent of families where wife in paid work)				
Marginal tax rate: Up to 10 per cent	26.3	26.0	26.0	26.6
11-20 per cent	-	0.3	0.3	-
21-30 per cent	0.4	0.4	0.4	0.4
31-40 per cent	66.9	66.9	66.9	66.5
41-50 per cent	3.8	3.8	3.8	3.8
51-60 per cent	2.4	2.4	2.4	2.4
61 per cent plus	0.3	0.3	0.3	0.3
Average marginal rate	29.1	30.6	28.5	27.5

heads of working families to be in this position (where the marginal tax rate is calculated assuming that benefits are re-assessed), or some 450,000 in total. The majority of these are families paying income tax (30 per cent), NIC (6.85 per cent or 9 per cent), and losing rent and rate rebates (35 per cent). It is clear that a reduction of a few per cent in the income tax rate will make little contribution to reducing the extent of the poverty trap. Policies P2 and P3 do however involve a cut in housing benefit, which narrows the range over which there would be entitlement (partly offset by the reduction in child benefit). From Table 4.6, Policy P3 would - by cutting benefits - reduce the number in the poverty trap by more than a third, to around 300,000.

Much of the discussion of incentives tends to focus on the head of the family, but the evidence from studies of labour supply (a recent survey is Killingsworth, 1983) suggests that the wife's earning decision may be more sensitive to taxation. In the lower part of Table 4.6 are shown the marginal tax rates faced by working wives. In some quarter of cases the rate is zero, since they are below the tax and NIC thresholds, and these people would not be affected by the tax cuts. Nevertheless, Policy P3 offers a reduction in the average marginal tax rate of 1.6 percentage points, compared with a rise of 1.5 percentage points under Policy P1 (reflecting the rise in NIC rate for married women).

Conclusions

By adopting Policy P3, rather than P1, the government would be able to reduce the tax rate paid by the working population by an average of 2.3 percentage points. The replacement rate would fall. The marginal tax rates faced by those in work would fall by some 3 to 4 percentage points on average, and the number in the poverty trap would fall by more than a third. This would be achieved at the expense of transferring £3.4 billion less to those not in the working population (under Policy P3 total taxes would be cut by £2.0 billion, compared with a £1.4 billion rise under Policy P1). The distribution of the tax cut would favour middle and upper income groups, and coupled with the relative fall in benefits, would reduce the share of lower income groups. It would favour those without children relative to families with children. The distribution within the family would shift away from the wife towards the husband.

Policy alternatives
The options open to the government are much wider than the simple choice considered in Section 3 between cutting tax rates (Policy P3) and maintaining benefits (Policy P1). We now consider a range of such alternatives. In each case they are standardised to yield the same revenue, where we have taken Policy P3 as the base (we could equally have taken another base for the comparison). It is important to note that the revenue neutrality is defined for the population of families with a working head, not for the whole population, and that the implications for other groups are not examined.

Alternative A: Income tax structure
Under Policy P3, the basic rate of income tax was cut by 2.3 percentage points, but the revenue handed back to the working population could have been used instead to raise the income tax personal allowances, and this is indeed the assumption in the Green Paper. In the alternative policy A, the basic rate is set at 30 per cent, and personal allowances are raised to £2275 (single) and £3590 (married), an increase of some 14 per cent. This, together with the other changes under P3, would generate the same net transfer, relative to the present policy, of £2.0 billion to the working population.

The average tax rate is therefore the same as under P3; the difference lies in the distribution of the tax burden and in the implications for marginal rates. The policy of raising the tax threshold concentrates most of the gain on lower income ranges. Analysis of the shares of total equivalent income received by different groups shows that the bottom half of the distribution does less well than with Policy P1 (although this only shows up in the second decimal place), but they do better than with the present policy, and decidedly better than with Policy P3. The latter comparison is shown in Table 4.7. The share of the bottom 10 per cent, for example, becomes 10.8 per cent rather than 10.6 per cent. Differences of 0.2-0.3 per cent may appear to some readers as of minor importance, but they represent quite sizeable changes, and the overall conclusion must be that the choice of tax structure can make a significant difference to the distributional consequences.

The alternative policy, like Policy P3, involves a reduction in child benefit, and it may be seen from Figure 4.4 (page 129) that the implications for different family types are very close. This diagram shows the differences in average income for different family groups, again taken cumulatively,

Table 4.7 Comparison of alternative policies

	Policy alternatives				
	P3	A	B	C	D
Shares in total equivalent income of:					
bottom 20 per cent	10.6	10.8	11.0	10.7	11.0
bottom 40 per cent	25.2	25.5	25.8	25.5	25.8
bottom 60 per cent	43.5	43.8	44.1	43.7	44.2
Percentage with wife's share of income:					
below 15 per cent	41.4	41.4	33.5	40.9	41.1
below 30 per cent	65.8	65.6	59.7	62.5	65.4
Marginal tax rate of head:					
average	35.6	37.4	37.6	36.5	39.7
per cent in excess of 60 per cent	1.9	1.6	1.5	1.9	1.8
Marginal tax rate of wife:					
average	27.5	27.7	33.5	24.9	28.9

Note: Equal revenue basis for families with working head
       See text for details of policies

where the differences are those from Policy P3. Differences of less than 10 pence a week are not shown, and since the alternative policy A departs by less than this in all cases the line is shown simply as horizontal (zero). As far as the within-family distribution is concerned, the policy of raising thresholds provides some additional benefit to working wives, via the increased wife's earned income allowance. But this is still not enough to offset the impact of the reduced child benefit: the proportion with a wife's 'share' of less than 30 per cent is 65.6 per cent, compared with 64.1 under the present policy. As may be seen from Table 4.7, there is little effective departure from Policy P3.

Concentrating resources on raising thresholds rather than cutting the basic rate may be expected to score less well in terms of reducing marginal tax rates, and the average for family heads is indeed 37.4 per cent, compared with 35.6 per cent under Policy P3. At the same time, the alternative policy will take a number of married women out of tax. The proportion with a marginal tax rate of 10 per cent or less rises from 26.3 per cent to 30.3 per cent; and the average is only a little above that with Policy P3. Moreover, the number of families whose head is subject to the poverty trap, with marginal rates above 60 per cent, is reduced even more than with Policy P3, to around 200,000.

Alternative B: Child benefit

The Policy P3 holds child benefit constant while earnings rise. Increasing child benefit has, however, been advocated both on distributional grounds and to reduce the poverty trap. In the latter context, the Treasury has argued (Memorandum on the Effects of Increases in Tax Allowances and Child Benefit on the Poverty and Unemployment Traps, House of Commons Treasury and Civil Service Committee, June 1984) that an increase in child benefit would in itself make no contribution. This is however based on the definition of the poverty trap as receiving FIS in addition to paying income tax and NIC (i.e. a marginal rate in excess of 86.85 per cent). This seems a rather restrictive definition, and it seems more reasonable to include, as we do here, all those with marginal rates in excess of 60 per cent. A great many of these families are receiving housing benefit, and a rise in child benefit will float some of them off dependence on means-tested benefits, thus reducing the size of the poverty trap.

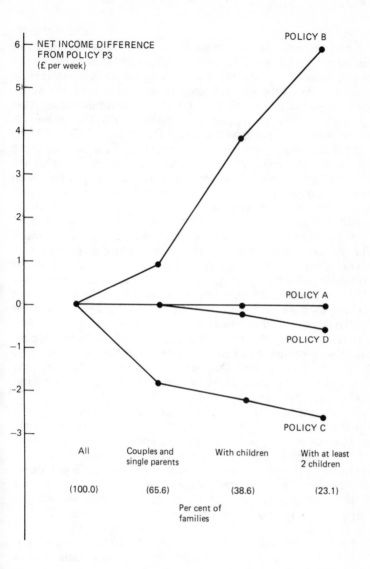

Figure 4.4: Average incomes of different family types

Child benefit is at present tax free, but it has been suggested that increases in benefit could be accompanied by making it subject to income tax. This proposal is often felt to be meaningless, on the grounds that most people face the same marginal rate of tax: for example, 'taxing child benefit is simply giving with one hand and taking with the other, a complete waste of time and money' (Hemming, 1984, p.186). This criticism both ignores the effect on the distribution within the family and fails to address the question as to whose income the benefit would be for tax purposes. If, in the case of married couples, the benefit were treated as the earned income of the wife, then it is not true that the basic rate of tax would be paid in virtually all cases. Some 40 per cent of wives with children are not in paid work, and a sizeable fraction of those who do work are below the tax threshold.

The alternative Policy B considers the effect of using the revenue which under policy A financed a higher tax threshold to raise child benefit, while making this taxable as the earned income of the wife. The level of benefit would be £11.00 (and one parent benefit would become £6.85). For the basic rate taxpayer, the net value would be £7.70, which would represent an increase of 18 per cent relative to present policy; for those not paying tax, the net gain would be 70 per cent (although this may be offset in part by reducing housing benefit).

The distributional impact in terms of equivalent income is such that the shares of the bottom groups are significantly higher than under the present system, and a great deal higher than with Policy P3, as may be seen from Table 4.7. For example, the bottom 40 per cent would receive 25.8 per cent, compared with 25.2 per cent under Policy P3. The policy would also have a major effect on the average income of different family types, in a quite predictable way - see Figure 4.4.

The implications for the distribution of resources within the family depends in part on the administrative arrangements for collecting the tax on child benefit. If the tax is levied on the husband, with the benefit being paid in full to the wife, then a sizeable transfer would take place. The calculations in Table 4.7 assume that this would be the mechanism, and the effect is evidently quite dramatic. The proportion of cases where the wife's 'share' is less than 15 per cent would fall to a third, compared with 41 per cent under Policy P3.

The marginal tax rate faced by family heads would be similar to that under Policy A, with an average of 37.6 per cent, compared with 37.4 per cent. Of particular interest, given the Treasury argument quoted earlier, is the estimate that the number taken out of the poverty trap, defined as marginal rates in excess of 60 per cent, would be close to that under the policy of raising tax thresholds. This is an aspect which needs to be examined more fully with a larger sample, preferably pooling the FES data for several years to augment the number of observations, but there appears to be little to choose between the two policies in this respect.

Where the Policy B has an evident disadvantage is that it would raise the marginal tax rate for wives in paid work. This arises because part of the wife's earned income allowance would in effect be absorbed by the child benefit. Indeed, for families with 4 or more children the wife would become liable for income tax from the first £ of earnings. Table 4.7 shows that the marginal tax rate on the wife's earnings would rise from an average of 27.5 per cent under Policy P3 to 33.5 per cent.

Alternative C: Tax treatment of husband and wife

The taxation of the wife's earnings is one aspect of the general issue of the tax treatment of husband and wife. The wife's earned income allowance, and the option of a separate earnings election for wives, mean that there is a substantial degree of independence. The move to fully independent taxation of earnings would require the abolition of the married man's allowance, and it is this that is considered as Policy C, with the revenue being used to raise the tax threshold. (It is assumed for the purpose of the calculations that investment income would be taxed as at present, although this would need consideration.) In practice, there may be pressure to make increased provision for those caring for adult dependants, either through tax allowances or cash benefits; and this would need to be considered.

This policy means that both husband and wife would have a (non-transferable) tax allowance of £2955, which would represent an increase of some 30 per cent over the single allowance under Policy A. Such a policy would have a distinct tilt against couples (and single parent families), and this is shown in Figure 4.4. Interestingly, the overall distribution in terms of equivalent income is quite close to that with Policy A (see Table 4.7). And the share of family income is shifted slightly in favour of the wife.

Changes in the tax treatment of husband and wife are usually discussed in terms of equity, or the financial incentive or penalty to marriage. The effects on marginal tax rates are however quite significant, particularly since separate election will now be advantageous in many more cases. The average tax rate on couples will rise, but for those currently paying higher rates and not choosing separate election (because of the existence of the married man's allowance) the marginal tax rate may fall for both husband and wife. The rate would on average be nearly 1 percentage point lower for family heads, and nearly 3 percentage points lower for wives, than under Policy A. The percentage of wives in paid work with a marginal rate of 10 per cent or less would be 37.4 compared with 30.3 per cent under Policy A.

Alternative D: Integration of NIC and income tax

The principle of independent assessment has long been accepted in the case of National Insurance Contributions (NIC). The increasing convergence of NIC with income tax has however led to proposals that they should be combined. (Here discussion is limited to employee contributions.) If they were to be integrated with the present form of income tax, then the consequence would be that contributions would differ according to marital status. This in turn leads to questions about the contribution conditions, which have not always been addressed by those advocating integration. It would presumably not be acceptable to relate benefits to amounts actually paid (which would mean, other things equal, that married men got lower benefits than single men). Under the proposal of integration, it is usually supposed that contribution conditions would be replaced by criteria such as residence, but this would not provide an answer in the case of the state earnings related pension scheme. These issues are not pursued here, although they are clearly important.

Under Policy D, we consider the effects of integration from the standpoint of contributors, it being assumed that NIC would be replaced by income tax at 39.1 per cent (and the present tax thresholds). The tax would fall on all kinds of income, not just earnings. One of the main arguments for this change is that it would reduce the burden on the lower paid (who at present are liable for 9 per cent on all earnings once they pass the lower threshold) and it would eliminate the apparently anomalous 'dip' in marginal rates between the NIC upper ceiling and the starting point of higher rates. From

Table 4.7, it may be seen that the overall distribution is close to that under Policy B of raising child benefit, although somewhat different groups benefit, as may be seen from Figure 4.4.

The proposal tends to raise marginal rates of tax in two ways: (i) those in the 'dip' would be paying 39.1 per cent, rather than simply the basic rate of income tax, and (ii) this rate of 39.1 per cent is higher than the combined NIC plus income tax rate (35.5 per cent) for those not contracted out on the assumptions of Policy P3 because of the exemption of earnings below the threshold. The average of the marginal rates faced by family heads is 4.1 percentage points higher than under Policy P3, although - as may be expected - there is little difference in the poverty trap. For wives, the marginal rate is on average higher by 1.3 percentage points.

Conclusions

In this paper we have described a range of policy options open to the government when it looks ahead to the mid-1990s. These options are in some cases alternatives and in others could be employed in conjunction. The policies A to D discussed in the previous section were compared with Policy P3 of restraining benefits, but they could have been combined with the Policy P1 of maintaining benefits in line with earnings.

The choice of options to examine has deliberately remained close to the structure of the present tax and benefit system. It would however be possible to take on board more radical departures. Suppose that the government wished to adopt a basic income guarantee scheme, of the kind developed by Parker (1982), whereby everyone receives a tax free cash payment and all income is taxed (at a rate of 45-50 per cent). As far as the working population is concerned, this could in large part be achieved by integration of NIC contributions (Policy D), abolishing the married man's allowance (Policy C), raising child benefit (Policy B, but not taxable), and raising the threshold and basic rate (Policy A). The one change which would remain to be made is the replacement of the wife's earned income allowance by a cash payment to all wives. Other radical proposals would require more extensive administrative changes. This would apply to a large-scale extension of means-testing, as proposed by Dilnot, Kay and Morris (1984). It would apply to proposals for a return to a graduated structure of marginal rates of income tax, coupled with an extension of National Insurance, as set out in Atkinson (1984).

The choice between these different options naturally depends on the objectives of the government; and one of the purposes of the analysis is to bring out the ways in which these need more careful consideration. We have seen, for example, that the pursuit of Policy P3 would allow the government to reduce the average tax rate, but we need to ask why this goal is pursued - if only because we have seen in the previous section that there is a range of ways in which this could be done, all with the same average tax rate. Does the government want to reduce the basic rate of income tax, as a 'high profile' policy parameter? Does it wish to reduce the tax burden on the average family? Does it wish to reduce the amount taken out of the pay packet? Each of these would have rather different implications. For example, a reduction in the basic rate can be achieved by keeping down the tax threshold: if the thresholds were indexed only in line with prices, not earnings, then the basic rate could be reduced to some 24 per cent by 1994-95. The deductions from the pay packet can be reduced by transferring income from wife to husband, as is brought about by cuts in child benefit.

Cutting taxes may not be an end in itself, but a means to reduce the disincentive effects. This means however that we must examine the source of such disincentives and seek to reduce the tax rates on those people, and on those decisions, which are most sensitive. If the work decisions of family heads are relatively insensitive to taxation, then it may be better to concentrate the reductions in marginal rates on secondary workers. This could, for instance, be achieved by abolishing the married man's income tax allowance and using the revenue to raise the (then common) tax threshold (Policy C). We need also to distinguish between the distortion of work decisions and the reduction of labour supply. A reduction in tax rates may reduce distortion but cause people to work less.

A policy of restricting benefits relative to earnings would have major distributional consequences. Many of these have not been explored here, since the paper has focussed on the working population, but even within families at work there are important distributional issues. Raising child benefit, under Policy B, has been shown as helping low income families, but the judgment about such redistribution depends on the view taken about the needs of different family types. Judgments are also necessary about the desirability of redistributing income within the family, an aspect which is not typically incorporated into statistical measures of income distribution.

The concepts of equity and distributional justice need to be further elaborated. We have not considered the role of time and the notion of the individual life-cycle. The distributional impact of the National Insurance system as a whole must take into account the lifetime aspects, and the relative treatment of different generations. We must consider ideas of 'fairness' and 'rights'. It may for example be that objections to the poverty trap are as much concerned with its 'unfairness' as with any disincentive. The policy towards the treatment of husband and wife for tax and benefit purposes may be significantly influenced by the notion of a 'right' to minimum financial independence which applies as much to individual family members as to the family as a whole.

Appendix: TAXPROJ model

The model provides projections of the tax and benefit position of families where the head is in paid employment. It is based on a 1 in 5 sample of families in the 1980 Family Expenditure Survey (FES), adjusted and grossed-up to represent the whole population of families with heads in paid work. The program is not intended to provide a substitute for analyses based on the full FES sample, but allows a readily accessible first-round examination of a range of alternatives. As noted in the text, the fact that a sub-sample is used means that the sampling error is enlarged. We have however made an approximate adjustment for the systematic sources of error in the income data, arising from differential non-response and recording bias. As a check on the validity of the methods, we have made comparisons with other sources, in so far as these are possible, but the reader should be warned that the program is only intended to provide a broad first look at the impact of different policies, and limited weight should be placed on the results for the smaller sub-groups.

The user can vary a wide range of policy parameters. These include the rates of income tax, personal allowances and the tax treatment of mortgage interest, and the rates and brackets for National Insurance Contributions. The benefits include child benefit, one parent benefit, Family Income Supplement (varying the prescribed amounts, taper and maximum), passport benefits, and housing rebates (varying the needs allowances, tapers, earnings disregards, and minima). The 'present policy' values are those in effect in July 1984.

The basic data employed from the FES are a 1 in 5 random sample of tax units interviewed in the period April-December 1980 where the head (male or female) was under the minimum retirement age and in paid employment, working sufficient hours to be eligible for FIS. The resulting sample consisted of 708 tax units. The income and housing cost variables have been up-dated to a 1984-85 basis using (i) the movement of earnings in the New Earnings Survey from April 1983, extrapolated using the monthly index of average earnings, (ii) investment income based on the changes in building society interest paid out and credited, and (iii) rent, mortgage interest and rates based on the relevant components of the Retail Prices Index. Differential grossing-up factors have been applied by type of tax unit so as to bring the sample composition into line with that for the whole population. This allows both for differential coverage of the FES and for sampling variation in drawing the 1 in 5 sample. (For further details, see Atkinson and Sutherland, 1984.)

The projection to 1994-95 allows the user to re-weight the different types of tax unit, distinguishing in the case of couples those where the wife is in paid employment. Table A shows the categories considered, and the composition of both the 1984-85 population and that projected in the paper to 1994-95. The projection is based on the following: (i) a 35 per cent growth in the number of one parent families (based on the projections of the Department of Environment in Social Trends, 1981, Table 2.5), (ii) an increase of 6.4 per cent in the number of families with children - see text - would be spread uniformly across families of different sizes), (iii) an increase of 5.4 per cent in the number of married women (based on OPCS Population Projections, Series PP2, no. 9), and (iv) changes of +1.7 per cent, -5.9 per cent, and +4.9 per cent, in the number of men, single women and married women

Table A: Composition of families: actual and projected

Type of family	Percentage in each category	
	1984–85	1994–95
Single man	23.2	21.1
Single woman	14.4	13.3
Single parent family	2.2	2.9
Couple without children: wife working	17.3	18.0
wife not working	8.4	9.0
Couple with 1 child: wife working	8.7	9.0
wife not working	4.4	4.5
Couple with 2 children: wife working	8.6	8.9
wife not working	7.0	7.2
Couple with 3 children wife working	2.4	2.5
wife not working	2.1	2.2
Couple with 4+ children: wife working	0.6	0.6
wife not working	0.8	0.8

Note: 'not working' means not in paid employment.

employed persons (based on the Government Actuary's estimates of the changes in the number of contributors from 1985-86 to 1995-96 in First Quinquennial Review, Table 8).

References

Altmann, R. and Atkinson, A.B. (1982), 'State Pensions, Taxation, and Retirement Income: 1981-2031', in M. Fogarty (ed), Retirement Policy: the Next Fifty Years, Heinemann.

Atkinson, A.B. (1984), Review of the UK Social Security System: Evidence to the National Consumer Council, Taxation, Incentives and the Distribution of Income Discussion Paper 66, London School of Economics, unpublished.

Atkinson, A.B. and Bourguignon, F. (1984), Income Distribution and Differences in Needs, Taxation, Incentives and the Distribution of Income Discussion Paper 64, London School of Economics, unpublished.

Atkinson, A.B. and Sutherland, H. (1984), TAXMOD: User Manual, London School of Economics.

Dilnot, A.W., Kay, J.A. and Morris, C.N. (1984), The Reform of Social Security, Oxford University Press.

Hemming, R. (1984), Poverty and Incentives, Oxford University Press.

Hemming, R. and Kay, J.A. (1982), 'The Cost of the State Earnings Related Pension Scheme', Economic Journal, Vol. 92, No. 366, pp.300-319.

Killingsworth, M.R. (1983), Labour Supply, Cambridge University Press.

O'Higgins, M. and Patterson, A. (1985), 'The Prospects for Public Expenditure: A Disaggregate Analysis', in R. Klein and M. O'Higgins (eds), The Future of Welfare, Basil Blackwell.

Parker, H. (1982), 'Basic Income Guarantee Scheme', Minutes of Evidence, House of Commons Select Committee on the Treasury and the Civil Service, The Structure of Personal Income Taxation and Income Support, HMSO.

5 Policy choices in the health sector

ALAN MAYNARD

Introduction

We are concerned with the 'present tension between needs and resources and the potential prospect of even more exacting policy choices in the years ahead'. This chapter examines the problems and policy choices which are emerging in the health field as technological and demographic changes increase the demand for resources at a rate in excess of society's ability to finance the provision of prevention, cure and care. These problems and choices are very similar to those faced by other societies (McLachlan and Maynard, 1982; Abel-Smith, 1984); indeed, as pointed out in a recent Brookings study (Aaron and Schwartz, 1984), it is possible that the semi-feudal nature of the UK health care system and the residual characteristics of the British class structure are such that rationing is carried out more easily here than it can be in many other societies.

This chapter is divided into four main sections. The first section analyses briefly the problems emerging from the production of health care (an input) and health (a desired outcome), concentrating in particular on the nature of efficiency, the health production process, the lack of evaluation, and the inadequacy of the incentive structure. The second section outlines the prospective pressures facing the UK health care system. The third section examines a sub-set of policy choices which emerge from these problems. In particular, choices with regard to incentives, evaluation and alternatives are emphasised. The conclusion in section four seeks to summarise the analysis and set out the characteristics of the choices facing policy makers. Inevitably this list is selective and reflects the biases of an economist. However it is argued that these choices will underlie policy for the next decade at least and that failure to define and appraise them precisely will ensure that the inadequacies of the health and health care systems will be preserved and resources will be misused.

Health and health care problems

In this section an attempt will be made to analyse the background characteristics of the health and health care industries. Inevitably this analysis will exhibit brevity and concentrate on the main issues arising from these markets.

Efficiency in health care

A request to most decision makers in the National Health Service to define efficiency may generate responses such as:

    (i)   a short length of stay in hospital;

    (ii)   the cheapest provision of care for a client group;

    (iii)   ten minutes at least for a GP consultation.

However, careful examination of such responses exhibits their inadequacies:

    (i)   a short length of stay in hospital may minimise the costs of the hospital service but gives the decision maker no information about the benefits of the hospital visit and ignores the costs of health care provision outside the hospital.

    (ii)   the cheapest form of care for a client group such as the mentally handicapped or the mentally ill is probably provided in institutions (the rightly much-denigrated 'bins'). By minimising costs, adopting the cheapest form of care for these deprived groups, the NHS decision maker is ignoring the substantive improvements in service provision and perhaps in patient outcome provided by good community care prospects and is failing to analyse the full opportunity costs of the alternative form of care.

    (iii)   the minimum of ten minutes for a GP consultation is a standard which ignores the costs of such provision and its benefits. It begs additional questions such as is there a cheaper alternative and what evidence is there that ten minutes is better or worse than nine or eleven minutes?

Such 'definitions' of efficiency and other measures of optimality in resource allocation such as naive use of performance indicators fail to distinguish between inputs, processes and outcomes. It is important to recognise the distinction between inputs, processes and outcomes, for example:

    (a)   health care inputs such as doctors, nurses, beds and expenditure;

(b)   health care <u>processes</u> or activities involving measures of throughput such as the number of cases, the number of patient days, length of stay or length of consultation;

(c)   health status <u>outcomes</u> which require a measure of the impact of inputs and processes on the patient's health in as much as it generates improvements or avoids declines in the length and quality of life.

It is easy to fall into the unfortunate trap of asserting unconsciously that increases in health care inputs and processes lead to increases in health status outcomes, that is, increased expenditure on health care which provides more doctors, hospital beds, consultations and operations may not always and everywhere lead to increases in the length and quality of life of recipients of such care. Such links that exist between inputs and outcomes have to be established by carefully designed trials which evaluate the costs and benefits of alternative ways of treating patients.

Unfortunately the evaluation of health care is imperfect and incomplete. Cochrane (1972) has argued that the failure to evaluate 'curing' therapies has led to a misallocation of resources to these unproven but apparently (as adjudged by provider rhetoric) efficacious techniques at the expense of resource allocations to care. Furthermore he asserts that the majority of therapies in use today have not been evaluated scientifically. His definition of the latter term is the advocacy of randomised control trials, preferably double blind to avoid practitioners biasing the results, and the incorporation of economic variables into such trials in the hope that the opportunity cost of the therapeutic gains, if any, can be identified.

The use of such evaluative techniques calls for the development of better measures of outcome. One crude level of outcome is survival one, three or five years after the medical intervention. Such a measure was used to evaluate the comparative therapeutic outcomes of care in hospital, including coronary care units, and in the home after a myocardial infarction (heart attack). This trial in Bristol and a subsequent one in Nottingham found that for the majority of patients there was little difference in outcome (Mather et al, 1976; Hill et al, 1978), in part because most infarction deaths occur in the first four hours after the outset of the attack when patients are outside the hospital system!

Such measures of outcome, survival after one year, are less than satisfactory. For instance, cancer interventions or amputation of the limbs of the elderly may generate additional years of life but these years may be of poor quality. What is required is a set of techniques to measure the quality of life and the duration of life. Such techniques generate measures of outcome, quality adjusted life years (or QALYs), for use in evaluating interventions within diagnostic categories and across such categories.

It is remarkable that though such techniques exist, their use is very limited. Much work has been done during the last fifteen years to develop and apply increasingly (for example to the heart transplant programme) techniques of output measurement. These techniques have been summarised and evaluated extensively (for example Rosser, 1983; Torrance, 1984) and, in work done by Torrance and his colleagues at McMaster University in Canada, these methods have been used in systematic and insightful manner (for example Boyle et al, 1983) to rank competing therapies in terms of the cost of generating a QALY: this shows, for instance, that coronary by-pass surgery is a 'better buy' than renal dialysis. Similar work in Britain by Rosser (Charing Cross Hospital), Williams (York University) and Buxton (Brunel) is gradually leading to the application of such techniques here.

Without such measures, clinical evaluation of therapies must remain rudimentary. However, the development and deployment of outcome measures alone is inadequate. Such measures of outcome (or QALYs gained by a medical intervention) have to be related to the full opportunity cost to society (not just the mere public expenditure consequences) of alternative therapies. Only if this is done can benefits (QALYs) be related to costs (the cost to society of achieving the benefit) and choice be informed.

The preceding argument is summarised in Figure 5.1A which highlights the sequential relationship between inputs, processes and outcomes. Efficiency is achieved when the cost of a given benefit is minimised and when that benefit is the most highly valued that can be achieved by the given resource (cost) input, that is the achievement of efficiency requires that costs be minimised and benefits maximised. Efficiency is an input-output relationship and only by evaluating carefully the costs and benefits of alternative therapies can policy makers be informed about what is 'good value for resources'. The use of performance indicators which obfuscate the input-

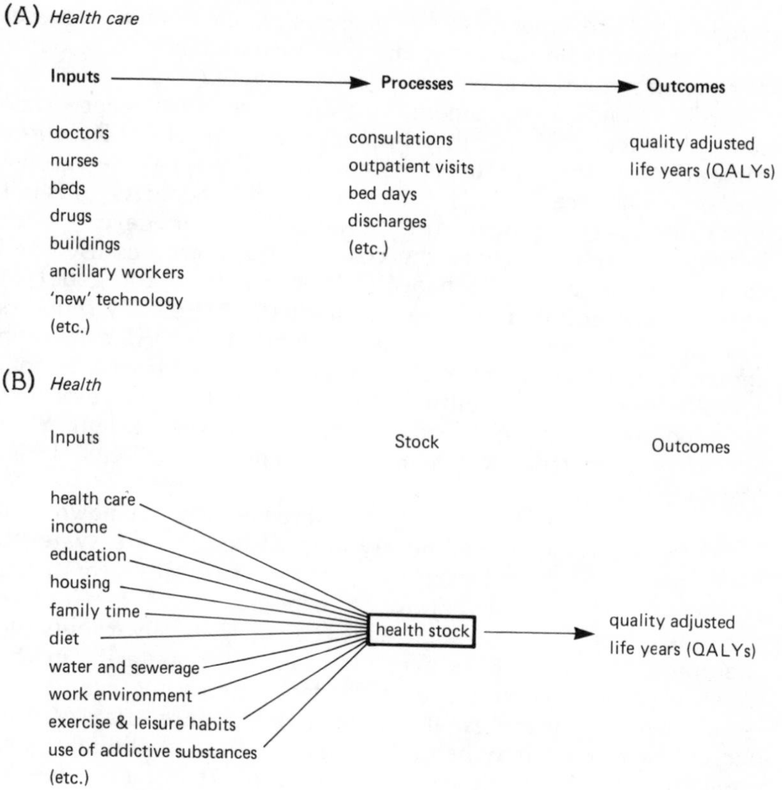

(A) *Health care*

Inputs ─────────────► Processes ─────────────► Outcomes

doctors   consultations   quality adjusted
nurses   outpatient visits   life years (QALYs)
beds   bed days
drugs   discharges
buildings   (etc.)
ancillary workers
'new' technology
(etc.)

(B) *Health*

Inputs   Stock   Outcomes

health care
income
education
housing
family time
diet   health stock ──────►   quality adjusted
water and sewerage   life years (QALYs)
work environment
exercise & leisure habits
use of addictive substances
(etc.)

Figure 5.1 The health care and health production processes

output link and emphasise the analysis of inputs and processes must inevitably be limited if the goal of efficiency in resource allocation is to be groped towards effectively.

The concept of economic efficiency is often ignored and poorly understood in the health care sector. Resource allocation in this sector is dominated by a provider group, doctors, who are trained to maximise the benefits of their therapies in relation to the patients in their care. Such behaviour tends to ignore the costs of the therapies used and to ignore the potential benefits (opportunities foregone) of care to non-recipients on the waiting list. Efficiency requires that practitioners maximise the production of QALYs within their available finite budgets. A failure to achieve this goal could be regarded as unethical: the inefficient use of resources by a doctor in the care of patient X deprives patient Y of access to care from which he could benefit (Williams, 1984; Maynard, 1983).

It is unfortunate that costs are usually unknown and benefits, if any, appraised poorly in most health care systems. Consequently it is not surprising to find case study material reviewing the 'rise and fall' of expensive and ineffective therapies (for example Bunker et al, 1977). Not only do therapies rise and fall as a result of initial popularity in the absence of evaluation and then condemnation when evaluation results appear, there is also now a belief that 'flat of the curve' health care may be quite common, that is, the marginal product of some health care may be zero, if not negative in some cases (see for example Evans, 1982, pp.380-382). Only detailed evaluation of health care practices can identify its marginal benefits in relation to marginal input cost. Such evaluation is essential if scarce resources are to be used efficiently.

Efficiency in health

To enable national policy makers and provider decision makers to use scarce health care resources more efficiently it is necessary to evaluate input (cost) - output (benefit) relationships. Ideally, cost-QALY relationships would be evaluated to generate a body of knowledge which informed decision makers about the costs and benefits of marginal (small) changes in resource allocations.

McKeown (1977, 1979) has argued that the major causes of growth in the size of Britain's population in the period between 1840 and 1970 were improvements in nutrition (diet) occasioned by greater affluence (income) and better public hygiene (water and sewerage). Similar arguments have been made in other developed countries and in connection with more recent population growth in less developed countries. A plausible hypothesis is that improvements in health (QALYs) may be produced more efficiently by inputs other than health care.

In terms of Figure 5.1B, the individual is endowed at birth with a health capital stock in part determined by genetic endowment and in part by the habits (for example, smoking, diet and exercise) of the mother. This health capital stock is augmented by a variety of inputs such as income, dietary habits and other factors over the life cycle. The stock depreciates over the life cycle due to use (the ageing process) and due to 'negative' factors such as 'junk food', poor work environment and use of substances such as tobacco. The health stock generates, provided it is above some minimum level, QALYs and this human capital model can be used to explore the relationships between the competing inputs and outcomes (QALYs or just LYs) (see Grossman, 1972, 1982).

This type of model permits exploration by economists of a variety of policy relevant puzzles, for example:

(i) analysis of the productivity at the margin of the various inputs which affect health (that is, what level of QALYs are produced by small (marginal) changes in the level of resources allocated to health care, altering diet, increasing income, or reducing work hazards?);

(ii) analysis of life cycle health (QALY) generating and degenerating activities to identify, for instance, if and when fluctuations in income affect QALYs;

(iii) analysis of inter-generational QALY generating and degenerating activities to identify for instance the links, if any, between parental income and the health (QALYs) of their sons and daughters;

(iv) analysis of inequalities in endowments and inputs and their impact on outcomes (QALYs), that is, exploration of the inequalities in health and health care identified in the Black Report (1980).

At present the impact of alternative inputs on health (QALYs) is explored inadequately. McKeown (1977, 1979) has provided an insightful historical analysis. Systematic exploration by economists and others of phenomena such as those illustrated in the Black Report (1980) is in its infancy. At present knowledge about the efficiency of alternative inputs into the health production process is lacking and knowledge about the causes and possible remedies for inequalities in health care are similarly absent. At present liberals tend to advocate increased access to health care for the poor, even though the marginal product of such care may be low and the resources used to fund such care might generate more benefits if used to educate (change the preferences) or increase the income of the poor, so that their time preference rates are changed and they behave as if they had a future (Fuchs, 1982).

Efficiency and incentives

A third problem besetting all health care systems is that of incentives or rather perverse incentives. It is generally accepted that private insurance and the National Health Service, by removing the price barrier to consumption, create moral hazard - that is, an incentive for consumers to ignore costs and utilise health care until their perceived marginal benefit from it is zero. The optimal level of consumption is where marginal cost equals marginal benefit and so the effect of insurance and NHS is to generate over-consumption. Patients, because they face, in the absence of copayments or user charges, only time costs in using health care facilities, have weak incentives to use health care facilities efficiently.

Thus in many health care systems the common problem is that patients and providers have no incentive to economise: the costs of their behaviour are imposed on the financing agencies either private or public. With little incentive for resource allocators to economise it is not surprising that all too little evaluation of health care therapies and the production of health takes place.

The basic incentive problem in all health care systems is the asymmetry of knowledge about costs and benefits. In the NHS treasurers know something about the financial characteristics, in terms of public expenditure, of primary and hospital care. Most of these data are aggregated and organised to ensure expenditure control rather than efficiency in resource allocation. Doctors in the NHS have some basic information about the benefits of their therapies but due to lack of scientific evaluation their awareness of processes and outcomes is very limited (for example, it is not known what the average GP does in terms of description of process). No one has information about the costs <u>and</u> benefits of health care.

Conclusions

There are three important problems which permeate all health care systems, with the NHS being no exception:

(i)   efficiency is ill-defined, there is a reluctance to distinguish between inputs, processes and outcomes in the health care production process, and the marginal product of health care is at best undiscernible and at worst zero or negative in some cases;

(ii) health (measured in terms of flows of quality adjusted life years QALYs) is the outcome produced by many inputs, only one of which is health care, and the marginal productivities of these inputs can be discerned only imperfectly;

(iii) incentives in the health care system are perverse with little incentive for consumers or providers to economise because of the asymmetry in imperfect knowledge about costs and benefits.

This lack of evaluation in health and health care, and these perverse incentives, are the primary causes of resource misallocation.

Prospective pressures facing the UK health system

During the next ten years the demand for health care will continue to expand rapidly. This section examines the causes of the growth in the expenditure on health care, indicates the nature of some questions which need further investigation, and outlines some possible responses to these pressures.

Demographic change

The Treasury (HM Treasury, 1984b) has indicated that the effects of demographic change are a major influence on public expenditure on the NHS. Using OPCS figures the Treasury document points out that between 1984 and 1994 the number of people of pensionable age will rise by 200,000 to 10.4 million (an increase of 2.0 per cent). In the same period the number of people over 75 years of age will rise by 300,000 to 3.8 million (8.6 per cent). Estimated gross expenditure per head in England on hospital and community health services (HCHS) in 1981-82 was £255 for all groups but £455 for the 65-74 year old group and £1,160 for the age group over 75 years of age (HM Treasury, 1984a). If these levels of expenditure were to remain constant, spending on HCHS would need to increase by 'somewhat under one per cent a year between 1983-84 and 1993-94 simply to keep pace with demographic changes' (HM Treasury, 1984b, para.36).

These forecasts tend to emphasise the demographic effects on the HCHS budget of just under one per cent and to gloss over the results of such pressures on the Family Practitioner Services (FPS) and Personal Social Services (PSS) budgets. The FPS budget is available only in aggregate terms and relatively little seems to be known about the impact of the elderly on the demand for primary care. Such data as are available indicate that the input mix may be changing; for example, from the General Household Survey it can be seen that there has been a significant increase in the use by the elderly of home helps, district nurse/health visitors, chiropodists and meals on wheels, but only a marginal increase in the use of GPs: for those over 65, GP consultations over the 1974-75 to 1981-82 period fluctuated but grew only marginally from 4.4 visits per person per year to 4.5. Whilst the FPS budget has expanded considerably over the last decade, the extension of care, measured in terms of consultations, appears to have increased slightly both for the elderly and the population as a whole.

So even the crude extrapolation of the FPS budget is difficult, due to poor data. The data which are available indicate that the expansion of care may be more significant in the PSS sector (meals on wheels, home helps, etc.). The 'just under one per cent' forecasts appear to exclude this sector and if this is the case the forecasts must, even within their existing crude methodology, be incomplete.

Concentration on such forecasts, even if complete, would be unsatisfactory. A considerable amount of care for the elderly is neither provided nor financed by the NHS. The DHSS, through its social security budget, finances care in the private sector for the elderly. Experiments, for instance in Kent, are being carried out with social workers using PSS monies to 'bribe' families to care for the elderly in private households. The elderly and their relatives pay for and provide care in a variety of institutions: for example, 25 per cent of carers of the elderly had given up work or reduced work effort as a result of caring for elderly dependents (Equal Opportunities Commission, 1980). A major question is the nature of the appropriate balance between health care and 'social care': what are the costs of the alternatives? Of course even when the most economic method of support for a given level of dependence in the elderly is identified there will be obstacles to the transfer of the patient to the best mode of care (Maynard and Smith, 1983). Such obstacles need to be charted and circumvented by appropriate incentives.

Any analysis of the effects of demographic change on resources should not be confined merely to a partial equilibrium analysis of public expenditure effects because of the interdependence between public, private and household provision and finance of care. There are two questions which require careful evaluation:

(i)　will the economic capacity of the care system (that is public and private production including non-marketed elements provided by households) expand to generate sufficient resources to fund care for the elderly?

(ii)　will appropriate mechanisms be devised to match the needs (dependency) of the elderly and care at lowest opportunity cost (that is, QALYs need to be maximised at least cost)?

Williams offers a tentative but optimistic answer to question (i), based on modest assumptions about economic growth and hopes for the avoidance of costly military adventures (Williams, 1983). Such a conclusion is at variance with current opinion but controversy about such issues has been around for a long time (see, for example, Paish and Peacock, 1954). Clearly these issues need more careful analysis and modelling. In particular it is necessary to determine who does what now, at what cost, and why existing patterns of care are as they are. Such analysis should examine the whole market of care for the elderly, not merely the role of the NHS. The need for NHS expenditure is determined by:

(i)　the demand for care. Demand is a function of numbers and illness patterns. It is possible that living longer merely delays the costly health care expenses associated with dying, costs which in the USA appear to consume one per cent of GNP. Alternative technical advances may increase QALYs by marginal amounts at high costs. If this is the problem it is one of access to technology rather than demography. Whatever the facts there may be a need to redefine who is old. Fuchs (1984) has pointed out that in the USA in 1935 life expectancy at the age of eligibility for social security benefits was 12.5 years. In 1984 the average 72-year-old had this life expectancy. Does old age begin in the USA at 72 years of age nowadays? Can a similar argument be used in the UK, and can labour force participation of these people be increased?

(ii)   the supply of care. What are the patterns of care provided for the elderly? To what extent do they vary and why? Evidence from the USA indicates that the costs of caring for the very ill vary significantly depending on the patient and the doctor (Garber et al, 1984). There is a need to evaluate alternatives and identify the least costly methods of caring for the elderly, especially the very ill elderly.

Technological change

The discussion of the impact of technological change on expenditure on health care has been analysed by government at a macro-level, with the Treasury (HM Treasury, 1984b, para.36) pointing out that this was another major pressure on resources and discussion of this matter indicating that at least half a per cent increase in (HCHS?) expenditure was necessary to meet these effects. Little is known about the generation, dissemination and adoption of new technology, however defined, in the health care sector. Unpublished work by Barbara Stocking for the Nuffield Provincial Hospitals Trust indicates that it is difficult to draw general conclusions about the adoption of new techniques in the NHS.

General points can be made about some innovations. For instance, the use of day case surgery for hernia repairs saves low-cost hotel days in hospital, offering alternatives such as reduced bed allocations and staffing, or increased throughput with higher expenditure, or stable hernia repair rates and the use of 'freed' resources to generate new provision of care. What actually happens is a matter of fact which is not generally known. Even if known, could it be controlled, how and by whom and at what cost? The evidence (e.g. Burn, 1983) indicates that the unexploited scope for day case surgery is considerable.

New diagnostic techniques, such as whole body CAT scanners and NMR scanners, may improve diagnosis, but the impact of such marginal improvements in diagnosis on prognosis is uncertain. The need to evaluate the costs and benefits offered by such new technology is acute because of their high costs.

Improvements in the treatment of renal failure (for example, CAPD) offer for many a new form of maintenance treatment. The expenses of this are considerable, but so are the benefits. Both costs and benefits require more careful evaluation as previous studies have been based on imperfect information. The adoption of new technology such as this seems to be influenced strongly by such individual qualities as the consultant's awareness and drive for resources.

Heart transplants appear to be declining in cost as technical expertise is improved and QALYs also seem to be improving. It is possible that this work may generate QALYs for a given budget superior to other treatments (for example, some cancer treatments). Only careful evaluation of the costs and benefits of all such innovations from an early stage in their use will provide the information base to improve control of technological change and its impact on resources.

Labour costs

The labour intensity of health care makes the expenditure on the NHS sensitive to wage changes over time. Expenditure forecasts have to make some assumptions about the price and quantity of labour that will be used. During the last ten years there have been changes in input mixes but there has been no systematic and extensive analysis of production functions, substitution possibilities and costs. This lack of evaluation restricts the basis for forecasting but crude extrapolations using alternative assumptions could be used.

For instance the process of tendering for contracts for cleaning, catering and laundry work seems to be showing a 'going rate' saving of up to 30 per cent by privatising. The causes of this outcome will have significant effects on employment and income (reduced wages and fringe benefits) but in terms of NHS expenditure there will be savings. The analysis of private care for the elderly of similar dependency levels seems to indicate further potential from privatisation. A logical extension of this is an NHS health authority which determines and finances patterns of care but provides nothing. Such changes in input mix and cost within and without the NHS require careful evaluation to provide the basis for more efficient forecasting.

Rising incomes

As real incomes increase this will increase the capacity of the economy to provide health care, public and private. Any decision to channel such increased capacity into the public or private sector will be determined by ideology. The advocate of the NHS seeks to maximise QALYs from the given budget regardless of an individual's willingness and ability to pay. Services to achieve this objective could be purchased from private or public institutions. The advocates of a market solution wish to determine access to care wholly or partially on the basis of willingness and ability to pay.

If the ideological decision is to privatise health care then the problems of modelling expenditure are no different and as complex as those of any other private sector activity. If, on the contrary, the decision is to maintain a public service then the impact of rising incomes on expenditure is more difficult to model, with demand diffused through political institutions. In this case the use of crude and unsatisfactory forecasting techniques, such as comparative income elasticities, seem unavoidable but perhaps capable of supplementation with carefully designed questionnaires.

Overview and responses

The factors discussed briefly above and listed by the Treasury (HM Treasury, 1984b) are not new and can be dealt with by better forecasting based on better evaluation of the microeconomics of the health care system and modest economic growth which will generate the capacity, together with the increased efficiency of the use of existing resources, to meet increasing health care needs.

Such need can be met either by public or private provision and finance of health care. The primary concern is to identify that mode of production which uses the least resources to produce the service demanded. The determination of demand will be via the market or the NHS with a clearly stated set of priorities. If the ideological decision is to allocate care, to some or a complete degree, on the basis of willingness and ability to pay, then consumers will buy those services they prefer. On the other hand, if care is to be provided in an NHS framework then politicians, the taxpayers' agents, will fix priorities and purchase care from those suppliers, perhaps public and private, who can provide it efficiently. The ends and means of the alternative scenarios have been explored extensively elsewhere (for example Culyer et al, 1981, and Maynard and Williams, 1984).

Whatever the form of finance and provision, the primary policy concern will be with efficiency. Demand will increase whether care is provided publicly and/or privately. So whilst demographic trends, wage costs, technological changes and increased aspirations associated with higher levels of income will continue to augment demand, the focus of analysis on the efficiency with which care is provided must be clarified and augmented. Choices between public and private provision and finance can be made on ideological or opportunity cost minimising grounds. The latter can be pursued only if the defects in the allocation system are mitigated by innovations such as those outlined below.

Policy choices

The problems outlined in the preceding section are accepted generally by most policy analysts. In this section an attempt will be made to examine in outline some policy choices which may mitigate these difficulties. Throughout this analysis the objective assumed for the system is that outcomes (QALYs) are to be maximised from the given finite budget.

Incentives

It was argued above that an important incentive problem is the asymmetry in knowledge about the costs and benefits of health care systems. Examples of this problem can be drawn from every health care sector but it manifests itself particularly clearly in the community care projects which are being developed for 'Cinderella' groups such as the mentally ill, the mentally handicapped and the elderly.

The development of community care for the mentally handicapped involves the closure of large institutions. The ward costs of these institutions appear to vary significantly, with higher public sector cost wards catering for patients with particularly serious problems (old age, handicap and propensity for disturbance) and low cost wards generally lacking resources to meet the observable demands of patients (Wright and Haycox, 1984). The saving from ward closures in this case varied from £10 to £48 per patient day; even the higher of these figures is probably an inadequate level of resource to finance good quality care in the community. In this type of unit the perception of benefits is often imprecise, with little attempt to measure dependency needs and match provision to such needs. Where dependency needs are linked to provision it is done generally in isolation from costs which are unknown at the patient/ward level and known at the unit level because of restricted interest of unit treasurers who are trained to stay within budgets and to pay little attention to efficiency in resource allocation.

The transfer of such patients into the community proliferates these problems. An enlightened health authority and a cooperative local authority can use Joint Finance funds to develop community care with the cost of provision tapering to the local authority. However, such an arrangement assumes that the local authority will accept the tapering arrangement. This they are often reluctant to do because of the costs to social services, education and possibly housing budgets: such patients in the mental handicap sector may involve expenditure of £10,000 to £15,000 per patient per annum.

The process of negotiating the transfer of patients into community care is very difficult, with rate capping and the equivocation of an Administration which advocates community care but limits the ability of local authorities to finance its provision. The local authority treasurer can see the costs of such policies but has little incentive to take account of their benefits. The providers, local authority and health authority, can see the benefits but find it difficult to mobilise funds because the scope for 'horse-trading' is limited. There is an obvious risk that the rate of deinstitutionalisation will outstrip the available community care resources, to the detriment of patient care.

The asymmetry in knowledge of costs and benefits is preserved by the compartmentalisation of the caring system: there are many separate 'empires' operating in relation to different but related goals, with independent budgets and with a reluctance to trade at the margins and induce efficiency. These problems exist in the sectors concerned with providing care for the mentally ill and handicapped. In the case of care for the elderly the uncoordinated rules and regulations in the differing public and private sectors offering care (Maynard and Smith, 1983) are further complicated by an enhanced flow of funds from the social security budget in the finance of private care; care which appears to be cheaper than NHS care for patients of similar dependence now but which may not be so if cartels emerge in the future.

How can the asymmetry in knowledge about costs and benefits which is protected by the compartmentalisation of the health care system, be challenged and reduced? Three possibilities will be considered here:

(i)   clinical budgets;
(ii)   client group managers;
(iii) a variant of the labour managed firm: Health Maintenance Organisations (HMOs).

At present clinicians and other providers of health care have little idea of the costs of their decisions. A system of ward or clinical budgets may concentrate the minds of resource allocators on the finite nature of the budgets and, with suitable shadow user charges for inputs, illuminate the opportunity costs involved in using these inputs. Suitable incentive systems might induce allocators to economise if they got a share of surpluses for redeployment on the ward. Various experiments are underway in the UK, the biggest of which is the CASPE study run by Iden Wickings at the Kings Fund. Another set of experiments, with seemingly little evaluation built into them, has been commissioned from accounting firms over the last twelve months. Are these schemes a success?

The answer to this depends on the definition of 'success'. Some observers seem to behave as if the objective of these schemes is to reduce expenditure. This view is deficient because it concentrates on inputs and exhibits the asymmetry of knowledge and the lack of concern about costs and benefits that is a major defect of the NHS. Merely cutting costs might not be efficient. Obsession with costs, as exhibited by the narrow-minded accountant, to the exclusion of any systematic consideration of what you get for these cost inputs, is not a sensible way to design and implement policy.

Furthermore, anyone familiar with the NHS would predict that 'cost savings' will be redeployed rapidly: demand is infinite, increasing in volume, and articulated with increasing sophistication by producer and patient groups. Thus the impact of clinical budgets would be predicted to be not in their effect on the total costs of clinical teams but on the processes of care and outcomes, that is, the litmus test of clinical budgets is whether the processes of providing care are 'better' (however defined) and QALYs are increased. To the extent that costs are altered by clinical budgets, the impact will be on average and, more importantly, marginal costs. Under a regime of clinical budgets total costs are unlikely to fall (indeed may rise) but marginal costs may be improved together with processes and benefits at the margin and in total.

The effect of clinical budgets in changing processes will arise, inter alia, from the ways in which they oblige clinical teams to work together to determine and regulate practice. This obligation is very involved and requires the participants to make and adhere to agreements about the budget's allocations and the processes of care, for example, work practices, volumes and type of activity. The experience of participants in the initial years of these trials is traumatic at times; its novelty requires the adoption and execution of new roles by doctors and nurses. Questions are asked about the rationale of existing practices and their advocates have to defend them. Thus clinical budgets socialise participants in that they have to exchange information and accept some level of peer review. The changes in behaviour and practice generated by clinical budgets would seem to be potentially worthwhile.

However the principal determinants of such arrangements are not just their impacts on processes but also their effect on benefits and the bridging of the cost-benefit gap or asymmetry. Proper evaluation of such trials requires careful attention to these effects. Concentration on the impacts of such arrangements on total costs is indefensible, if it is accepted that efficiency means that:

a)   total benefits (i) exceed total costs (ii)

b)   marginal benefits (iii) equal marginal costs (iv).

Only if indicators, however crude, of magnitudes (i) to (iv) are available can the efficiency of clinical budgets or the work of accounting/management consultant work be judged.

If clinical budgeting arrangements induce resource allocators to collect information on the magnitude of (i) to (iv), they will be a significant development. To determine whether they have such effects will require careful evaluation. However, even if such beneficial outcomes are achieved, this offers no unambiguous solution to the problem of compartmentalisation of the network of health inducing systems in the NHS, the local authorities, private voluntary agencies and the family. Some of these boundaries can be bridged by broad definition of the clinical budget.

A natural development of clinical budgets is the client group manager. Thus, to take the example of the Cinderella services, the designation of a client group manager in each locality for the elderly, the mentally ill and the mentally handicapped to manage the budget and buy in caring services from the various providing agencies, health-care and nonhealth-care, public and private, would create a mechanism to challenge and reduce these boundaries. Such a procedure would require the designation of all relevant budgets into elderly, etc., elements on which the client group manager could call. He or she would assess dependency/need and match it to provision across institutional boundaries. Such a person would identify the relevant client population, review continually their needs and press for the development of resources to meet these needs.

This is generally regarded as a radical step, but its costs and benefits need to be compared to those attributes of existing arrangements and alternatives. Modest experiments with virement (for example, some Kent social workers buying family support to reduce hospitalisation) enables boundaries to be bridged and the asymmetry of knowledge of and concern for costs and benefits to be reduced. The logical extension of such modest innovations is arrangements where a decision maker (for example, a client group manager) has the responsibility to detect needs, detect the benefits of alternative patterns of care, match them to client needs, and finance that care out of the 'clinical' budget.

But who is to be the client group manager? Who is to manage the collectivity of labour (a labour managed firm) responsible for meeting the needs of clients? Can 'lay' professionals manage 'health care' professionals such as doctors? Such broad questions can generate broad answers but here the response will be narrow and specific: an analysis of the nature of a Health Maintenance Organisation and how such a structure might be used within or without a state-provided and financed health care system.

The essence of the HMO is that for an annual subscription of a fixed amount, the practitioners contract to provide a comprehensive range of health care for the patient. The HMO itself, a collective of medical practitioners and related professionals and support staff, provides primary care in a 'health centre' and buys in those services, such as hospital care, which are not available on site. This buying in could be done from the cheapest source, public or private.

Such organisations are analysed at length by Luft (1981) and Brown (1983). Alain Enthoven (1980) has incorporated them into his health plan whereby subscribers are required to be offered a choice of providers (HMOs and others) and asked to recontract every year. Choice of alternative providers and the recontracting clause offers the possibility of introducing uncertainty into providers' lives and inducing them to look to the quality and quantity of their product in competing for patients.

The internal incentives of the HMO may offer a potential solution to the asymmetry problem. The HMO managers, doctors, have an incentive to minimise costs as the difference between revenue and expenditure is 'profit' for their firm. In an effort to reduce costs the practitioners may be induced to evaluate practice to improve process and outcome and identify cheaper alternatives such as health education and health promotion. Of course such incentives to cost minimise may lead to reductions in the quality of care. Evidence as to the quality, process and cost effects is an empirical matter and, like the effects of clinical budgets, a matter for dispute, although some of the evidence seems to suggest major cost savings (see e.g. Manning et al, 1984).

However, such mechanisms offer the potential of effective peer review with, for instance, in England the health centre or GP partnership acting as the HMO and buying in care, as necessary, for the patients. The patients' subscriptions could be paid by the state, perhaps in the form of a voucher and perhaps of higher value for low income or high dependency patients. Such a form of organisation might overcome the asymmetry problem and create a health authority which owns and provides nothing, merely giving patients the chance to choose between competing HMOs which would provide and buy in a comprehensive range of care for competing providers in the diagnostic and hospital sectors.

Whether the asymmetry in knowledge of and concern for costs and benefits is dealt with by clinical budgeting, client group managers or HMOs, the potential of these devices seems to be considerable and to merit further study as relevant policy choices for the next decade. The obsession with cost minimisation which permeates public decision-making must be mitigated by consideration of such developments as this if efficiency considerations are to predominate and the blinkered concerns of cost-minimising accountants and benefit-maximising clinicians are to be put in their proper place.

Evaluation
Let us assume for the moment that the improvements in incentives discussed above prove to be too radical to contemplate and that the policy debate is about the improvement of evaluation. The asymmetry in the knowledge

and concern for costs and benefits is well illustrated by a consideration of the evaluation of new technology in health care. The 1968 Medicines Act lays down strict procedures which drug manufacturers have to follow to test the safety and efficacy of new chemical entities (NCEs). However, NCEs also have costs and it is noteworthy that these same companies are not asked by the state to demonstrate that their products are cost effective (the cheapest way of achieving a given therapeutic goal). This is a good example of benefit maximisation regardless of cost being tacitly encouraged and asymmetry in thinking about costs and benefits being reinforced.

Consideration of this legislation also raises another paradox. The 1968 Act delays the issuing of product licences to avoid thalidomide-type episodes. Representatives of the industry point out that this delays the use of efficacious products: for example, in the United States it is claimed that the delayed introduction of beta-blockers due to the Food and Drug Administration (FDA) caution led to thousands of avoidable deaths. The FDA, like the Medicines Division of DHSS, has powers to delay the introduction of new drugs. The benefit-risk trade off is adjudged to necessitate the delay in use of new procedures.

New procedures such as transplantation, whole-body CAT scanners, NMR scanners and other innovations also involve benefit-risk trade offs and substantial resource costs. At present many innovations are disseminated with all too little regard to costs and benefits. The need for evaluation and control have been expressed in a variety of places (for example, Council for Science and Society, 1982) and there seems to be a clear need to have in the UK an Office of Technology Assessment similar to that which existed briefly in the USA. The US institution (killed off, inter alia, by an administration reacting to the antipathy of strong industrial pressure groups) evaluated new technologies by commissioning original work and critical reviews of existing literature. The mere creation of such an agency would be insufficient; it would have to be funded (perhaps as part of a Health Research Council as discussed in the report of the Merrison Royal Commission) and its output appraised by independent experts according to agreed criteria.

The policy choice is clear. Ad hoc evaluation can continue and the great pressures of the medical establishment can be permitted to introduce new technologies and exceed limited budgets. Alternatively a strategy to evaluate and permit widespread dissemination only in the light of supporting evidence about the relative costs and benefits of the new technology can be adopted. Such a strategy is half applied to new pharmaceuticals and could be applied more systematically to a wide range of new technologies.

Systematic appraisal of the impact of inputs other than health care on health (that is, health education and health promotion) is needed also. The familiar asymmetry is present: the costs of improving nutrition, cutting alcohol and tobacco use, and increasing exercise fall on many disparate but articulate producer groups. The benefits arise in the future, later in the life cycle of the individual who munches bran, gives up tobacco and jogs to work; many people prefer jam today (junk food, the benefits of addiction and an easy life) to jam tomorrow! In economic terms peoples' time preference (benefits now, costs tomorrow please) may lead them to depreciate their health capital in a way which does not maximise QALYs. To what extent should individual liberty be curbed to enhance the quality and quantity of life?

The evaluation of health education/promotion policies is even more limited than that of health care. There are the familiar problems of designing trials which evaluate the benefits, in terms of alterations in behaviour (processes) and outcomes (QALYs), and the costs, opportunities foregone for society. However an added complication with evaluation in this area is that benefits may accrue over long periods: a decision to give up the use of tobacco now may generate additional QALYs in 40 years time and the impact of a teenage drug education programme may accrue over decades.

These problems are not insurmountable in theory: the problems of evaluation in this area are defined and techniques are available to generate results which will increase knowledge and inform policy making. The major problem is one of managing and executing these trials: the scarcity of trained scientists with the requisite statistical and social science (for example psychology and economics) skills. It is not surprising that the design and execution of some health education programmes have been naive and yielded little new knowledge. There is no health education profession to lobby for funds to train scientists and ensure that campaigns, such as that about alcohol in the North East and financed by the Health Education Council, are designed, implemented and evaluated efficiently.

This problem can be ignored, in which case no surprise should be exhibited by policy makers who are presented with poor results for poor trials, or the problem of training scientists to evaluate health and health care can be tackled systematically. First, an increased input of economics, statistics and related skills into the curriculum of medical schools and over the medical career seems essential. The former suggestion will be countered by statements to the effect that curriculums are full and such inputs can only be provided at the expense of others. Such opportunity costs are unavoidable. The relevant question is whether the benefit at the margin involved in the acquisition of such evaluative skills is greater than the marginal cost. Perhaps the acquisition of some surgical skills which, after graduation, may be used by only a minority of practitioners, should be replaced by evaluative skills which will be used throughout their career!

Not only should people be trained and specialise in the use of such skills, a general awareness of the powers and pitfalls of clinical trials and cost-benefit analysis should also be inculcated in the policy makers, who will have to make decisions about resource allocations in the light of these results. These people need to be 'immunised' against the results of defective trials!

The process of evaluation in the health system and the NHS is seriously defective. The asymmetry of knowledge about costs and benefits is perpetuated by an education system which trains evaluators, sometimes poorly, to conduct trials to identify benefits. This 'one-eyed' view of the world is encouraged by legislation (for example, the 1968 Medicines Act). The policy choices on evaluation are:

(i) to control the dissemination of new technologies until the results of systematic evaluation are available (for example, hold investments in NMR scanners until their costs and benefits in relation to alternatives are clear);

(ii) to create an organisation to initiate such evaluation of health services (rather than bio-medical science which is the domain of the MRC) and to collate and disseminate the results of such work;

(iii) to initiate improved training of scientists in statistical, economic and related skills, and to raise the general awareness amongst those who allocate resources of the strengths and weaknesses of these techniques in principle and in practice.

What are the policy choices?

Improving efficiency

The present policy on efficiency in health care and health is heavy on tactics and weak on strategy. The government has adopted a Maoist approach, continuous revolution, with two 'redisorganisations' of the NHS (1982 and 1984), Korner reports on information, advocacy of investment appraisal (for example HN(81)30), the production of 'performance indicators' and the Griffiths report. Many of these proposals have merit but they are not related systematically to the task of mitigating the confusion of inputs (for example health care, nutrition, education) and outputs (quality adjusted life years, QALYs) and the asymmetry of knowledge of and concern for the costs and benefits of decisions. A primary objective of reform should be the identification of budget holders who are induced not to be mere cost (input) minimisers (accountants?) or benefit (output) maximisers (doctors?) but who are concerned with efficiency: minimising costs and maximising the benefits of those services which are most preferred by society.

Such a budget holder, if provided with adequate incentives (see above) could be persuaded to seek out the efficient options and induce the system's providers to adopt them. This might permit the more effective pursuit of policy targets such as redistribution as it might enable decision makers to identify efficient patterns of care and target them on particular (for instance low income) groups. At present it is known that the distribution of health care and health is unequal (Black Report, 1980). However, the usual liberal response of seeking to make the distribution of inputs such as health care more equal is less than satisfactory if this merely results in the poor getting access to more low productivity health care. Redistribution needs to be informed by evaluation of efficiency if resources are to be used sensibly.

The tendency to throw resources at problems, the 'drunken sailor syndrome', and to fail to evaluate the outcomes permeates decision making in the public and private sectors. The belief that management/administration/evaluation is 'burdensome' and to be avoided without regard to the costs and benefits of such a policy choice is a fact of life that requires challenge. Sophisticated and systematic processes of management, public and private, require uncertainty and competition to 'concentrate the mind', but these mechanisms cannot be done without!

A coherent strategy about health can be pursued in the long term if these policy choices about the pursuit of efficiency are resolved. The questions inherent in the strategy have been elaborated elsewhere (McLachlan and Maynard, 1982, pp.548-50):

(i)   what are the objectives of the health system in terms of efficiency and distribution?

(ii) who really controls the health system, especially resource use at the boundaries of the component parts of the system (for example, the NHS-local authority interface, the DHSS-addiction industries interface, etc.)?

(iii) what incentives are there for resource managers in different parts of the <u>health</u> system to use resources efficiently?

(iv) who rations what health-inducing inputs (not just health care) and how?

(v)   who decides and how, about investment in health-promoting activities and disinvestment in health-destroying activities (for example tobacco)?

Alternatives to health care

Inherent in the preceding questions is the requirement that health-inducing policies are considered across the responsibilities of many Whitehall departments; for example the (unpublished) CPRS report on alcohol policies identified 16 Whitehall departments with responsibilities in alcohol, such as the Home Office, the Ministries of Agriculture, Trade and Industry, DHSS, Customs and Excise, and the Inland Revenue. The joint approach to social policy of yesteryear has to be very joint!

A policy to improve health (QALYs) by, for instance, reducing tobacco consumption, may offer few benefits other than enhanced QALYs (for example, Leu and Schaub (1983) show that the reduction of smoking merely redistributes health care expenditure across the life cycle rather than reducing it). Furthermore the inherent paternalism in such policies is a matter objected to by some liberals (for example Littlechild and Wiseman, 1984): what right have I to force you to live a longer, better quality life if you wish to die at 60 from lung cancer and enjoy a lifetime of tobacco use?

If problems such as this are resolved, then the opportunity cost of proposed changes in policy requires careful study. A policy to change diet (for example less fat, less salt, more bran, etc.) requires changes in industrial structure, profits and employment. Proposals to alter tobacco and alcohol usage more rapidly will induce vigorous responses from the few multi-national firms that operate in these markets. The implications for tax revenue will be significant also. The opportunity costs of attempts to maximise QALYs will be significant and distributed right across the economy. Decision making, informed by evaluation about the costs and benefits of alternative ways of creating QALYs, will inevitably involve a diverse collection of industries and ministries, and mechanisms for these groups to 'trade' may require radical change in existing attitudes and institutions.

Improving human capital

Existing institutions generate perverse incentives which perpetuate resource misallocation and a continuation of the asymmetry in knowledge about the costs and benefits of competing policies. These problems cannot be resolved easily because of the lack of knowledge about relevant input-output relationships. This ignorance can be remedied in time by investment in the training of scientists, practitioners and policy makers who have to translate the results of evaluation into changes in policy.

Such training must not be one-sided (for example concerned with benefit evaluation) but must include careful consideration of the costs of generating desired outcomes, both in total and at the margin. Division of labour in medicine and in the production of health has led to the division of responsibility to consider costs and benefits. Such schizophrenia is not helpful in that it perpetuates the asymmetry of knowledge of costs and benefits and the inefficiency in the use of inputs which can create health.

Conclusion

The policy choices in health and health care are subtle, but obvious when appreciated by the discerning observer. The debate about the public-private mix is irrelevant because similar problems exist in all health care systems. Competition, by which is meant the challenge of rival notions and people for power to determine resource allocation in private or public enterprises, can be helpful in generating alternative ideas and mechanisms which may mitigate the existing problems in the finance and production of health and health care.

To achieve improvements in the use of inputs to create health (QALYs) it is necessary for policy makers to bear in mind some simple ideas:

(i) the distinction between inputs, processes and outcomes;

(ii) efficiency is concerned with maximising benefits and minimising costs, not merely minimising costs (controlling expenditure) or maximising benefits (improvements in health);

(iii) the asymmetry in knowledge of, and concern for, costs and benefits encourages inefficient behaviour by cost minimisers (for example accountants) and benefit maximisers (for example doctors);

(iv) to make choices about efficiency, information is required about costs and benefits, in total and at the margin, and this can only be created by more evaluation;

(v) competing incentive mechanisms, to remedy the asymmetry and encourage economy, include clinical budgets, client group managers and HMOs;

(vi) evaluation of the marginal productivity of all inputs (not just health care) into the health production process will generate major policy problems because costs are imposed on small groups of powerful producers and benefits accrue (many of them in the future) to diffuse groups of patients;

(vii) health education/promotion policies may generate more QALYs than health care and if this proves to be so, how will the DHSS 'buy' such benefits (outcomes) from rival ministries who will face their costs in terms of industrial restructuring and other effects?

It will be difficult to improve efficiency in the health care sector because of its impact on providers' incomes and employment. It will not be easy to improve efficiency in the production of health because of its impact on industrial incomes and profits. All policies which generate QALYs have costs: the challenge is to identify these in relation to benefits and to induce decision makers to grope towards more efficient practices across the broad range of activities that involve improvements in health status.

References

Aaron, H.J. and Schwartz, W.B. (1984), The Painful Prescription: Rationing hospital care, Brookings Institution.

Abel-Smith, B. (1984), Cost Containment in Health Care, Occasional Papers on Social Administration, Number 73, Bedford Square Press.

Black, D. (Chairman) (1980), Inequalities in Health: report of a Research Working Group, DHSS.

Boyle, M.H., Torrance, G.W., Sinclair, J.C. and Horwood, S.P. (1983), 'Economic evaluation of neonatal intensive care of very-low-birth-weight infants', New England Journal of Medicine, Vol. 308, pp.1330-1337.

Brown, L. (1983), Politics and Health Care Organisations: HMOs as Federal Policy, Brookings Institution.

Bunker, J.P., Barnes, B.A. and Mosteller, F. (eds) (1977), The Costs, Benefits and Risks of Surgery, Oxford University Press.

Burn, J.M. (1983), 'Responsible use of resources: day surgery', British Journal of Medicine, Vol. 286, pp.492-93.

Cochrane, A.L. (1972), Effectiveness and Efficiency: Random Reflections on Health Care, Nuffield Provincial Hospitals Trust.

Council for Science and Society (1982), Expensive Medical Techniques, CSS.

Culyer, A.J. and Horisberger, B. (1983), The Economic and Medical Evaluation of Health Care Technologies, Springer-Verlag.

Culyer, A.J., Maynard, A. and Williams, A. (1981), 'Alternative systems of health care provision: an essay on motes and beams', in M. Olsen (ed), A New Approach to the Economics of Health Care, American Enterprise Institute.

Enthoven, C.A. (1980), Health Plan: the only practical solution to the soaring cost of medical care, Addison-Wesley.

Equal Opportunities Commission (1980), The Experience of Caring for the Elderly and Handicapped Dependants: Survey Report, EOC.

Evans, R.E. (1982), 'Health Care in Canada: Patterns of funding and regulation', in G. McLachlan and A. Maynard (eds), (1982).

Fuchs, V. (1982), 'Time preference and health: an exploratory study', in V. Fuchs (ed), Economic Aspects of Health,

National Bureau of Economic Research, University of Chicago Press.

Fuchs, V.R. (1984), '"Though much is taken": reflections on aging, health and medical care', Milbank Memorial Fund Quarterly, Vol. 62, No. 2, pp.143-166.

Garber, A.M., Fuchs, V.R. and Silverman, J.F. (1984), 'Case mix, costs and outcomes: differences between Family and Community Services in a University Hospital', New England Journal of Medicine, Vol. 310, No. 19, 10 May.

Grossman, M. (1972), The Demand for Health: a theoretical and empirical framework, National Bureau for Economic Research, Columbia University Press.

Grossman, M. (1982), 'The demand for health after a decade', Journal of Health Economics, Vol. 1, No. 1, pp.1-3.

HM Treasury (1984a), The Government's Expenditure Plans 1984-85 to 1986-87, Volume II, HMSO.

HM Treasury (1984b), The Next Ten Years: Public Expenditure and Taxation into the 1990s, HMSO.

Hill, J.D., Hampton, J.R. and Mitchell, J.R.A. (1978) 'A randomised trial of home versus hospital management for patients with suspected myocardial infarction', Lancet, 22 April.

Littlechild, S. and Wiseman, J. (1984), 'Principles of public policy relevant to smoking', Policy Studies, January.

Lue, R. and Schaub, T. (1983), 'Does smoking increase medical care expenditure?', Social Science and Medicine, Vol. 17, No. 23, pp.1907-14.

Luft, H.S. (1981), Health Maintenance Organisations: Dimensions of Performance, Wiley.

Manning, W.G., Leibowitz, A. Goldberg, G.A., Rogers, W.H. and Newhouse, J.P. (1984), 'A controlled trial of the effect of a prepaid group practice on use of services', New England Journal of Medicine, Vol. 310, No. 23, pp.1505-10.

Mather, H.G. et al (1976), 'Myocardial infarction: a comparison between home and hospital care for patients', British Medical Journal, Vol. 1, pp.925-929.

Maynard, A. (1983), 'Privatising the National Health Service', Lloyds Bank Review, April.

Maynard, A. and Smith, J. (1983), The Elderly: Who Cares? Who Pays?, Nuffield-York portfolio, Number 1, Nuffield Provincial Hospitals Trust.

Maynard, A. and Williams, A. (1984), 'The privatisation of health care', in J. Le Grand and R. Robinson (eds), Privatisation and the Welfare State, Allen & Unwin.

McKeown, T. (1977), The Modern Rise of Population, Edward Arnold.

McKeown, T. (1979), The Role of Medicine, 2nd edition, Blackwells.

McLachlan, G. and Maynard, A. (eds) (1982), The Public/Private Mix for Health: the Relevance and Effects of Change, Nuffield Provincial Hospitals Trust.

Paish, F. and Peacock, A.T. (1954), 'The economics of dependence, 1952-82', Economica, pp.279-299.

Rosser, R. (1983), 'Issues of measurement in the design of health indicators: a review', in A.J. Culyer (ed), Health Indicators, Martin Robertson.

Torrance, G. (1984), Health Status Measurement for Economic Appraisal, paper to the Health Economists Study Group, July.

Williams, A. (1983), Improving the Care of the Homebound Elderly: A UK View of the Economic Issues, Commonwealth Fund conference (conference volume forthcoming).

Williams, A. (1984), Medical Ethics: health service efficiency and clinical freedom, Nuffield-York portfolio, Number 2, Nuffield Provincial Hospitals Trust.

Wright, K. and Haycox, A. (1984), Public Sector Costs of Caring for Mentally Handicapped Persons in a Large Hospital, University of York, Centre for Health Economics, Discussion Paper 1.

6 Incomes of the elderly: the future of state provision

J. A. KAY

State expenditure on income maintenance is dominated by provision for the elderly. About three-quarters of all national insurance benefits go to the old, even at current exceptional levels of unemployment. DHSS figures show that just over half of all households in receipt of supplementary benefit, and about half of households with incomes still below the supplementary benefit line, are over pension age.

Moreover, the dependence of the elderly on state support is increasing. In 1951, 42 per cent of the income of the elderly came from state benefits; that figure is now 60 per cent (DHSS, 1984). The growth of occupational pensions has been more or less exactly offset by the fall in income from savings, and the total of privately provided income in retirement has remained at just under one-third of the total. The balance is the sharply diminished contribution of earnings to the incomes of the elderly. Table 6.1 shows the composition of pensioner incomes. Most pensioners are almost wholly dependent on state benefits; better-off old people are better off because they have occupational pensions or investment income, or, more commonly, both.

Thus the last thirty years have seen an increasing number of people of pensionable age (18 per cent of the population as against $13\frac{1}{2}$ per cent in 1951), with incomes increasingly large relative to those of the rest of the population (personal disposable income 69 per cent of that of non-pensioners as against 41 per cent in 1951), and deriving an increasing proportion of that income from the state. Will these trends continue, or will the incomes of the elderly cease to be a principal element in the growth of social security spending and indeed in public expenditure as a whole?

The current position
State support for the elderly takes a bewildering variety of forms. There are cash benefits directly related to the contingency of old age. There are cash benefits which,

although not specifically age related, accrue substantially to the elderly because the criteria used in defining need bring relatively large numbers of old people into the net. There are tax allowances which are aimed directly or indirectly at supporting incomes in retirement. There is a complex set of financial relationships between the state and the private sector consequent on provisions for contracting out of the state earnings related pension scheme. These are in addition to support in kind and in services which fall outside the scope of this paper.

Table 6.1 Composition of pensioner couple incomes by source

Percentages

	Up to £75	£75– £100	£100– £150	£150+
	Income Range (pw, 1982)			
State pension	75	58	40	23
Other pensions	8	21	34	35
Earnings	1	10	14	21
Other benefits	12	2	1	1
Investments	4	9	11	21
% of all pensioner couples in range	58%	18%	15%	9%

Source: IFS estimates based on 1982 Family Expenditure Survey.

Much the largest expenditure on the elderly is on national insurance pensions, which amount to £15.5 billion in 1984-85. This is about three-quarters of all expenditure on national insurance benefits. In addition, there are commitments to very substantial increased expenditures even on unchanged policies.   These arise from two main sources. One is the growth of entitlement to earnings related pensions, which have arisen since 1978.   The provisions of the 1975 Social Security Pensions Act give entitlement to an additional pension based on one-quarter of average revalued qualifying earnings in the best 20 years of a working lifetime subsequent to 1978. Qualifying earnings are weekly earnings in excess of a floor set by the single person's retirement pension and below a ceiling roughly $7\frac{1}{2}$ times that amount.   The floor is at present £34.50 per week and the ceiling £250; thus someone on average earnings of £180 per week (in real terms) would, at maturity of the scheme,   acquire (also in real terms) an additional pension of approximately £37 per week.

The 1975 Act also made significantly more generous provision for married women; in particular, it allows for up to twenty years of home responsibilities to be counted as satisfying contribution conditions for an individual pension. The result is that a woman who exceeds the lower earnings limit for national insurance contributions for around half her potential working lifetime can expect in future to obtain a full national insurance pension in her own right.

The distinction between benefits which are contingent on old age and benefits which although not explicitly directed accrue substantially to them is not a rigid one because the two most important - supplementary benefit and housing benefit - are awarded on a more generous basis to the old. Although the distinction between long term and short-term supplementary benefit rules is not explicitly based on age, most of those who receive the long term rate are pensioners and most non-pensioners are in receipt of short-term benefit.   Housing benefit incorporates different rates of withdrawal for pensioner and non-pensioner households.

There are two types of tax allowance favouring the elderly: age allowance and exemption for approved pension schemes. Age allowance gives increased personal income tax allowances to tax units where one or other member is over 65. It was introduced in 1957 and, although criticised by the Labour Party at that time, was considerably extended in scope in 1974.   Age allowance is a provision which, at first inconsequential, has become significant as a result partly of policy decisions but also because of the real increase in pensioner incomes since initial implementation. It offers no advantage to low income pensioners - who would pay no tax in any event - or to high income pensioners, from whom it is withdrawn through a tapering mechanism. It has some administrative rationale; because the tax threshold has recently been close to the level of national insurance pension, while the age allowance figures are well above it, the effect of age allowance is to keep a large number of tax units who would otherwise be just inside or just outside the tax net clear of the tax system altogether. The 1984 budget reduced the real value of age allowance by confining the increase in thresholds over and above the statutory indexation requirement to personal allowances alone.

Table 6.2 Net revenue effect of changes in the tax treatment of pension funds

£ billion

	1984	2004
30% tax on contributions	4450	4400
30% tax on fund income	1350	5000
10% tax on fund income	500	1550
Phased 10% - 30% tax on income	-10	5700
Phased charge on lump sums on retirement	0	1000

Source: Fry et al (1985).
Note: Calculations based on assumption that pension benefits would be maintained.

There are also tax concessions to private provision for retirement saving. A wide variety of estimates of the 'cost' of these concessions is in circulation; no less than four of these estimates are due to the Inland Revenue (Inland Revenue, 1983). Although it is frequently argued that the costs of tax expenditures of this kind should be treated in the same way as direct budgetary changes, a view of what a tax expenditure is demands a view of what the tax treatment of the activity in question would be, or ought to be, in the absence of the existing regime; and in the case of pension schemes neither of these things is at all obvious. Table 6.2, based on Fry et al (1985), shows the revenue impact of a variety of possible changes to the tax treatment of pension funds. Although it is misleading to describe these numbers as tax expenditures or the cost of tax reliefs, it is evident that the tax treatment of retirement savings is more favourable than that of many other kinds of savings and that the magnitudes involved are substantial, even in relation to total state expenditure on incomes in retirement.

Tax concessions apply not only to occupational schemes but also to retirement annuities taken out by the self-employed and by those in non-pensionable employment. Self-employed retirement annuities have increased considerably in significance since the upper limits on contributions were removed in 1980 and the flexibility of contracts increased by the development of associated 'loanback' schemes. Take-up of contracts by employees outside occupational schemes remains insignificant.

A final means by which the state supports retirement savings is through the contracting out provisions of the earnings related scheme. Contracting out means that both employer and employee pay a reduced rate of national insurance contribution in return for a commitment by an occupational pension scheme to meet a part of the individual's state pension entitlement - the guaranteed minimum pension. It can be most straighforwardly seen as a means by which the state lends money to the private occupational pension sector and, since the guaranteed minimum pension is based on earnings revalued to the date of retirement, the loan is an indexed one (see Hemming and Kay, 1981, for a fuller explanation of the economic impact of contracting out). The real rate of interest payable on the loan is designed to be around one half of one per cent.

The financial costs of this arrangement to the state are twofold. At a real rate of interest of around zero, the cost of contribution rebates would, once the scheme reaches steady state, more or less balance the savings on guaranteed minimum pensions. For the first fifty years or so, until steady state is reached, the loss of contribution income will be greater than the amount paid in guaranteed minimum pensions. The national insurance fund would make substantial savings if the scheme, on having reached maturity, were then to be wound up; but this is not likely to happen. If a public sector balance sheet recorded future pension commitments as a liability, then the savings bought with contracting out rebates would reduce that liability; but this too does not happen. The mismatch between the cash basis of public sector pension accounting and the accrual basis of private sector pension accounting means that the impact of contracting out on public sector finance is permanently adverse.

All this would be true even if the terms of contracting out were actuarially fair. But they are a good deal better than actuarially fair. The real return of $\frac{1}{2}$ per cent at which the national insurance fund is lending money may be contrasted with the current cost of raising index-linked debt which is between 3 per cent and 5 per cent, depending on maturity. The gap is not as wide as this suggests because contracting out terms are earnings linked and index linked gilts are price linked, but is nonetheless substantial. Additionally, the terms of contracting out give occupational schemes a range of options under which liabilities for guaranteed minimum pensions can be passed back to the state. Through these options, the government significantly underwrites both the risk of a rapid acceleration in inflation and of a poor investment performance by the occupational pension sector.

Future cost trends
Over the next fifty years the incomes of the elderly, expressed as a percentage of the earnings of those at work, will almost double (Table 6.3). This is partly the result of demographic changes. The support ratio - the number of persons of working age per person of pensionable age - is currently 3.3. This will improve slightly over the next 20 years but falls very rapidly from the beginning of the next century, as those born in the 20 years after 1945 begin to leave the labour force and enter retirement.

About 20 per cent of the cost increase shown in Table 6.3 is the result of these adverse demographic movements. Similar, or more commonly worse, demographic problems are faced by most countries in the western world over the same period, and although the implied rises in social security costs and contributions are very substantial they are not necessarily insupportable.

They do, however, invite a critical examination of the efficiency of the projected expenditure. In the private sector, the part of the increase in cost which is not demographically induced is the result of the growth to maturity of the occupational pension sector. In the public sector, the major cause is the provisions of the 1975 Act.

The principal beneficiaries of SERPS will be those without occupational pensions of their own. At low income levels, the earnings related component of the pension will simply eliminate entitlement to supplementary benefit on a £ for £ basis. Only if entitlement is not claimed, or if the

Table 6.3 Total pensions and benefits to the elderly as a proportion of total wages and salaries

Percentages

	1981	2005-6	2025-6
National insurance benefits			
- flat rate	$9\frac{1}{2}$	10	$12\frac{1}{2}$
- earnings related	0	$2\frac{1}{2}$	$5\frac{1}{2}$
Occupational schemes	$4\frac{1}{2}$	6	8
Total	14	$18\frac{1}{2}$	26

Source: DHSS (1984), Table 9.
Note: Calculations assume flat rate benefits are linked to earnings.

additional pension is sufficient to take the pensioner over the supplementary benefit level (broadly, if it exceeds household rent and rates) will there be a net gain. It should be noted that a curious by-product of the growth of owner occupation is a reduction in the cost of support for the elderly since most owner occupier pensioners have only rates as housing cost. In a similar way, any independent pension due to the wife will simply count against total household income for supplementary benefit purposes. Thus the largest gains are made by those with higher earnings, up to the contribution ceiling, and no occupational pension. The pension for a man on average earnings will be approximately doubled and, if his wife acquires rights to a pension of her own, total household income may double.

Most employees with occupational pensions are contracted out of the state scheme. This does not imply that they receive no state earnings related pension. Rather their state pension is reduced by a 'guaranteed minimum pension' and the occupational pension scheme must provide them with benefits of at least that amount. Thus they will gain the difference between their earnings related pension and their guaranteed minimum pension. There are two main sources of this difference. The GMP is based on average lifetime earnings but the state entitlement on a 'best twenty years' rule, thus benefiting (eventually) those with uneven earnings profiles. The GMP is not indexed after retirement but SERPS is; thus SERPS partly compensates private sector pensioners for deficiencies in the degree of indexation provided in their occupational scheme.

Although the costs of SERPS are substantial, much of this expenditure results from misdirected elements (Hemming and Kay, 1982) and considerable pressure for additional expenditure will remain. One source of this is the failure of SERPS to do more for the poorest pensioners. Others are consequent on the design of SERPS itself. How easily can the planned build-up over 20 years be defended? On the one hand, there may be pressure to credit entitlements over a period less than 20 years. On the other, the question of whether it will be acceptable for people who have 'contributed' over 30 years from 1978 to acquire rights only marginally greater than those of individuals who have 'contributed' over only 20 years is bound to arise when its implications are understood and effective, especially when this feature is not mirrored in the occupational schemes which substantially substitutes for SERPS for many employees.

Basic principles
What should be the role of the state in supporting retirement provision? Old age is predictable, and a contingency for which extremely well-developed private insurance markets exist. Why should the government become involved at all? One obvious retort is that if people make grossly inadequate provision for retirement, either by imprudence or because things have gone wrong, we are not prepared to let them starve in the streets in consequence. We can respond to this either by guaranteeing people some minimum level of retirement income regardless of what they themselves choose to do, or by requiring them to measure up to that minimum level whether they want to do so or not.

Each of these alternatives has its difficulties. The problem with the minimum income guarantee is that it provides a very substantial disincentive to provision slightly in excess of the guarantee. If I am promised £35 per week whether I save anything or not, and the income which I would ideally like in retirement is £36 per week, then I have to save sufficient to obtain £36 in order to benefit by an additional £1. The practical consequence is that I will not do so, overall savings will be reduced, and the retired population will be polarised into one group who are reliant on the minimum income guarantee and another with substantially higher incomes who have found it worthwhile to make provision for themselves. Elements of this scenario are familiar.

Compulsory insurance up to the level of a minimum income guarantee could be achieved either by requiring that people take out appropriate private contracts, or by the government implementing the insurance scheme itself. One difficulty is that the cost of such insurance will be more than many people are willing to pay which is, after all, why it is necessary to make the scheme compulsory in the first place. If we respond - as we have - by breaking the link between individual contributions and receipts we simply succeed in transferring the cost of a universal benefit to public expenditure, and transforming the insurance premium into a hypothecated tax. Another problem is how to achieve insurance based benefits which will achieve a guaranteed income level varying according to household needs, especially if these are taken to include housing costs.

A solution which appears to make little sense is that of a minimum income guarantee combined with compulsory insurance to a level below the minimum income guarantee. This achieves most of the disadvantages of both solutions, combining most of the incentive problems of the pure guarantee system with most of the cost disadvantages of the purely insurance based proposal; but it is a broad characterisation of what has been done.

These arguments would support a basic level of state provision, but would not justify earnings-related state pension provision. Most individuals would aim at a retirement standard of living which reflected their earnings while at work, but may fail or be unable to do so for themselves. A paternalistic view that households will thank the state, in their retirement, for having obliged them to make greater provision than they had intended might acquire some justification from the low response to current opportunities for retirement saving by those outside the private occupational sector. But it is puzzling that the myopia which is apparently experienced in making individual savings decisions should fall away when collective savings decisions are made. An alternative hypothesis would note the inflexibility of tax-favoured individual provision for retirement, combined with the tax disadvantages and uncertain returns of personal saving - particularly in the absence of indexation. These factors together with the readiness of politicians to promise that our children will pay us more generous pensions than we are willing to pay our parents, have combined to enable the state to offer retirement saving provisions on considerably more attractive terms than individuals could provide for themselves.

This argument suggests that the shape of state pension provision is very much influenced by failures in the market for private pension provision. Many of these failures are the result of other policy choices or could be remedied or relieved by other policy choices. A shift from the taxation of income towards the taxation of expenditure, for example, would enable individuals to make less distorted choices between present and future consumption. Other difficulties are characteristic of the operation of the private pension sector itself. The incorporation in occupational pension schemes of features which impose penalties on early leavers seems to be a world-wide characteristic of such schemes and one which tends to re-emerge whatever legal steps are taken to outlaw it. Considerable uncertainty about the real value of pensions after retirement remains. There is no significant control of the solvency of private occupational schemes; a matter which has not been of much significance so far because of the magnitude of the net cash inflow into the sector and because inflation confers substantial discretion about the real value of the benefits to be paid. Both of these features are likely to be of diminishing significance in future and the probability of some major pension schemes facing financial problems is a real one.

The greater flexibility of individual provision has its corollary in the greater administrative cost of individually designed arrangements. Some of these costs are the result of excessive misleading sales efforts, which are already the subject of increasing concern within the insurance industry itself. Thus a more individualist solution to the provision of incomes in retirement requires the support of sympathetic tax policies and an appropriate regulatory regime for the private sector. A number of developments of this kind are likely in any event.

Arguments against this individualist direction of change may be social as well as economic. It is frequently suggested that a universal system is more likely to win popular esteem and support for high benefit levels than a selective or minimalist one. This argument may have more plausibility in relation to provision for retirement than it does for a social security system which taken as a whole neither commands such esteem nor induces willingness to finance high levels of benefit.

These questions about the objectives of state pension provision require answers if we are to suggest the broad lines of development of future policy in this area. But the elements of answers are also required if a range of immediate and specific policy issues are to be considered. What should the rate of state flat-rate pension be? Should there be differential rates of short and long run benefit; if so, what should be the qualification criteria and what should be the gap between them? The present gap is one which is the historical product of the effects of two different indexation formulas and which has now been frozen in real amount by the move to a common indexation formula. Should benefit rates be derived from a poverty standard or a target replacement rate? All these are questions which ultimately turn on a view of the proper role of the state in benefit provision.

The design of state pension schemes

Even if the basic structure of state provision remains unchanged, a number of issues inevitably arise within it. The question of retirement age has receded from the immediate focus of attention but is certain to return to the debate. The difference between male and female retirement ages remains an anomaly. There is also a desire for increased flexibility of retirement age and it is probably through this mechanism that the objective of equality of retirement age for men and women can be ultimately achieved without either excessive cost or abrupt disappointment of established expectations.

The treatment of women raises several issues. There is no rational way of reconciling demands for equality of treatment, equality of contribution and equality of benefit for men and women with substantial and predictable differences in their mortality experience. This problem arises immediately in the context of EEC directives and while it can to some extent be concealed in the majority of EEC states in which insurance-based provision plays a relatively minor role, the partnership of public and private sector in the UK makes the inconsistency impossible to conceal. The provisions of the 1975 Act appear to start from the premise that pensions should be provided on an individual basis but then, recognising that the consequence of this would in practice be very poor pensions for women, turns round and provides them on a dependency basis as well. And the inconsistency between individualism, symmetry of treatment, and adequate provision leads to the half-hearted institution of largely unwanted and unnecessary benefits such as widowers' pensions.

The argument is characterised by a certain unwillingness to face up to a reality whose most important feature is that so long as the earnings records of women are typically so markedly inferior to those of men, i.e. for the foreseeable future, an individual basis is unsustainable. The corollary of this would be that rights earned by either partner would accrue to the unit rather than to the individual and this principle is one which is capable of application in the private as well as the public sector. The underlying problem of how a government which wished that men and women were treated equally should react to a world in which they are not remains, and it is not resolved, or much helped, by resounding declarations of principle.

Indexation of public sector pensions - both state and occupational - is likely to remain an issue. It should hardly need repeating that the burden of indexed pensions is what the burden of unindexed pensions would be if inflation stopped and that the difficulty is not so much that indexation is expensive as that it removes an arbitrary mechanism for reducing the real value of pensions in payment. The mechanics of indexation have not worked well, with consequent repeated changes to them. This is partly the result of the 1975 better-of-earnings-or-prices formula, which owed more to the heart than the head, and partly to the dilemma that a forecast basis is inevitably subject to error and a historic basis inevitably irrelevant by the date of implementation. This is a consequence of annual uprating and it is difficult to see why pensions fixed in units of a variable currency rather than in cash could not be readjusted more frequently and by smaller amounts.

The mismatch between indexation formulae in SERPS seems unsustainable, and none of those who have made projections of the future impact of the scheme have felt able to assume that the current legislative provisions could continue for an extended period. Earnings are revalued using an earnings index while the ceiling and floor against which these revalued earnings are measured are indexed to prices. So are pensions in payment. The most obvious solution is that the flat rate retirement pension, at least, will be de facto indexed to earnings and hence the national insurance floor and ceiling will move in line.

Funding of state pension liabilities was effectively abandoned when the national insurance fund came under financial pressure in the late 1950s, although there has since been a considerable increase in the extent of funding of pensions for the government's own - mostly indirect - employees. The principal arguments for funding in the private sector - tax benefits and a promotion of pensioners' claims in the event of liquidation of the employer's business - are evidently irrelevant to the public sector. Funding does demand immediate recognition of the cost of pension promises - a recognition which is both a discipline on these promises and a necessary element in the calculation of the price of goods and services which are currently being used in the public sector or elsewhere. Evidence on its effects on capital formation are inconclusive. It is hard to believe that a resumption of funding of state pensions will ever prove politically popular, but the absence of any regular quantification of liabilities is breathtaking, especially in a context in which fiscal policy is dominated by measures of change in the accrued liabilities of the public sector. The variety of provision for public sector employees - with some liabilities unfunded, some 'notionally funded', and others modelled on private sector arrangements, is also a proper subject for review.

Integration

Issues of integration arise in considering both the relationship between taxation and benefits and in the relationship between the public and private sectors. The strange characteristics of the income tax age allowance have already been noted and it is difficult to believe that anyone would have set out to devise a benefit which accrued neither to poor or rich pensioners but only to those in between. The Inland Revenue is now responsible for the collection of national insurance contributions but record keeping remains with DHSS and the interaction between the respective tax schedules of income tax and national insurance remains absurd. There is scope for tension between the government's desire on the one hand to stimulate personal pension provision and on the other to trim the tax concessions which make it attractive.

A second kind of integration is that between public and private occupational sectors. Contracting-out arrangements are in a sense a form of integration; but they are perhaps more accurately viewed as a sort of armed truce in which both state and occupational sector have agreed to occupy distinct territories with a narrow but carefully defined strip of territory between them. Indeed one of the sources of pressure on employers to contract out of SERPS has been the practical difficulty of constructing a genuinely integrated scheme, i.e. one in which the employer tops up state benefits to a defined level. The outcome is one in which, both for contracted out and not contracted out employees who are members of occupational schemes, the level of benefits ultimately obtained is not determined or known by either the state or the employer. Among other disadvantages, the result is to aggravate considerably the difficulty which the employee has in making rational retirement plans. Indeed it is difficult to overstate the degree of uncertainty about retirement income to which most people not on the immediate point of retirement are now subject - an uncertainty which is the result of a potential multiplicity of sources of retirement income, of the complexity of design of both the state scheme and occupational schemes, and of the extent to which benefits may prove to be contingent on both macroeconomic and microeconomic events prior to retirement.

Conclusions

Consider two possible views of the future of pension provision in Britain. In one, there is a minimum income guaranteed in retirement, probably means-tested with a gentle taper phasing out state support from the many old people whose needs are more than adequately met by private pensions. The income guarantee is administered in some relatively automatic way and although discretionary payments and provisions exist they operate only for smallish numbers of people who are typically in need of forms of support other than financial.

If private pension provision is to be the dominant form of saving for retirement income, then it is necessary that it should deal more widely and more adequately with the half of the labour force who are outside the coverage of occupational pensions schemes. It is also necessary that the occupational sector should deal more adequately, and more fairly, with those who do not engage in lifetime employment with a single firm. It is therefore unlikely that occupational schemes will dominate the sector as they do now; the move to portable pensions is probably a first element of this change. Other countries have already gone further in allowing individuals - in or out of occupational schemes - to make tax-sheltered provisions which they are free to shift between institutions or to manage themselves.

A second picture is one in which the state replaces a high proportion of pre-retirement incomes of all but the most affluent. It is probable that occupational pension schemes continue to exist but they are integrated into and essentially subordinate to the state scheme. The pension they provide is matched more or less £ for £ by offsetting reductions in state benefits and the same is true on the contribution side. Taxation rates make long-term personal saving (other than through house purchase) both difficult and unattractive and, except in the top decile of the income range, not very much of it takes place.

Each of these scenarios represents a possible - indeed plausible - line of development for pension provision in the UK and the elements, and to a considerable extent the reality, of each of them can already be seen in other countries. Britain, with its unique, uneasy and complex mixture of private and public sectors, lies somewhere in between - capable of moving in either direction or of absorbing the best or worst of each.

The advantages of the first of these scenarios are its considerable flexibility, its low cost in public expenditure, and its stimulus to savings and investment, particularly by individuals. The advantages of the second are the high degree of security and certainty of relevant income which it offers. It is, of course, probable that we shall end with an element of each. But what we should seek to avoid is a compromise which combines the disadvantages of both - the uncertainties of the individualist outcome in a context in which there is enormous variability in provision for retirement, mostly the result of factors which are outside individual control, and with a very large pensions bill on public expenditure without a corresponding degree of security in retirement.

References

DHSS (1984), Population, Pension Costs and Pensioners' Incomes, HMSO.

Fry, V.C., Hammond, E.H. and Kay, J.A. (1985), Taxing Pensions, IFS Report Series 14.

Hemming, R. and Kay, J.A. (1981), 'Contracting out of the state earnings related pension scheme', Fiscal Studies, Vol. 2, No. 3, November.

Hemming, R. and Kay, J.A. (1982), 'The costs of the state earnings related pension scheme', Economic Journal, Vol. 92, No. 366, June.

Inland Revenue (1983), Cost of tax reliefs for pension schemes: appropriate statistical approach, mimeo, Inland Revenue.

7 Care of elderly people

ALAN WALKER

The 'welfare state' is chiefly a welfare state for elderly people. A large proportion of its benefits and services go to them. They are the main client group of the Department of Health and Social Security, which has primary responsibility for implementing government social policy and planning. Elderly people rely overwhelmingly on the state for income, but this large-scale economic dependency is not matched by physical or social dependence on the state. Nevertheless, public health and personal social services make a crucial contribution to the quality of life and often the very survival of the minority of elderly people who use them and, in turn, just under half of public expenditure on these services goes to elderly people (CPRS/CSO, 1980, p.85). Considerations about the future of the 'welfare state' and social policy, therefore, are inevitably concerned with the well-being and status of elderly people. Changes in the demands for and availability of resources for the social services over the next 10 to 15 years are likely to have a profound impact on them.

The purpose of this chapter is to set the scene for a discussion of the care of elderly people and the need for further research. What is the scale of need? What can be predicted with certainty about changes in the need and demand for services in the near future? What pressures will continue to influence the development of policy in this field? What principles should underpin policy? How, if at all, can the supply of resources for care be increased? How far can the preoccupation of policy-makers and the needs of elderly people and their families be reconciled in the development of social care policy? What priorities might be identified for policy and research? Because of shortage of space and time I have concentrated on the issue of care rather than treatment (see Abrams, 1978a, p.78) although the distinction between the two is often blurred.

The elderly population and their need for care

Discussions about social policy with regard to elderly people usually start with an account of the recent and projected growth in their numbers and, while this one is no different, three cautions should be borne in mind.

It is now commonplace, in both official and independent documents, to describe Britain's ageing population in terms which often border on alarm. Descriptions such as 'the growing burden of dependency', 'social disaster', 'flood' and 'rising tide' create the impression that we are being swamped or taken over by multiplying hoards of frail elderly people (see, for example, Health Advisory Service, 1983). The fact that this is not the case, as I will go on to show, is difficult to establish in the face of such exaggerated language. This caricature of old age, which is at best restricted and at worst downright degrading, has its origins more in social and political institutions, particularly the labour market, than in demographic facts. We are encouraged to believe that the social problem of dependency exists just because the numbers in a particular age group are increasing, by the simple but mistaken translation of demographic projections into social realities. But dependency is a socially rather than a biologically constructed status. It is primarily the product of a particular social division of labour and structure of inequality rather than a natural concomitant of the ageing process. So, the description of ageing by means of demographic statistics has largely substituted for social analysis of the changing meaning and experience of old age. As a result, the extent to which we have created a dependent status in old age has been obscured. This is not to say that people do not grow old and suffer from disabilities some of which might entail dependency (see below), but rather, what we regard as old age is of our own manufacture and not a function of demography or the biological ageing process (for a full account see Walker, 1980, 1981a, 1983; Townsend, 1981a).

The practical implication of this sort of structural analysis is that since age and dependency are social institutions, they can be altered, as they have been in the past, through social and economic policies such as those affecting the age of retirement. In the health and personal social services there is a wide range of powerful groups and interests that may have unwittingly encouraged the myth that old age and dependency are synonymous. Staff of domiciliary services and residential homes alike, health and social services unions, social services managers and directors, local politicians, the medical profession and Department of Health and Social Security officials and ministers have all no doubt stressed the worrying implications of the rising numbers of elderly people in their wholly honourable pursuit of better services, conditions of service or more resources for the health and personal social services (Walker, 1982a, pp. 124-5). But in doing so they have helped to spread and legitimate an inaccurate picture of elderly people and the true origins of their needs. There is a continuing danger, therefore, that policy will be formulated in a climate of alarmist speculation, following the path of least resistance, rather than on the basis of a careful analysis of actual needs among the elderly. This emphasises the fundamental role of independent research in the planning of social care.

Secondly, to conceive of increases in the numbers of elderly as a threat or burden is paradoxically, as Titmuss (1963, p.56) pointed out, to undervalue the social progress British society has made, and particularly the achievements of public welfare, in putting an end to many of the causes of premature death.

Thirdly, increases in the population in need do not necessarily result in increased public resources. As Ermisch (1983, p.283) has shown, expenditure on the health and personal social services has not been sensitive in the past to increases in the need for care but, instead, has been determined by what the government has decided to spend. So, it seems that whatever pressures derive from rising numbers of elderly people in the future, the crucial factors in the allocation of resources to the health and personal social services will be political. Whether or not elderly people themselves become a more concerted political force in the battle for resources, as in the USA, is an interesting matter for speculation beyond the scope of this paper.

Demographic changes
Bearing in mind these cautions and Abrams's (1978b, p.5) warning that 'predictions and projections based on demographic data are, of all types of social prediction, the ones most likely to go wrong', what can be said with confidence about the size and composition of the elderly population over the coming decade or so? Continuing growth in the numbers over 65 can be expected until the early 1990s, when a slight fall will be followed by a steep rise in the first

part of next century. Between 1983 and 1991 the population aged 65 and over is expected to rise by 7 per cent to 8.8 million. This follows a growth in this age group of 360 per cent since the beginning of the century (Wicks, 1982).

Britain shares this expansion in the population of elderly people with its EEC partners and, with the exception of Ireland, has a similar proportion of its population aged 65 and over: the proportion of the population of EEC countries in this age group varies from 13.2 per cent in Greece to 15.1 per cent in West Germany, with the UK figure at 15.0 per cent (Eurostat, 1984, pp.76-77). However, it is the projected increase in the number of elderly people aged 75 and over and especially those aged 85 or more that has been the chief focus of attention in recent years (Ermisch, 1983, p.282). The numbers aged 75 and over are expected to rise by 14 per cent by 1991 and 21 per cent by 2001, those aged 85 and over by 22 per cent and 69 per cent respectively.

Disability and the need for care
The major factor of importance to social policy-makers in the ageing of the population and particularly increasing longevity is the rising incidence of disability in successively older age groups (Townsend, 1979, p.706). Although there are no up-to-date official estimates of the full extent of disability in old age - a major deficiency that should be rectified by the Office of Population Censuses and Surveys survey currently under way - some indication of variations in incapacity between different groups of elderly people can be given. For example, the proportion of elderly people who are unable to go out of doors and walk down the road unaided increases by ten fold between the 65 to 69 and the 85 and over age groups. The proportion of those aged 85 and over who are unable to bath, shower or wash all over alone is seven times higher than that for those aged 65 to 69 (OPCS, 1981).

As well as indicating the existence of a significant proportion of elderly people who suffer from restricted mobility or who are unable to perform certain self-care tasks - 12 per cent of all elderly people or 990,000 people are unable to go out of doors unaided and 7 per cent, 577,000, are housebound - these statistics show that the vast majority are not troubled by illness or disability which restricts their activity to any significant extent. The most recent national survey of elderly people living in the community (Hunt, 1978, p.73) also found that the majority were not functionally impaired: only four per cent could not manage to go upstairs and eight per cent could not bath themselves. Again it is among the older age groups that the greatest need and, therefore, the main demand for social services occurs. For example, those aged 75 and over are six times more likely than those in the 65 to 74 age group to have a home help (OPCS, 1982, p.154). Even so less than one in five of the 75 and overs receive a home help service.

A similar picture emerges from more recent research among those elderly people taking part in innovatory home care and neighbourly help schemes and even among those in residential care. For instance, 55 per cent of those in the community care schemes, and 55 per cent of a sample of people in residential care, are able to wash without help or with only minimal support. Three-quarters of those in the special schemes and four-fifths of those in residential care are able to dress adequately without supervision (Tinker, 1984, p.67). This emphasises the importance of not attributing disability, let alone dependency, to the elderly population in general.

The distribution and composition of the elderly population also has important implications for social service planning. Regional variations in the distribution of elderly people mean that the potential demand for services is higher in some areas, particularly the south coast and inner city areas of the north and north west. Then there are important differences between age groups in the proportion living alone. There has been a substantial increase in the numbers of elderly people living alone over the last 20 years to some three in ten of the elderly population. The higher mortality rate among men than among women means that the majority of those surviving alone to advanced old age are women and the provision of care to this group is one of the main challenges facing social service planners over the next two decades.

This arises from two separate factors. Not only are a large number of elderly people, and elderly women in particular, outliving their spouses for long periods but also there are a significant number of elderly people who have either never had children or who have none surviving (Abrams, 1980). Thus household composition has an important bearing on the use of social services: those aged 75 and over living alone are nearly three times as likely as those in the same age group living with a spouse to receive a home help and five times as likely to receive meals on wheels (OPCS, 1982, p.154).

On the basis of official demographic projections, then, there is likely to be an increase in the numbers needing care over the next two decades and beyond. An approximate estimate has been made of some of the increases in the need for care implied by these population changes (Henwood and Wicks, 1984, p.16). Between 1981 and 1991 the numbers of people over 65 who are unable to bath themselves might increase by 16 per cent (122,000 persons), those not independently mobile by 17 per cent (183,000) and those living alone by 9 per cent (258,000), although there would be considerable overlap between these groups. If these estimates are projected forward to 2001 the increases over 1981 would be 23 per cent, 25 per cent and 9.5 per cent respectively.

Family care of elderly people
The need for care on the part of elderly people is likely to go on increasing, but not at an alarming rate. However when rising levels of need are coupled with the existing shortfall in formal service provision (see below) it is reasonable to express concern about the adequacy of care for a substantial minority of elderly people in the near future. Who is likely to meet the need for care?

Despite the fact that elderly people are the largest client group in the health and personal social services, the vast bulk of care is not provided publicly but privately by the family. In turn, family care is a euphemism for care by female kin (Land, 1978; Finch and Groves, 1980; Walker, 1981b). Women carry out most of the help, assistance and support or 'tending' (Parker, 1981) that caring tasks consist of. As well as doing most of the unpaid labour women bear the main burden of guilt and worry that the other side of the caring coin, love or affection, usually entails (Graham, 1983; Ungerson, 1983). A survey of carers by the Equal Opportunities Commission (1980, p.9) found that there were three times as many women carers as men. A more recent study of elderly people using short-term residential care found that 85 per cent had female carers (Allen, 1983b). A detailed study of a very small sample of families caring for severely disabled elderly relatives found that the average time spent on care activities on weekdays was 3 hours 24 minutes, of which 3 hours 11 minutes was spent by wives and 13 minutes by husbands (Nissel and Bonnerjea, 1982, p.21).

The burden of care on women appears to be increasing. In a survey of women's employment, Hunt (1968, p.109) found five per cent of women aged 16-64 were responsible for the care of at least one elderly or infirm person in their household and six per cent were responsible for at least one person outside of the household. In the recent Office of Population Censuses and Surveys survey of women's employment, 13 per cent were found to have caring responsibilities for sick and elderly dependents. This sort of finding and the absence of any national data on carers points to the need for large-scale research into the factors which encourage or inhibit the provision of care in the family.

Thus the future supply of care for elderly people is primarily a question of how far women will be prepared to continue shouldering the main responsibility for providing care.

Certainly there are powerful normative, ideological and marital pressures on women, and especially daughters, to care for elderly relatives. Preliminary results from a pioneering piece of research in this country, which has examined the caring relationship from the perspective of both elderly people and their principal carers, have confirmed the continuing strength of the normative structure underlying the hypothetical decision-making process about which relatives from an available pool will provide care (Qureshi and Walker, 1986). It is possible to predict, with a high degree of accuracy, the outcome of decisions about which relatives will care, even within large close-knit kinship structures. One of the most potent influences on the 'selection' of carers is that female relatives are preferred to male relatives. The majority of carers themselves believe that they are the right person to provide care and that care for elderly people is women's work. At the same time the preference for relatives as against non-relatives by both elderly people and their relatives may set limits on the involvement of friends, neighbours and volunteers in the care of elderly people, a point I return to below.

The supply of informal carers

Against the demonstrably powerful influence of norms concerning the distribution of caring functions there are several factors which might have an increasing bearing on the availability of family carers, resulting in a widening 'care gap', which must be considered in planning future policies.

It has already been noted that a significant proportion of elderly people are surviving without any children or other relatives. In addition there are likely to be changes in the pool of potential family carers. The decline in fertility during the 1920s and low fertility in the 1930s mean that the generation who are now 75 have fewer children than any previous generation (Ermisch, 1983, p.283). The generation who will become the elderly of the 1990s produced slightly more children but their families were still relatively small. So the ratio of potential family carers per person aged 75 and over has declined steadily over the course of this century (Eversley, 1982). There is no evidence from the recent survey of family care in Sheffield that the size of the pool of potential family carers has a significant influence on the provision of care; the crucial elements are the sex and proximity of carers (Qureshi and Walker, 1986). It must be pointed out, however, that Sheffield is an area of traditionally low migration and geographical mobility might increase the importance of the size of the pool of possible carers.

Increasing longevity has made the aged carer a more common phenomenon. Again precise information is not available, but we do know that some 49 per cent of all elderly people and 35 per cent of those aged 85 or over live with other elderly people in different types of household (Hunt, 1978, p.16). In one local study it was found that 30 per cent of elderly people were receiving help from others of their generation (Green et al, 1979). While the existence of elderly carers is not a cause for concern, it is likely that in advanced old age carers will be less able than younger people to stand up to the strains of caring.

Family breakdown too is likely to have a small impact on the future availability of carers. It is not possible to predict the consequences of divorce and family reconstruction on the supply of family care and Parker's (1981, p.21) question about who will look after the dependent step-grandmothers and grandfathers of the next century remains an open one. On the basis of the differences in obligations towards the care of elderly relatives felt by daughters-in-law compared with daughters it is likely that increases in divorce will weaken the impact of the normative pressure to care. It is estimated that by 1999 5.1 per cent of women and 2.9 per cent of men aged 65 or more will have experienced divorce.

Economic changes may affect the supply of care, if not the numbers available to provide care, by restricting the ability and propensity of family members to help elderly relatives. It is sometimes suggested that the growth of unemployment might have a beneficial spin-off in freeing more men to take a greater share of caring tasks. On the face of it this is an appealing argument, entailing benefits for elderly people, female carers and unemployed men. But it contradicts all that we know about the debilitating, isolating and psychologically damaging effects of unemployment (see, for example, Hakim, 1982). What little evidence there is suggests that unemployed men are _less_ likely than those in work to provide care to elderly relatives or to support the caring activities of their wives (Qureshi and Walker, 1986). While this points to a pessimistic view of unemployed people as a potential resource for the care of the elderly, there is one group among the newly economically insecure some of whom do not suffer the same high level of stigma, loss of status and acute poverty as the unemployed: the early retired. Large numbers of men, predominantly in their fifties and early sixties, are leaving the labour market and might be encouraged to take part in caring activities.

It is probable too that the continuing growth of family poverty (Townsend, 1984) with all its attendant anxieties, both financial and mental, will not contribute to the willingness of family members to care for elderly relatives. There is very little information on the relationship between economic status, income levels and the supply of informal care, a deficiency that might be felt acutely by policy-makers in the near future. The evolving relationship between the market, especially the growth of part-time work, and informal care is another important focus for research.

It is sometimes suggested that the increased involvement of married women in the labour market - in 1983 over half of married women aged 25 to 35 and two-thirds of those aged 35 to 54 were economically active - will reduce their commitment to care. There is no evidence that this is the case. On the contrary, what is remarkable is the extraordinary lengths that many married women go to - often sustaining three separate roles at great physical and mental cost to themselves - in order to care for elderly relatives and keep them in the community (Nissel and Bonnerjea, 1982; Allen, 1983a; EOC, 1980).

The gender division in care
This brings me to what is perhaps the greatest long-term challenge to the structure of norms and values on which the present pattern of care is based: the growing opposition on the part of women to sex-based inequality and the questions it

raises about the unequal division of domestic labour, including the provision of informal care. Some feminists and female carers are directly confronting questions concerning the justice and fairness of sexist forms of care and the possibility of alternative approaches which do not exploit the low status of women (Wilson, 1982; Finch and Groves, 1983; Finch, 1984), questions which will emerge in a different form in many families caring for elderly relatives in the future. Although opposition to sex-based inequalities is unlikely, under its own steam, to have a major impact on the provision of informal care in the medium term, planning for the longer term is essential if we are to respond to the effects of changes in the roles of women which may challenge their normative designation as carers.

While the effects of these developments are uncertain, even in the long term, the feminist critique of care does emphasise the important question: should women be the primary source of care? Policy-makers might prefer to approach this question from a different angle: what are the implications of a continuation of the present unequal sexual division in informal care?

Caring entails a number of costs - financial, social, psychological and physical (Nissel and Bonnerjea, 1982; Allen, 1983a) - which are not only unfairly borne predominantly by women, but because of this, they are forced to give up caring prematurely. For example, Isaacs and his colleagues (1972) found:

> 'The factors which made the burden of caring for an ill, old person overwhelming were, above all, the personality of the patient, the distortion of personality and behaviour caused by mental illness, and to a lesser extent the physical burden of providing night-and-day nursing care for the helpless'.

If carers do give up full-time care it is usually because they are no longer able to bear the huge emotional and psychological costs or because they have been worn out by the sheer physical costs in terms of sleepless nights, illness and exhaustion from lifting and taking care of their relatives. It should be a matter for concern to policy-makers not only that the breakdown in informal care results in the demand for formal services but also that individual carers should be driven to breaking point before these services are made available on a casualty basis.

The caring capacity of the community

What is the potential of the informal sector to meet the rising needs of elderly people for care? A simple answer would be misleading because it depends on the quality of care and caring regarded as desirable for elderly people and their relatives. On the one hand there is no doubt that, in the short term at least, female kin will continue to meet the needs of their elderly relatives extremely effectively until they are no longer able to do so. In the medium and long terms the pressures I have outlined above will come to have an increasing influence on the provision of care. Thus to the roughly one in three of over 75s who have no children there will be added an unknown number with children or other relatives who for whatever reason cannot or will not provide care.

If, on the other hand, we are seeking to promote and support informal caring networks which do not exploit the duty felt by families, and above all by women, to provide care and which does not impose enormous financial, physical, social or psychological costs on carers, then we must look to the formal sector for policies which contribute to this development. In practice this means that more resources will have to be put into helping and supporting informal care and, as the Department of Health and Social Security (1981a, p.55) study of community care pointed out, a greater official recognition of the existing burden on informal carers. The Social Work Service Development Group project on support for informal carers is a step in the right direction (SWSDG, 1983) but shifts in resources are required to put this sort of policy into effective practice. The interdependence of the formal and informal sectors has been underlined most recently by the authors of a study of carers of confused elderly people in the community:

> 'Something can be done to alleviate most of the problems these supporters face but it will not be done if resources are not earmarked for this purpose. Care by the family in the community does not do away with the need for services: rather it can be promoted by them' (Levin et al, 1983).

This study also demonstrated the importance of the health and personal social services in preventing the build up of physical and emotional strain and thereby increasing the capacity of those supporting even the most difficult elderly people to care for them informally.

There is no evidence of large unused human resources in the current system of family care (DHSS, 1981a, p.54). Those regarded by both elderly people and carers as the most appropriate persons to provide help are for the most part doing so and often working at full stretch. Of course there are instances of friction within families where, for example, one daughter is providing a great deal of assistance and another is not, and one of the more sensitive tasks for social scientists is to investigate not only why some people provide care but also why others do not. The only substantial untapped resource within the family is that of male kin, particularly sons and sons-in-law. Policy-makers might turn their attention to ways of increasing the willingness of men to share caring tasks. This is not a matter for the family to resolve privately because of the enormous costs that continue to fall on women and the costs that might fall on society if there were a breakdown in care. There is a need, then, for <u>preventive</u> action which would have the beneficial effect of promoting sex equality and reducing the need for formal services. Moreover, when we consider the financial benefits to the state of the unpaid labour of families (Moroney, 1976; and below) the case for material support for the caring activities of the family is very strong - perhaps taking the form of a social security benefit or tax concession for those who take part-time work in order to provide care.

While the family is undoubtedly the main source of care for elderly people there is a danger, to be guarded against, of constructing policy on the assumption that this is <u>necessarily</u> the best source of care. This approach is based on an over-idealised view of family life and family-based care, uninformed by either historical or contemporary research, which sometimes results in policy-makers casting longing looks back to a supposed golden age of the family (Moroney, 1976, p.125). The same 'ideological naiveté' (Whittaker and Garbarino, 1983) underlies the similar tendency to idealise the whole of the informal sector as a preferable alternative to the formal sector (Walker, 1985). But just because the family provides the bulk of care it is not always the best and most effective source (Qureshi and Walker, 1986). The provision and receipt of family care can be a difficult and mutually painful experience for both carers and elderly people. Moreover the standard of care provided in such difficult circumstances is not likely to be very high.

Long overdue measures to improve the quality of life of carers and attempts to draw into caring those on the sidelines would not increase the supply of informal care to elderly people who do not have close kin, or none living nearby. Here the role of neighbours, friends and volunteers assumes greater significance.

A great deal of interest has been focussed on the activities and potential role of neighbours and volunteers in care. While this is undoubtedly an important resource for care, its potential as a substitute for family or formal care is doubtful. The pioneering work of Abrams (1978a, 1981) on neighbouring has questioned the existence of spontaneous neighbourly care based on locality. Paradoxically it requires formal organisation to promote and sustain it. In some small close-knit communities the contribution of friends and neighbours to care can be significant (Seyd et al, 1984; Wenger, 1982) but even in this setting it is secondary to the contribution of the family (Seyd et al, 1984, p.33). Other research in more typical locations confirms that neighbours and friends rarely fulfil a principal carer role for disabled elderly people needing considerable daily support (Charlesworth et al, 1983, p.60; Tinker, 1984; Qureshi and Walker, 1986). The future contribution of neighbours to the care of elderly people is likely to be confined to the secondary, but nonetheless important, role of supporting family carers rather than substituting for them.

For similar reasons - the need for secure, reliable and durable assistance - the potential of volunteers also needs cautious consideration. There have been a number of important experiments in collaboration between formal and voluntary services which give cause for some optimism about their wider use in a supportive capacity (Johnson and Challis, 1983, p.111). Working in conjunction with statutory services, volunteers can make a modest contribution to filling the gap in the care of the elderly (Power and Kelly, 1981). Again the use of volunteers cannot be seen as a substitute for formal services; the latter are required in order to make the most of voluntary help:

> 'In only a few situations is the voluntary sector an alternative to the statutory sector, either in the sense of offering a choice of services or in the sense of being able to do the work now done by the statutory services. Thus voluntary organisations are not a challenge to the state in the sense of being able to supplant it or carry on in parallel to it' (Hatch, 1980, p.148).

In sum, the successful provision of care by the family to the vast majority of elderly people who need it should not be taken as a cause for complacency. There is no sign of the family being less willing to care, though it may become less able to care. There is no general crisis of care on the horizon, though individual carers will increasingly experience personal and family crises unless policy is geared to their needs. But there are factors which are likely to limit the supply of potential carers and, perhaps, inhibit the willingness of family members to care. These are likely to result in a widening of the care gap over the next two decades. This brings us to the crucial role of the formal services in filling that gap and in supporting the caring activities of families and the rest of the informal sector.

Community care

'Community care' of elderly people has been a stated goal of governments of both political parties since the Second World War. But the precise meaning of the concept has varied considerably in practice and has recently been the focus of critical attention (Abrams, 1978a; Walker, 1981b, 1982b). Indeed the history of community care policy provides a powerful lesson for policy-makers and planners of the dangers, to paraphrase Titmuss, of employing idealistic terms to describe aspects of public policy (for a full account see Walker, 1982b). The most recent emphasis of policy rhetoric has swung firmly behind care by the community: 'care in the community must increasingly mean care by the community' (DHSS, 1981b, p.3). As we have seen, the community or the family is already providing most of the care and there are limitations on the ability of informal carers outside of the family to deliver the same level or intensity of care as either the family or the formal sector. Is there scope in the formal sector to fill the growing care gap?

Again the answer depends on the aims and priorities underlying policy. If the overriding concern is with a narrow form of economic efficiency in the public sector - the provision of services at the least cost to the Exchequer - then the answer will be straightforward: privatise the care of elderly people in the formal sector, providing the subsidy to the private sector is less than the cost to the public sector. If there is strong ideological opposition to the public sector then the final caveat might also be dispensed with (Minford, 1984). But the hallmark of public provision and one of the key differences between the public and private sectors, is concern with social efficiency as well as economic efficiency (Hirsch, 1977; Walker, 1984), though it may reasonably be argued that this dual concern has not always been translated successfully into practice. This means that policy-makers in the public sector are interested in the impact of policy, or policy effectiveness, as well as in cost efficiency (DHSS, 1981a, p.16). Assuming that this balanced approach continues to influence policy development then critical questions must be asked about efficiency and effectiveness in both public and private sectors. There has been a rapid growth in recent years in studies of relative cost efficiency between the two sectors, but as the Department of Health and Social Security study of community care recognised, research on the effectiveness of provision, particularly (I would add) from the clients' perspective, is less developed (DHSS, 1981a, p.16).

The current emphasis on care by the community stems primarily from a desire to limit the cost of care to the public sector. Total anticipated expenditure for all age groups on the personal social services in 1984/5 is £2,260 million, with about half going to services for the over-75s. Health service expenditure in this group is higher, at approximately £3.6 billion, and the transfer of resources from 'treatment' to care offers one of the best hopes of improving the quality and scope of caring services while remaining within or close to existing resource allocations. In the personal social services too, over half of expenditure is taken up by residential services, with only one-fifth going to community care. So the long-standing policy of shifting resources from residential to community services has not made much impression on the actual distribution of expenditure on these services.

In order to put it in context, public expenditure on the care of elderly people might be compared with estimates of the hypothetical financial contribution made by family carers. Assuming a relatively low rate of pay and small number of hours worked, Henwood and Wicks (1984, p.12) put the annual 'cost' of such care at between £3.7 and £5.3 billion (depending on the number of hours worked).

Restrictions on expenditure are worrying not only because increasing numbers of frail elderly people will face a growing care gap in the informal sector but also because, as Table 7.1 shows, there is already a substantial shortfall of services because expenditure has failed to keep pace with need.

Table 7.1 Elderly population and the PSS: indices of change 1975/6 to 1981/2

	1975/6 (=100)	Indices of change					
		1976/7	1977/8	1978/9	1979/80	1980/1	1981/2
Total elderly population (000s)							
aged 65+	6,811	102.8	102.8	104.6	105.3	107.6	108
aged 75+	2,446	103.3	103.3	107.2	109.0	113.0	115
Total elderly in residential care (000s)	120.3	104.0	105.5	104.8	104.1	101.6	105
Per thousand population 65+	17.7	101.1	102.9	100.0	98.9	94.4	97
Per thousand population 75+	49.2	I01.0	102.0	97.8	95.5	89.8	87.3
Home helps (whole time equivalents) (000s)	50.1	93.0	97.2	99.2	96.9	100.2	102
Per thousand population 65+	7.4	90.5	94.6	94.6	91.2	93.2	94.6
Per thousand population 75+	20.5	89.8	94.2	92.7	88.8	88.8	88.3
Meals (000s)	41,276	100.2	99.1	97.5	103.9	99.9	99.4
Per thousand population 65+	6,060	99.9	96.8	93.1	98.1	92.9	92.2
Per thousand population 75+	16,872	99.4	96.2	91.0	98.4	88.4	86.5

Source: Henwood and Wicks (1984), p.14.

Home help provision nationally averages only half of the (now defunct) guideline figure of 12 home helps per 1000 population (DHSS, 1977). There is evidence too that increases in the number of clients helped have been at the expense of a reduction in the average hours per client, and that only just over half of elderly people classed as being in severe, considerable or moderate need actually received a home help (Bebbington, 1981). Expenditure cuts have contributed to this shortfall and, as the Department of Health and Social Security (1981a, p.67) study of community care pointed out, this has inhibited the development of community care as a replacement for residential care:

'In the personal social services, some elements of the package of care which might be provided as an alternative to long-term hospital care do seem to have been held back as a result of expenditure constraint. The growth in the number of home helps for example, had not kept pace with the increasing number of elderly people'.

Insufficient weight appears to have been given to the impact of demographic changes on the health and personal social services. An allowance of 2 per cent per annum is made in planning public expenditure to meet demographic and other pressures in the personal social services. This does not match the increases in population shown in the table and the figure has been criticised as being, at best, 'a well-informed guess' (Webb and Wistow, 1983). Furthermore there is considerable variation between local authorities in the extent to which even this level of growth has been maintained.

Reallocating resources to community care
The substantial shortfall in community care services in the face of rising need represents a powerful argument for increased resources for the personal social services in the annual public expenditure round. But are there possibilities for freeing resources to meet the needs of elderly people more effectively from within the existing allocation to the health and personal social services? There would appear to be three main ones: a diminution in hospital and residential care, increasing cost effectiveness and privatisation. Each will be considered briefly.

Although the current interest in community care derives primarily from financial considerations, it coincides with a long-standing critique of the detrimental impact of residential care on elderly people. Ever since the pioneering work of Townsend (1962) there has been a long series of research studies confirming his findings that significant proportions of residents of old peoples' homes are physically and mentally capable of living more independently in the community, and that for a large number of people admission to a home rests on social factors such as the lack of alternative forms of care, rather than physical or mental disability. (For a summary of research see Townsend, 1981b.) There is some indication too that, once people have been admitted, residential homes can increase their dependency (Walker, 1982a) but further research is required on this important issue. Coupled with criticisms of residential care is the continuing finding of research that elderly people and their families are extremely reluctant to contemplate admission to a home (Qureshi and Walker, 1986).

There is evidence that the need for residential care can be delayed by innovative schemes like the Kent Community Care Project. But there are few examples of attempts to replace residential care with an intensive community-based package. Where this has been attempted there are doubts whether it would prove a cheaper option in the long run (DHSS, 1981a, p.30), although the evidence does not point only in that direction (Tinker, 1984). As usual this depends on the way in which costs are calculated and further research is required on cost comparisons. One important focus for this sort of research will be the Elderly Person Support Unit's innovation in Sheffield. Sheffield Family and Community Services Department is replacing the traditionally divided structure of services for elderly people - into domiciliary, day care and residential care - with an integrated and flexible form of provision which includes a new sort of all-purpose community support worker (MacDonald et al, 1984). An evaluative project has been funded by the Joseph Rowntree Memorial Trust (Qureshi and Walker, 1983).

The development of a concerted community care policy to replace traditional long-term residential care would require careful planning and preparation. It would be intended to foster independence and inter-dependence rather than dependence. It would require the cooperation of health and housing authorities. It would however meet with powerful opposition from those that have a strong interest in residential provision. Even if it proved feasible it might not be cheaper than residential care; however it might meet the needs of elderly people more effectively. These are issues for further research and policy debate.

Similar questions might be asked about long-term hospital care for elderly people and the possibilities for its replacement with community care and community nursing (the EPSU innovation includes provision for community nursing) and also about the further development of segregated, sheltered and very sheltered housing provision. But in each case issues of cost-effectiveness must incorporate consideration of the effectiveness of care in meeting the needs of elderly people.

The potential for developing alternatives to residential care and treatment has yet to be explored fully. But whatever initiatives are attempted locally, they are unlikely to be successful without a firm foundation of community care services (Webb and Wistow, 1983).

Secondly, there is likely to be some scope for improving cost-effectiveness in the health and personal social services in order to free resources for community care; although it would be mistaken to expect that substantial resources would result from this source and misleading to underemphasise the difficulties involved in securing such savings. A recent study of social services to the elderly, by the Audit Inspectorate (1983), suggested that savings might be made, for example, by improving the priority allocation of hospital beds, replacing residential care for some with community-based services, improving the operation of the home help and meals services and improving the coordination between residential and domiciliary care. Although these recommendations cannot necessarily be put into practice quickly and easily in all authorities, they do suggest that it is possible to improve the cost-efficiency of the public sector and thereby, perhaps, provide some resources to help to fill the care gap. The study concluded that authorities should seek more information about the clients of services in order to support effective allocation to individuals (Audit Inspectorate, 1983, p. 20).

Thirdly, there is privatisation, a major subject in its own right (Le Grand and Robinson, 1984). As I have already indicated, a simple way of freeing health and personal social service resources would be to privatise care. Indeed this seems to have been proceeding quietly in the residential sector over the last few years. There has been a substantial increase in private residential accommodation in response to the inability of local authorities to keep pace with need and the active promotion by the government of the private sector - private and voluntary homes now represent about one-half of all registered places (Johnson, 1983).

This growth has <u>not</u> taken place on the basis of careful policy formulation and evaluation. Quite apart from the fundamental differences between public and private services in motivation and accountability and the implications of the creation of a residual public sector for the poorest, there is very little information on the comparative effectiveness and quality of care in the two sectors on which to plan the development of policy. There is some evidence that private care operates at lower cost than public care, primarily due to the lower levels of wages in the former (Judge et al, 1983), but there are no measures of the <u>outcomes</u> of different forms of care. In the absence of more detailed research it would be wrong to recommend a policy of privatisation in order to provide resources for community care. While we wait for this information, the public sector has important lessons to learn from the private residential sector, such as the effectiveness of smaller units and flexible regimes. It must be pointed out, equally, that although the privatisation of residential care would shift some costs to the private sector it would contradict the current policy of care in the community. Privatisation is not a response to the need for policies which promote community care and support the work of informal carers. Moreover there is no evidence that rapid growth of the private sector in recent years has resulted in the allocation of any extra resources for the public sector.

What scope is there for the possible further spread of privatisation in the public sector in the form of charges for services, which contributed £306 million to the personal social services in 1981/82? There are important objections on universalistic and efficiency grounds, which must continue to be weighed in policy (Le Grand and Robinson, 1984, pp. 25-54). In addition there is little possibility of increasing revenue from charges for the care of the elderly without considerable social costs because of the widespread poverty among this group (Walker, 1980, 1981a) and their detrimental impact on the take-up of services among those most in need (Judge and Matthews, 1980, p.120). Research on the impact of charges on those receiving a home help also suggests that they operate to reduce the living standards of some of the poorest elderly people (Foster, 1983, p.155).

Conclusion
This review of some aspects of the social care for elderly people shows that there will be a growing need for care within

both the informal and formal sectors over the next 10 to 20 years, on top of the existing major shortfall in the provision of domiciliary services. There will be some scope for increasing the supply of human resources for care, in the form of male kin and volunteers, but to achieve this requires promotional policies and formal organisation. The 'Helping the Community to Care' initiative is indicative of the sort of programme required, but it is too modest. There is scope too for financial savings resulting from greater efficiency in the delivery of care. But even if these extra resources are secured, an increasing public expenditure commitment to domiciliary services is necessary if the promises of community care and support for the carers are to become reality.

What should be the aim of policy over the next 10 years? The central requirement is for policies which share care more effectively with the family and more equally within the family. This means moving from a casualty service, which substitutes for the family following breakdown, to a supportive and preventive role. Failure to adopt this position in the past may be explained by the twin fears about the resource implications and the supposed threat that state interference might discourage the family from caring. There is no evidence whatsoever that the existence of public services has made the family less willing to care and it is hoped that research has dispelled the fears of policy-makers on this score (Moroney, 1976, p.125). In fact recent research shows that formal services can actively encourage and support the provision of care by the family. It may well be that shared care will be more expensive in the short run, but against this must be weighed the benefits of an improved quality of life for elderly people and their carers and the relatively small total cost involved.

Because in so many aspects of social care we are entering uncharted waters, a partnership between research and policy-making is essential. Some suggestions for research have been made already. There are likely to be three priorities in the medium term:

- a large-scale study of family care, focussing primarily on the dynamics of reciprocity within the family, and variations in caring arrangements; this would involve close study of the processes underpinning stability in informal networks or which precipitate breakdowns and crises;

- evaluation of formal care delivery in both the public and private sectors, especially client preferences, the outcomes of care and the relationship between service delivery and dependency;
- continual monitoring and evaluation of promising innovations in social care, particularly alternatives to residential and hospital care.

This sort of research programme would ensure that policy-makers have a sound basis on which to develop policies to provide care efficiently and effectively to elderly people.

References

Abrams, M. (1980), Beyond Three Score and Ten, Age Concern.
Abrams, P. (1978a), 'Community Care: Some Research Problems and Priorities', in J. Barnes and N. Connelly (eds), Social Care Research, Bedford Square Press, pp.78-99.
Abrams, P. (1978b), Work, Urbanism and Inequality, Weidenfeld & Nicolson.
Abrams, P., Abrams, S., Humphrey, R. and Smith, R. (1981), Action for Care, The Volunteer Centre.
Allen, I. (1983a), 'The Elderly and their Informal Carers', in DHSS (1983), Elderly People in the Community, HMSO, pp.69-91.
Allen, I. (1983b), Short Stay Residential Care for the Elderly, Policy Studies Institute.
Audit Inspectorate (1983), Social Services: Provision of Care to the Elderly, HMSO.
Bebbington, A. (1981), 'Appendix' in E.M. Goldberg and S. Hatch (eds), A New Look at the Personal Social Services, Policy Studies Institute, pp.65-7.
CPRS/CSO (1980), People and Their Families, HMSO.
Charlesworth, A., Wilkin, D. and Durie, A. (1983), Carers and Services, University of Manchester.
DHSS (1977), The Way Forward, HMSO.
DHSS (1981a), Care in the Community, HC(81)9, DHSS.
DHSS (1981b), Growing Older, Cmnd. 8173, HMSO.
Equal Opportunities Commission (1980), The Experience of Caring for Elderly and Handicapped Dependents, EOC.
Ermisch, J. (1983), The Political Economy of Demographic Change, Heinemann.

Eurostat (1984), Demographic Statistics, Statistical Office of the European Communities.

Eversley, D. (1982), 'The Demography of Retirement - Prospects to the Year 2030', in M. Fogarty (ed), Retirement Policy: The Next Fifty Years, Heinemann.

Finch, J. (1984), 'Community Care: Developing Non-Sexist Alternatives', Critical Social Policy, Issue 9, pp.6-18.

Finch, J. and Groves, D. (1980), 'Community Care and the Family: A Case for Equal Opportunities?', Journal of Social Policy, Vol.9, No. 4, pp.487-514.

Finch, J. and Groves, D. (eds) (1983), A Labour of Love, Routledge & Kegan Paul.

Foster, P. (1983), Access to Welfare, Macmillan.

Graham, H. (1983), 'Caring: a Labour of Love', in J.Finch and D. Groves (eds) (1983), pp.13-30.

Green, S., Creese, X. and Kanfert, J. (1979), 'Social Support and Government Policy on Services for the Elderly', Social Policy and Administration, Vol. 13, No. 3, pp.210-18.

Hakim, C. (1982), 'The Social Consequences of High Unemployment', Journal of Social Policy, Vol. 11, No. 4, pp.433-68.

Hatch, S. (1980), Outside the State, Croom Helm.

Health Advisory Service (1983), The Rising Tide, DHSS.

Henwood, M. and Wicks, M. (1984), The Forgotten Army, Family Policy Studies Centre.

Hirsch, F. (1977), The Social Limits to Growth, Routledge & Kegan Paul.

Hunt, A. (1968), Women's Employment, Vol. 1, HMSO.

Hunt, A. (1978), The Elderly at Home, HMSO.

Isaacs, B., Livingstone, M. and Neville, Y. (1972), Survival of the Unfittest, Routledge & Kegan Paul.

Johnson, M (1983), 'Private Lives', Health and Social Services Journal, 28 July, pp.901-903.

Johnson, M. and Challis D. (1983), 'The Realities and Potential of Community Care', in DHSS, Elderly People in the Community, HMSO, pp.93-117.

Judge, K., Knapp, M. and Smith, J. (1983), The Comparative Cost of Public and Private Residential Homes for the Elderly, Kent, PSSRU.

Judge, K. and Matthews, J. (1980), 'Pricing Personal Social Services', in K. Judge (ed), Pricing the Social Services, Macmillan.

Land, H. (1978), 'Who Cares for the Family?', Journal of Social Policy, Vol. 7, No. 3, pp.357-84.

Le Grand, J. and Robinson, R. (eds) (1984), Privatisation and the Welfare State, Allen & Unwin.

Levin, E., Sinclair, I. and Gorbach, P. (1983), The Supporters of Confused Elderly Persons at Home, NISW.

MacDonald, R., Qureshi, H. and Walker, A. (1984), 'Sheffield Shows the Way', Community Care, 18 October, pp.28-30.

Minford, P. (1984), 'State Expenditure: A Study of Waste', Economic Affairs, Supplement, April-June, pp.i-xix.

Moroney, R.M. (1976), The Family and the State, Longman.

Nissel, M. and Bonnerjea, L. (1982), Family Care of the Handicapped Elderly: Who Pays?, Policy Studies Institute.

OPCS (1981), General Household Survey 1980, HMSO.

OPCS (1982), General Household Survey 1981, HMSO.

Parker, R (1981), 'Tending and Social Policy', in E.M. Goldberg and S. Hatch (eds), A New Look at the Personal Social Services, Policy Studies Institute.

Power, M. and Kelly, S. (1981), 'Evaluating Domiciliary Volunteer Care of the Very Old', in E.M. Goldberg and N. Connelly (eds), Evaluative Research in Social Care, Heinemann, pp.214-234.

Qureshi, H. and Walker, A. (1983), Elderly Persons Support Units Evaluation Project 1984-1987, Department of Sociological Studies, University of Sheffield.

Qureshi, H. and Walker, A. (1986), The Caring Relationship, Routledge & Kegan Paul.

SWSDG (1983), Supporting the Informal Carers, DHSS.

Seyd, R., Simons, K., Tennant, A. and Bayley, M. (1984), Community Care in Dinnington, University of Sheffield.

Tinker, A. (1984), Staying at Home, HMSO.

Titmuss, R.M. (1963), Essays on 'the Welfare State', Second Edition, Allen & Unwin.

Townsend, P. (1962), The Last Refuge, Routledge & Kegan Paul.

Townsend, P. (1979), Poverty in the United Kingdom, Allen Lane.

Townsend, P. (1981a), 'The Structured Dependency of the Elderly: Creation of Social Policy in the Twentieth Century', Ageing and Society, Vol. 1, No. 1, pp.5-28.

Townsend, P. (1981b), 'Elderly People with Disabilities', in A. Walker and P. Townsend (eds) (1981), Disability in Britain, Martin Robertson, pp.91-118.

Townsend, P. (1984), Fewer Children, More Poverty, University of Bristol.

Ungerson, C. (1983), 'Why Do Women Care?', in J. Finch and D. Groves (eds) (1983), pp.31-50.

Walker, A. (1980), 'The Social Creation of Poverty and Dependency in Old Age', Journal of Social Policy, Vol. 9, No. 1, pp.45-75.

Walker, A. (1981a), 'Towards a Political Economy of Old Age', Ageing and Society, Vol. 1, No. 1, pp.73-94.

Walker, A. (1981b), 'Community Care and the Elderly in Great Britain: Theory and Practice', International Journal of Health and Services, Vol. 11, No. 4, pp.541-57.

Walker, A. (1982a), 'Dependency and Old Age', Social Policy and Administration, Vol. 16, No. 2, pp.115-135.

Walker, A. (ed) (1982b), Community Care, Blackwell/ Robertson.

Walker, A. (1983), 'Social Policy and Elderly People in Great Britain: The Construction of Dependent Social and Economic Status in Old Age', in A.M. Guillemard (ed), Old Age and the Welfare State, Sage, pp.143-68.

Walker, A. (1984), Social Planning, Blackwell/Robertson.

Walker, A. (1985), 'From Welfare State to Caring Society?', paper presented to the Conference on Support Networks in a Caring Community, The Hague, January.

Webb, A. and Wistow, G. (1983), 'Public Expenditure and Policy Implementation: the Case of Community Care', Public Administration, Vol. 61, Spring, pp.21-44.

Wenger, G. (1982), 'Ageing in Rural Communities', Ageing and Society, Vol. 2, No. 2, pp.211-229.

Whittaker, J.K. and Garbarino, J. (eds) (1983), Social Support Networks, Aldine.

Wicks, M. (1982), 'Community Care and Elderly People', in A. Walker (ed) (1982b), pp.97-117.

Wilson, E. (1982), 'Women, the "Community" and the "Family"', in A. Walker (ed) (1982b), pp.40-55.

Index

DATE DUE

GAYLORD			PRINTED IN U.S.A.

HV244 .C38 1985   c.1
100106 000
Challenges to social policy /

3 9310 00074031 4
GOSHEN COLLEGE-GOOD LIBRARY